*Photography by* Ann Cary Simpson    The University of North Carolina Press    Chapel Hill

# The Inner Islands

A CAROLINIAN'S SOUND COUNTRY CHRONICLE   BLAND SIMPSON

Set in The Serif types by Keystone Typesetting, Inc.

Manufactured in the United States of America

This book was published with the assistance of the Blythe
Family Fund of the University of North Carolina Press.

The paper in this book meets the guidelines for permanence
and durability of the Committee on Production Guidelines
for Book Longevity of the Council on Library Resources.

Portions of this book initially appeared, in slightly different
form, in *Wildlife in North Carolina* and *North Carolina Literary
Review*; permission to use these materials in *The Inner Islands*
is gratefully acknowledged.

Visitors to North Carolina's Sound Country may seek
information about regulations and restrictions pertaining to
the inner islands from one or more of these agencies:

National Audubon Society
North Carolina Coastal Island Sanctuaries
3806-B Park Avenue
Wilmington, NC 28403

North Carolina National Estuarine Research Reserve
North Carolina Department of Environment and Natural
Resources
1601 Mail Service Center
Raleigh, NC 27699-1601

North Carolina Wildlife Resources Commission
1722 Mail Service Center
Raleigh, NC 27699-1722

U.S. Fish & Wildlife Service
<southeast@fws.gov>
and the North Carolina Field Offices of our
National Wildlife Refuges

Library of Congress Cataloging-in-Publication Data

Simpson, Bland.

The inner islands : a Carolinian's sound country chronicle
/ Bland Simpson ; photography by Ann Cary Simpson.
   p. cm.

Includes bibliographical references and index.

ISBN-13: 978-0-8078-3056-7 (cloth: alk. paper)

ISBN-10: 0-8078-3056-9 (cloth: alk. paper)

1. Islands—North Carolina. 2. Islands—North Carolina—
History. 3. Natural history—North Carolina. 4. North
Carolina—History, Local. 5. North Carolina—Description
and travel. 6. North Carolina—Geography. I. Simpson, Ann
Cary. II. Title.

F262.A19S56 2006

975.6—dc22    2006014017

10 09 08 07 06  5 4 3 2 1

For

Susie Spruill Simpson      John Robert (Tad) Kindell Jr.

Sherri Simpson Million     Carolyn Elizabeth Kindell

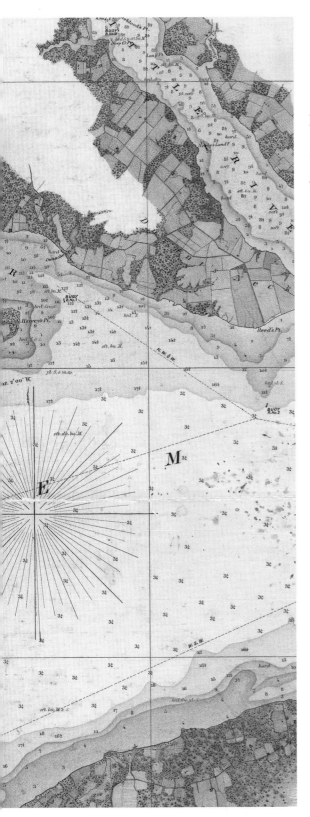

But the next day I went exploring around down through the island. I was boss of it; it all belonged to me, so to say, and I wanted to know all about it; but mainly I wanted to put in the time.

—Mark Twain,
  *Adventures of Huckleberry Finn*
  (1884)

# Contents

Scores and scores of inner islands lie scattered about the many waters of North Carolina's river and sound country, yet less than a century hence our grandchildren's grandchildren will wonder over what and where these islands were, so many of them will have gone under and disappeared in that single hairbreadth of time. The land subsides and sinks and the seas rise. Were it not for the slender barriers, the Outer Banks, Core Banks and Bogue, scarcely holding back the rising ocean as they are, many of these inner islands would not be extant today.

I have boated to them, beached small craft upon them, worn my trousers rolled and walked their small shores, listened always for notes from ancient flutes and shell-shakers, snatches of song in the wind, and, knowing I was there but for a slip of time, probably never to return to most of them, I have loved them all—from the little mossy islands of Pembroke Creek near Edenton to those at the mouth of Deep Creek into Bull's Bay; from Colington in the sound behind Kitty Hawk, where my cousin the high sheriff of Tyrrell County as a young man used to beach his boat and make his way with kin through the liveoak woods over to Leroy's old family-style hotel on the seabeach, to the marshy Abigails between Swanquarter and Rose Bays; from Great Island off Fort Landing, which my grandmother passed on the ferryboat bound for East Lake, to Eagles Island in the Cape Fear River, where my grandfather caught the ferry after work back over to Wilmington, town and home, before he moved upstate and turned his builder's hand to stadium and belltower and library; from Monkey Island, near which my father shouldered his twelve-gauge, to Durant Island, where my son climbed the big sandy bluff; and from shellbank Harbor Island in Core Sound, where Ann played as a child, to Bird Shoal and Carrot Island not far south of Harbor, where our own children trailed after horseshoe crabs.

Many must have felt such a fondness for these little bits of land, for just regard the traces, the names left behind upon them—names to honor travail: the Hard Working Lumps; and those who did it: Sam Windsor's Lump; a name to ward off pain: No Ache Island; names to make an often-harsh landscape more tender, or personable, somehow: the Bunch of Hair, the Maiden Paps; names for women we loved: Kathryne Jane, Cora June; names, half an alphabet and more, of all manner of beasts, fish, and fowl: Bird, Brant, Buck, Cat, Clam, Cow, Dog, Duck, so many Goats, Goose, Gull,

*Beyond this Island [Roanoke] there is the maine lande, and over against this Island falleth into this spacious water, the great river called Occam [Albemarle Sound] by the inhabitants . . . and in this inclosed Sea there are above an hundreth Islands of divers bignesses.*
*—Philip Amadas and Arthur Barlowe,*
Report to Sir Walter Ralegh *(1584)*

Herring Shoal, so many Hogs, Horse, Louse, Raccoon, Sheep, Sow, Steer, Swan, Teal, even Penguin and Little Penguin; names of growing things: Bean, Carrot, Cedar, Cotton, Flax, Myrtle, Pilentary, Pine, Rice, and Wood; and names of former inhabitants and all but forgotten honorees: Campbell, Huggins, Phillips, Piver, Rumley.

Indian.

All these and more have I loved.

One summer day some years ago, my son Hunter and I sat out on the broad deck of a Pasquotank River restaurant at Elizabeth City's Narrows, upon a wide wooden planking stretched out over the dark waters from a brick warehouse where old-time produce agent R. C. Abbott once brokered potatoes and peas. A few slips, there to serve Betsy Town's transient boating trade, lay mostly empty nearby. As the August evening deepened and the red-lit summer clouds faded to ash and it grew dusky dark, across the black river that snakes down out of the Great Dismal Swamp lights in the apartments and the topdecked marina restaurant twinkled on and shone through the far shoreline's cypress trees.

I couldn't take my eyes off any of it, must have gone adrift in time and wandered off into a trance.

"What are you looking at?" Hunter finally asked.

"Oh, just that island over there on the other side of the bridge—it's one of the most familiar sights in the world to me—I can't remember a time when I didn't know it."

"What's it called?"

"Machelhe," I said.

"Mu*shell*y?" he said after me, with just a hint of apprehension. "What do you see?"

The first of North Carolina's inner isles that I ever laid eyes upon and knew it was this one, Machelhe Island in the Pasquotank, lying inside a severe bend in the river long called The Narrows, where a ferry-flat once tied Elizabeth City to its eastern neighbors and where a bascule drawbridge like the one at London's Tower now did the honors, flowering open to the heavens to let through tugs, trawlers, the double-decked passenger yacht *Bonny Blue*. A mile or so long, very low, and in plain view straight out from the foot of Elizabeth City's East Main Street, Machelhe Island was, like the river itself, an inescapable daily sight in this old town, a swampy elongation stretching from Camden way toward us in town, pinching the river at The Narrows and then letting it—maybe *making* it—spread out to the southeast and quickly widen and become a bay.

Here, for me, the past was everywhere, and everywhere I could see it as clearly as if it stood alive before us, for Hunter in asking me about it might just as well have handed me a strange and wondrous telescope, for

*Any one viewing the Pasquotank from its wharf . . . is apt to think that he is overlooking some bay having immediate connection with an ocean instead of standing on the banks of a river.*
*—George I. Nowitzky,* Norfolk and the Sound and River Cities of North Carolina *(1888)*

*Cypress trees, 1998*

suddenly I was staring on down the long shaft of time. Machelhe Island once claimed local fame for its magnificent oyster shuckings, 100,000 gallons a year, and though the commercial oyster houses were long gone when I was a boy, their pilings along Machelhe's shore near several oiltanks in the river betrayed them and gave them away. Even as late as the 1940s a big three-masted wooden-hulled schooner lay dead in the water and a quarter submerged hard by the island just upriver of the bridge, the bowsprit of this ship aimed proudly downriver as if she were still anchors aweigh, full of lumber, and to the Indies outward bound.

I wish I could have shown Hunter those Texaco tanks, three big silver steel cakes set out there by Miles Clark the millionaire oilman among the short cypress on Machelhe's townward point. This was what I saw as a boy, walking down East Main toward the water and looking downriver toward the Albemarle Sound—the tanks, and the small black-hulled tankers—

among them the *Valencia*, built by the Elizabeth City Shipyard in 1927, and the *Carolinian*, crafted in Charleston as the first-ever all-welded ship in 1929—that brought oil to those tanks and then tied up in their lee.

Now the tanks and tankers, too, are long gone from the western tip of Machelhe Island, and oilman Clark, whose bounty fueled the Elizabeth City High School band with buses and yellowjacket uniforms and instruments, has long since joined the minority. His tankers, as many as seven of them in his fleet, plied the Dismal Swamp Canal long after most commercial traffic had given it up, and his yacht *Doris II* lay moored in a cut off the Pasquotank along Riverside Avenue all the while I was growing up there.

Machelhe Island was the backdrop for the International Cup Regatta, a set of astonishingly high-speed hydroplane races held out on the river each fall. The furious high whining and motorific keening we heard all day while we were in school a few blocks away, and then heard up close when class let out and we raced to the riverside to see what daring men in boats almost two-dimensionally flat could do on our river as they cut its surface at speeds in excess of a hundred miles an hour and threw rooster-tail plumes of water into the sky. We saw and marveled at all the derring-do before our eyes—till one day we also saw where the vivid edge really was, as Speed herself intervened and dissolved one contestant. Boat and man were rent in a moment's explosion of water and wood, blood and lacquer all admixed, a young racer's instant death and burial in the dark waters of the Pasquotank, leaving all of us spectators on the brick-rubbled mainland shore stunned and agape, Machelhe Island beyond simply a mute witness, a stoic wilderness, its ranked cypress bemused and waiting patiently in the shallows for whatever might happen next, and if next took a thousand years they could wait that long, too, and they would.

So thin a landform was Machelhe Island that one could see clear through it to the looming, tawny-brick shell of Dare Lumber that for decades lay out on the river's edge across the Pasquotank north of Machelhe. Once this plant covered nearly forty acres, its saws and hundreds of sawyers roaring and singing over the lowlands as they turned pine and cedar and gum logs, barged up across the Albemarle Sound from deepest Dare County, into floorboards, wainscoting, and trim for the North. For half a century the shell of a plant stood after Dare Lumber's demise, and this relic gave mute testimony of the long-gone timber years when men labored in outlier colonies like Buffalo City back on Milltail Creek in the Alligator River swamps of the Dare mainland way to the south. And if the Mill-spirit could have found a voice within its flooded ruin and told what all it had seen with its vacant windowed eyes, it would have had to speak of the true ingenuity of all those Buffalonians who, after cutting the logwoods supported them no more, turned to the business of refining shelled cracked corn that they then shipped north in glass canisters through Elizabeth City, though to different mills and these in a larger port town (Norfolk) and at much greater risk, danger and profit than sawdust and timber ever gave them.

Who and what else has journeyed and taken their turns around this little island?

The natives, the Algonkians in their cypress dugouts, who skirted Machelhe for a thousand years or more before they ever glimpsed a European, before the island ever had a name in English. Moses Grandy the slave freightboat captain who bought his freedom once, twice, *thrice* before it took and he could claim himself as his own and go off to England and tell and publish his story and try thereby to purchase the rest of his family, his own people. Wilbur Wright in 1900 alone and, later, with his brother Orville as well making their way in the bugeye *Hattie Creef* around the head of Machelhe Island bound for the Outer Banks and bound, too, for an astonishing glory that would surely change the world. Mothboat men and women racing the small sailboat first crafted by Cap'n Joel Van Sant and put before the wind right here. Farming lads and their daddies in little one- and two-masted schooners full of May peas, or watermelons maybe, bound for the wharfside trainyard of the late 1800s and early 1900s where forwarding agents like R. C. Abbott would get their truck crops vaulted north in boxcars on rails. Thespians from the lumber-barge playhouse, the *James Adams Floating Theater*, which lay up winters at the foot of Water Street and stormed both the Carolina Sound Country and the Chesapeake Bay by summer. And my father and I, setting out in 1956 or '57 from Machelhe Island's modest Causeway Marina in a dark gray or green rented skiff and hugging the island's south shoreline, our 1 $1/4$-horse engine chugging lightly and pushing us agreeably upstream, my right hand behind me holding the throttle and setting our course. If the thrilling times of being out on big water and having a nautical command could never be any more vivid than this in a man's life, they would still often match its joy and intensity, simply because of this one first moment: a man and a boy, looking for nothing more than the next stob to point her toward as we stood upriver for the great grain elevator that would one day blow up, its soybeans gone mad in a dusty combustion.

Back then in the 1950s I rarely thought, as summer or fall we drove east on our way to some spot on the barrier islands, to the Outer Banks villages Kitty Hawk or Nags Head, that the first place over the Pasquotank River bridge along our lane to the beach was our town's own island. Incredible that we were driving upon it at all. What a task it had been in the early 1920s for Engineer McNutt and his men to take a long island bog like

*Window,*
*Pelican Marina,*
*Machelhe Island,*
*September 2004*

Machelhe and try to succeed at putting a concrete road overtop of a float-ing corduroy of logs—"McNutt's Floating Road sank more than it floated," my aunt once told me. Another woman who had been but a girl during World War II remembered picnicking on the Pasquotank before crossing the bridge and enduring, though frightfully and queasily, the rippling un-steadiness and the underwater portions of the Floating Road. When, late in World War II, the state of North Carolina in the form of Engineer Ham Overman gave up on all that and brought in the big pumps and dredges, he and his men blew in a long mat of sand and laid atop it a tarmac road that worked.

Here men and women had long turned their stock out free-range, and for a hundred years the isle was called Goat Island. Then Charles Hall Robinson, a man come down all the way from Jefferson County in upstate New York first to be a lumberman before building the giant cotton mill west of town, bought it and named it for his children, pulling the first two letters off each of their names—*Ma*ry, *Ch*arles, *El*oise, *He*len—and putting them together: *Machelhe*, spoken not in a brisk hard Scottish mode like

*Machelhe Island,*
*about 1905*

Mack-Hell-he but rather in a softer coastal way, Mushelly. Not Macheel, nor, as the 1908 Sanborn map termed it, Marchella. Since Robinson's re-naming a century ago, the appellation *Goat* had moved upstream and lodged on a small cut-off island, a mile above which was Shipyard Landing and, above that, a Pasquotank ever more serpentine and in late summer slathered shore to shore with bright green duckweed as the river headed for its source, its upper reaches and bends bearing the name "Moccasin Track."

With Ham Overman's highway coup, Machelhe Island became popularly known, then and now, as the Camden Causeway.

Nowhere do ghosts come forth and consort any better than they do over water, and so, there on the riverfront with Hunter, I watched a line of boys—fathers and sons decades apart—joining me in looking out at their island in the stream.

In 1929, my father at seven stood in a crowd at the Water Street wharf watching a Taft floating biplane named *Kingfisher* that lumbermen Fore-man and Blades had teamed up to build. In their homegrown Taft Airplane Corporation across the Pasquotank over on Machelhe Island, planks that might have floored riverport homes or coastal cottages lay together tacked and glued into a form not at all dissimilar from the one the Wright Brothers

had made legendary only twenty-six years before. Propelled by a roaring rotary motor, now *Kingfisher* went lumbering along the river's surface, spreading a fan of foam behind it till it lifted slowly, the undersides of its fuselage and wings mirrored in the river as it throttled up and soared and went aloft. The boy who would one day fly shielded his eyes as he looked up into the bright Sound Country skies, and, though he could see the waving airmen and sunglints off their goggles, he could not see what they were taking in as they circled and buzzed the waterfront in their cypress aircraft, their flying boat: how small was the town, how large was the river, how enormous the great sound to the south!

In 1905, my father's father, just twelve, stood in this same spot scouting a pair of tugs plying the river, pulling a log raft 150 yards long and turning round the bend of The Narrows between Machelhe Island and the town, towing the raft to the mill. Four years earlier, just after Christmas 1901, two fishermen working the river straight out from Machelhe downriver of town came upon a dead woman in the water. They had found Beautiful Nell Cropsey, whose disappearance from the front porch of her riverside home just before Thanksgiving had engendered a national search, and woe to the man who was the last to see her alive. As she was being autopsied in a barn with a throng of men 2,000 strong outside looking on, boys ran through the streets of town, down to the waterfront, astonished by the wildness of their elders, my grandfather at age eight among them. Later, on the night before Nell Cropsey's funeral, her body lay in a casket in the Methodist Church, and Granddaddy Simpson would drift off to sleep in his home just across Church Street from that sanctuary, though his older sister would be too frightened by the ghostliness of it all to surrender, and rest.

*And what kinsman made his way down to the riverside in February 1862?* I wondered.

Roanoke Island had fallen, and Federal gunboats now moved inexorably across the sound from Roanoke Island and upriver to take Elizabeth City, pouring fire onto the Confederacy's mainland battery and then sinking several Southern ships within sight of the port town's wharves. One of them—the two-gun schooner *Black Warrior*—went down hard by Machelhe Island, disabled by Federal shelling and then torched by her fleeing crew.

Before this Civil War, before Captain Grandy and his canalboats made this transit many a day and night, working the Pasquotank and the Dismal Swamp Canal up and down, fifty years before him, little man-made was here to stare at. There was no north and south riverine commerce because no Dismal Swamp Canal yet existed—no communication yet connected Albemarle and Chesapeake, making it possible for bacon, brandy and tobacco to move through the great morass. Nothing here yet at this backwater way far up the Pasquotank but Betsy Tooley's tavern, though the town-to-be would soon take her spot and her name.

I could see every bit of this from the riverside deck, all of it vivified, and I felt hypnotized seeing small lights across dark water and hearing once again the memory-sound, the echoed drone of our skiff's little engine as Daddy and I coursed so long ago beneath the drawbridge tying Betsy Town and Machelhe Island together. The bridge, the boat-motor, the sound of the one reflecting upon the other, these ties and many another were cords around my heart, binding it here forever.

"What're you *staring at*, Dad?" Hunter asked again.

No one had ever told me how to explain to my son what I was regarding just then, how to let him know, and have him also *see*, that each small waterside lamp cast a light on some portion of the past and set it shimmering in full view before us—giving us some glimpse of men who bore his name, too, along with whom once worked mules and dredges scraping at the absolute mud to ditch it and dry it and run water off it so that a roadway on an island or through a swamp might be, that a farm or a hamlet might exist, and subsist; some glimpse of women and other men in over-the-river, islandside warehouses twisting knives with stout blades and rounded points into the muscle end of oysters and shucking them out, a fortune of them every year; and some glimpse of men aboard schooners

and skiffs, bugeyes and tankers, ferryboats and flying boats, all enterprising, all moving life's flotsam, jetsom and real stuff around this old river-
bend between swamp island and swamp town, all of which Neptune,
leaning east, gave us long ago and will spare for a spell yet before claiming it all for his own once again and then washing on to the west over
Pasquotank, then Perquimans, and then Chowan.

"Just Machelhe," I said.

"Mu*shelly*," Hunter repeated. "People around here sure come up with
some strange names."

"Yes," I said, "we sure do."

# Durant Island

*Miller withdrew;
but learning
that Mr. Durant,
leader of the hated
opposition, was
on board Gilliam's
ship, he went back
late the same
night, boarded the
ship, and arrested
Durant at pistol
point charging him
with treason. This
was the crisis, the
occasion for which
the restless had
been waiting. The
revolt broke out the
following morning.
—John Elliott Wood,
"On Culpeper's
Rebellion" (1677),
in Brief Sketch of
Pasquotank County*

Just before Christmas in the late 1990s, when Elizabeth City's blue water-tower had holiday lights zigzagging festively about its tanktop, a young man came to town and stashed his red kayak at the Pasquotank River wharf near the old R. C. Abbott warehouse, planning to return for it later that day. He then drove his truck down the coast to Morehead City, 110 miles away, and left it in that more southerly port, locking his wallet, money, ID and all in the glovebox, carrying only what he needed, then catching a northbound bus to get him *back* to Elizabeth City where he would begin his real adventure.

At The Narrows in Elizabeth City the kayaker put in, and made his late afternoon way down the great, dark, now bay-like river—passing in turn the points Cottage, Cobb, Brickhouse, Pool, Bluff, and Bank on the Pasquotank County side—toward Wade Point and the mouth of the Pasquotank, where it meets and joins the legendarily rough waters we have called, variously, the Carolina River, the Sea of Roanoke, the Albemarle Sound.

It was late, and he had had a full day, so the kayaker looked for a down-river spot to camp, finding one on shore within sight of a small cruising boat that was anchored out.

In the morning he took off, passing the anchored craft, the wind at his back, the confident north wind rising at his back as he skipped and skittered along toward God's own open waters and, then, as much as he was enjoying himself near the beginning of his ten- or twelve-mile crossing toward the mouth of Alligator River, he dumped. Off went the kayak, still on holiday, without him.

Even in his sleek, efficient craft, the kayaker had only gone so far before this misfortune befell him—he was still within sight of the anchored cruiser, and so swam for it, against the rising wind and the waters running hard at him, and only after a long hard time did he near the craft.

The pair aboard, a man and a woman, were ready for him. They had been watching his southerly progress, his swamping, and his swimming back their way in distress. Certainly they should have fired up their engine and gone to his aid, and they would have, too, were they not stuck on this sandbar, as they had been for a day and a night. When the swimming kayaker, his own red craft and orange drybag long since out of sight, reached the cruiser, the boaters pulled him in, helped his hypothermic self as best they could, and called the Coast Guard.

Now, the Elizabeth City Coast Guard Air Station is one of the maritime treasures of eastern America—it comprises the Hollowell family's old Bay-side Plantation on the south and west shore of the Pasquotank River, possibly the first place in America to grow an exotic bean named *soja*, or soy. From this open spot many rescues-at-sea are staged, launched, effected. Its lumbering C-130s, its orange-and-white copters, its lit-up runways and flashing riverside tower beacon all bespeak safety and good sense.

When the boaters called the Coast Guard, they were doing so for the second time in twenty-four hours. They had already made an appeal the previous day, but the Coast Guard, having ascertained that the boaters were safe, though stuck, couldn't come out in high winds for a mere grounding and thus left the boaters and their craft high, though not dry—the kayaker, after all, had judged them to be anchored.

This time, though, they had a genuine emergency—the kayaker was suffering from exposure. The Coast Guard must come.

A helicopter appeared at once—the Coast Guard Air Station was less than five miles upriver. The airmen dropped a rescue line and lifted the kayaker into the copter, and in the process the propwash felicitously blew the cruising boat off the shoal where it had sat forlornly and set it free—into churning and bombastic winter waters, mind, but still free.

Upriver to the hospital flew the copter carrying the near-frozen kayaker, who had nothing other than his blanket-enshrouded self, no wallet, no identification, certainly no money or insurance card, when he arrived at the emergency room. As the medics were thawing him out and back into the human race, there to help him came a woman who was the hospital's Patients' Advocate. And if ever anyone needed patience and advocacy— why, it was nearly three o'clock in the afternoon, now, on Christmas Eve!— here was that man.

She sized him up, literally—the first thing he would need once he returned to 98.6 degrees Fahrenheit would be clothing, for the kayaker's dry clothes, though safe, were somewhere not immediately accessible, way downriver.

Where does one shop for clothes in Elizabeth City as the afternoon wanes on Christmas Eve? Don't ever do this, she thought, even as she did it, later saying to all and sundry, "I don't advise it."

In the melee that was Wal-Mart on Christmas Eve, the Patients' Advocate found for the kayaker the only thing left in his size, a lime-green jumpsuit. Beggars, we know, cannot be choosers, and must by needs thank heaven for small favors. Gratefully he donned his holiday vestment, and then she checked him out of the hospital and found him a room at the Holiday Inn and drove him there.

And there she left him and drove on home to join her husband and change to go out for a traditional Christmas Eve dinner with friends. Something tugged at her, though, something decidedly uncheerful—it was the sight of the adventurer as she had left him, hunkering down in his motel room, a lime-green warrior now on crusade touring the yellow pages looking for rental vehicles, U-Hauls, buses, something to get him back to Morehead City, to his truck, his money, his identification on this earth.

But it being Christmas Eve with an ice storm brewing, there was nothing for rent, and no buses were running south down the Carolina coast.

When she finally broke through the kayaker's cascade of hapless, hopeless outgoing calls with a call of her own, the Patients' Advocate found him discouraged, though comfortable, and so ventured a bit of holiday cheer by inviting him to come along to the Christmas Eve dinner and join in. Would he?

He would!

At the dinner, the kayaker was a hit—he had the most unusual story, and he certainly had the most unusual outfit. All of the folks at the table were boaters, experienced on these their home waters, and if there be one thing that mariners love to do and must love to do, it is to speculate upon the wonders of wind and wave.

Where would his unsinkable red kayak and his orange drybag finally wind up?

The Coast Guard had suggested that the kayaker might best search for his goods at one point or another at the mouth of the Pasquotank, but the talk flowed strong on this matter. The boaters all agreed that, given the blow they were having, his gear would most likely fetch up somewhere on the south side of Albemarle Sound, somewhere near the mouth of the Alligator River, most probably on the long north shore of Durant Island.

This was all very interesting to the kayaker, though somewhat theoretical just then, given his isolation in Elizabeth City and his separation from his truck and wherewithal down in Morehead City.

"Oh!" a sister-in-law of the host spoke up. "Is that where you need to go? Morehead's my home, and I'm driving back down in the morning, once the ice's melted. Would you like a ride?"

Life in the Sound Country was starting to look up for the kayaker—new clothing, new friends, new home for a night, a portage in the offing from one river town to another in the car and company of a lovely woman. One might almost begin to think him lucky for having been dumped down the river, but let us not go overboard just yet.

Christmas Day in Carolina, and the roads were clear! The woman from the dinner party called at the Holiday Inn for the kayaker, and off they went. Three hours later and the pilgrim was reunited with his truck, whereupon he turned around and drove back up to Elizabeth City and began his new life as a searcher and a salvor.

Once he realized that he could not drive his truck to any of the potential places where the dinner guests had suggested he might find his boat, his heart sank, for he also realized that the task of locating it in this big, wide, wet territory was going to require an aircraft, and he could scarcely afford to hire one for the job.

A miracle was occurring, though—his story was going around Elizabeth City, ahead of him, as it were. This fact of smalltown life gave him pause, though, as he began to fear that word might get beyond the borders of the Sound Country and hurt his livelihood—he was a whitewater kayaking guide up in the North Carolina mountains. Then someone got the kayaker in touch with a pilot who worked out at the Coast Guard Air Station. The pilot needed to keep his flying hours up, and, when they spoke, he offered to take the kayaker along with him and they would fly around for a few hours and see what they saw, and the pilot would only charge him for the gas they used. This was a good deal, to which the kayaker agreed.

*When could they do this?* he wondered.

"Well, I get off today at noon," said the pilot. "How about meeting me at the airport, beside the base, say about twelve-thirty?"

Up and away they flew, right down the river and, seeing nothing there, right on over the sound, where, on the north shore of Durant Island, exactly where on the night before Christmas, the dinner guests had predicted they would be, lay the red kayak and the orange drybag. The two men had been aloft less than twenty minutes, and when the pilot returned the excited kayaker to the ground, he said, "We were hardly up anytime at all—I'm not going to charge you for the gas after all—go on and see about getting your boat."

How would he do that, though? There were no roads to, or on, Durant Island. Well, he knew that he would have to get near it, for starters, so he lit out in his truck, driving east from Elizabeth City to Camden, Bellcross, Barco, Coinjock, Grandy, Jarvisburg, Powells Point, Mamie, Harbinger, Point Harbor, Kitty Hawk, Kill Devil Hills, Nags Head, Whalebone, Manteo, Manns Harbor, East Lake! Which is way out yonder where there ain't nobody never is.

Especially in the dead of winter, when all the backcountry shacks and cabins are boarded up and closed.

What was the kayaker thinking as he drove up a long lane to the north of U.S. 64 toward the body of water, East Lake itself? The nearest commercial establishments, the nearest places he could even talk to someone about where and from whom to rent a boat, were back in Manns Harbor, or on across the other side of the broad, three-mile Alligator River. He didn't know what he was driving toward, only that the general direction was correct—he might or might not even get a glimpse of Durant Island from the end of this lane. And if he did, he would be looking at the south side of it, the wrong side.

At the end of the sandy lane there sat, as one might have expected, a cabin.

The surprise was that the owners were in.

When they heard the kayaker's tale, they said, "Why, take the skiff there, it's all gassed up, you just go on out the cut and . . ."

Not five minutes after he'd arrived, the kayaker was on his way again, bobbing and boating about East Lake, the well-known epicenter of white-liquor-making seventy years ago. East Lake, where a drunken moonshiner once happened upon a river baptism and got grabbed by the preacher conducting the service and sure enough got baptized, though he had no notion of what was going on, the preacher shouting at him as he pulled the moonshiner up from beneath the water,

"Have you found Jesus?"

Then dunking him again before he could respond, then pulling him up,

"Say, have you found *Jesus*?"

Slamming him back under rapidly yet again, yanking him up,

"Tell me, have you found JESUS?"

To which the moonshiner asked desperately,

"No, preacher, hold it, hold it—are you sure this is where he fell in?"

Now over this same legendary East Lake coursed the kayaker, cutting now through the shoal thoroughfare, the Haulover, and on out to Albemarle Sound where, in short order, he found his quarry on the north side of Durant Island, the red kayak and the orange drybag, which he loaded into the skiff and started back.

By the time he made it down the sound shore and through the cut at the Haulover and on into the canal back to the little cabin, it was late that December afternoon. He tied up the skiff, got his goods to his truck, and turned to thank the cabin owners.

And then it was that the kayaker truly felt the full power of eastern Carolina generosity and fellowship and helpfulness toward the troubled traveler—the enduring spirit of the Albemarle was abroad in the land. Because the kayaker then saw the firebarrel and smelled the fruits of the sound and sea and the next words he heard were these:

"Found your kayak, good . . . good . . . good—now, come on, we're just taking the first oysters off, and we got aplenty, a whole bushel and a half—so dig in. And the cooler's right over there—go on get yourself something to drink! Pilgrim, you have come to the right place!"

---

If there were determination ever made about who was source, symbol and sign of this long-vaunted Albemarle hospitality, those who established it and set it up to endure may well have been the multifaceted pair George and Ann Marwood Durant, who about 1661 started living down in extreme southeastern Perquimans County, in an area long since then called Durant's Neck and in whose home was a Geneva Bible, published in 1599, the book thought to have been in what is now North Carolina longer than any other.

Ann Marwood Durant, so a silver historical marker near the east bank of the cypress-fringed Perquimans River will tell you, was the first woman attorney in the history of North Carolina—she first went to court speaking for a sailor who was owed back pay, and she represented her husband as well.

In his will George Durant called himself a mariner, but that understated his interests somewhat, for he was also a planter, a merchant, and a hotelier, for after some fashion he and Ann operated an inn, or operated their household as if it were an inn. Ann billed people for "accommodations," for "attendance in sickness," for selling them rum and cider, for making their blouses and breeches and their coffins, and for setting up their last rites. A full service family.

And George was highly political—he was a revolutionary, bringing guns from England into Carolina to help kick off Culpeper's Rebellion in 1677, his home for a spell even serving as the seat of the rebel government. Then he was a law-and-order leader, becoming attorney general of the colony once the revolt was over and the Lords Proprietors relented to the positions of Durant and the original Carolina colonists, and installed rebel leaders in the new government.

So these were involved, engaged people, and beyond their active public lives lay a great consanguinity—they had nine children. Doubtless they would have known my eight times great-grandfather, William Drummond, the first governor of Albemarle, whose name is forever married to the huge, ruby-water lake he discovered at the heart of the Great Dismal Swamp and who called the first colonial assembly together, in February 1665, beneath a tree on the banks of Hall's Creek in present-day Pasquotank County, only a few miles away from the Durants. Durant's Neck and Hall's Creek were proximate indeed—today they share the very same inshore nautical chart, number 7, in the *GMCO Chartbook of North Carolina*, and we should remember that in the days of Drummond and the Durants boats were the only practical way to move from place to place and avoid the vast, lonesome pine barrens, the interminable bogs and dismals, the jungles of Carolina.

Neither George nor Ann Durant, I feel fairly sure, ever made their ways into the Carolina colony's interior way back when—that would be left for the prodigiously energetic early American explorer John Lawson to do, only a handful of years after the Durants had both made their last trek. Still, if one lives in a house by the side of the river and makes oneself a friend—possibly even an undertaker—to man, one's fame and one's name may well be broadcast about the province, and in a few spots over time it may stick.

And it must be something good for a name to live on as theirs has—not only on the Neck, but at Durant Island; at Durants Coast Guard Station near Hatteras village on the Outer Banks and Durant Point in Pamlico Sound just to its north; at the Boy Scout Camp Durant, now Durant Nature Park in north Raleigh. Seeing Durant and Durants all over Carolina creation should give one a strong sense of endurance beyond the normal mortal span, though all of these locales, excepting the park in Raleigh, do sit within easy reach of the rising Atlantic Ocean, and some transformation of the names may soon be in order—Durant Island may ere long become Durant Reef or Durant Shoal, and then later, when the shorewaters are lapping at the power plant in Rocky Mount, a well-submerged spot for divers of the thirtieth century, Durant Shelf.

---

My son Hunter and old friend Jake Mills and I boated out to Durant Island for a circumnavigation in June of '99, crossing the Alligator River in our seventeen-foot Boston Whaler, dodging a raincloud or two, then rounding Sound Point on the island's western end, the mouth of Alligator River, and coming on into the sandy beach with the high liveoak dune a quarter-mile farther along the northwestern shore. This was a grand, bold bluff, facing endless waters that look just like a sea. Strewn as it was with logs and the bones of whole trees, this long unpeopled beach, one knew, took God's own glorious pounding in the winter.

But this was summer.

So we climbed the high banks, walked beneath the canopy of the fifty-yard-wide liveoak forest that held the high ground and formed a band between blufftop and marsh, strode the boneyard beach of Durant Island, all these pine and liveoak logs bleaching in the sun. Here on this hot late June day, with only a light wind out of the southwest, we pondered other weathers, other vessels than our own, and other fates. And we ate turkey sandwiches, then weighed anchor and headed slowly east along Durant's north shore.

Soon we were passing a hunting lodge set back in on Tom Mann's Creek, a shooters' haven called the Durant Island Club, which has been an outpost here and held hunting and fishing rights to the island for about a hundred years. One story had it that the club was started by a man from Pennsylvania who had accidentally shot a friend on a deer hunt and who then wanted to get as far away from people as he could to hunt. He found Durant Island and put up the original caretaker's lodge, and folks from Rocky Mount favored the spot, joined the club, and would travel to Elizabeth City and from there boat across the sound to Tom Mann's Creek, a narrower piece of water three-quarters of a century ago than the open cove it has become since then.

We saw the gray granite of the Wright Brothers Memorial shining in the afternoon sunlight beyond Big Colington Island ten miles away, and we then coursed the extreme shallows of the Haulover, a marshy thoroughfare channel by which the Albemarle Sound and East Lake communicated, engine tilted up and us poling, and made our way back across the big river to the Little Alligator and our coveside camp at Willy and Feather Phillips's Fort Landing home. There Willy's softshell crab shedder trays out over the water and his wholesale operation, Full Circle Crab Company, were both in high gear and great form. Feather was a Pennsylvania girl and Willy a Hewlett's Creek boy from down Wilmington way, and, having honeymooned in the wilds of Browns Island in Carteret County, they had lived in Bath till 1987, when they moved on out here to the end of the Soundside Road— she ran a homegrown studio and gallery, Pocosin Arts, in town, and he ran crabs.

On this night we fished, just really yanking them in for an hour or so, from their long dock. One could see Durant Island way out big and dim as a headland on the horizon, far past the cove islet Great Island, which is called Goat Island locally after a brief, now defunct population of omnivores. Big pines throve on it, though four years hence Hurricane Isabel would blow through here and take them all down, leaving Great Island still green but a hundred acres of rootball with peaty ground so fragile one could fall right through most anywhere. Though it still appeared on charts, the tiny spot of land just off Great Island's southeast point was now drowned, as were such other nearby islands as Charles and Goose Pond and Mill Point.

*Lodge at Durant
Island, 1940s*

We ate fried soft crabs that night till we were soft in the head, enjoying the most authentic of Carolina vespers as distant Durant disappeared in the gloaming and we all felt an extraordinary sense of Sound Country well- being. Gazing eastward, Willy reflected: "Durants ... just the last name of perhaps dozens from forgotten tongues of people gone before us. Dunes built on the tide line of salt water from the ocean and waters from vast swamps and rivers. The site for lookouts, rituals and celebrations. There the currents pull you into a ... time of wonder ... truly a mortals portal."

From this stalwart waterman we then heard the tale of a shipwreck off Durant's, the wreck of the *Sun Chaser*, a Florida boat.

Not only a Florida boat, but Florida operators, a man and a woman plying north on the Intracoastal Waterway along about 1990. By the time they reached the Alligator River marina on the west side of the three-mile bridge, a nor'easter was blowing, and the marina folks told the Floridians no way could they cross the nearly twenty miles of open Albemarle Sound waters in the face of such a blow. So they hunkered down and lay up at the little harbor, set up for a dozen boats or so, a gas station and convenience store (and a large-scale model of the ubiquitous Hatteras Light) the only entertainments for such mariners for miles in any direction. Had they only known of the Bear Lady of Little Alligator River's nearby wilds, perhaps they might've disembarked and gone off and witnessed if not joined in with her bizarre practice of longstanding: feeding dogfood to a band of black bears whose members she has nicknamed and coddled. But the Flo- ridians were spared that, and knew not what they missed.

Instead they sat out in their trawler for a day or so, very bored, very frustrated, dying to go on and cross some of the roughest inside waters in the American east (and deservedly famous for it), the weather too windy even to allow them to sploosh about indolently in the relative luxury of the *Sun Chaser*'s upperdeck jacuzzi. Finding such a stalled-out situation oppres- sive, what were they to do after a full day and a half except get their dander up and say "Damn the storm, we're heading north!" And so, against the better judgment of all Alligator Riverians, the Floridians threw off *Sun Chaser*'s lines, slid out of their perfectly safe harbor and moved slowly north, running against the wind the last three miles to the double beacon at the mouth of mighty Alligator River.

Now, the hydrodynamic of a nor'easter hereabouts is such that, as the storm rages down, it blows all the Currituck Sound and eastern Albemarle waters down toward Pamlico and west toward the Roanoke River. The net effect is a lowering of the water level in the Albemarle system, one that sucks water up out of the Alligator—perhaps just the opposite of what one might suppose would happen—so that right at the river's mouth, right where the double beacon is, the channel there being but thirty or forty yards wide, right there the southbound waves during such a blow smack hard in relative shallows against the Alligator River's northbound flow and those waves stand straight up tall, with very short fetch.

The Floridians made it several waves' worth north past the double beacon, whereupon the Albemarle's high waves met that beamy, top-heavy trawler with its water-filled jacuzzi, and chop-chop the *Sun Chaser* just plain heeled on over, all the way over—the people got off her all right, but the sad craft herself sank there at the mouth of the Alligator River. The nor'easter's wind and waves blew her onto the north shore of Durant Island, where she lay a shipwreck and was soon set upon for salvage by the locals.

"We got there right after the boys who'd taken all the stainless steel fittings, screws and such, off her," Willy Phillips told us that evening out there at Fort Landing. "Got a few things, a pretty good boat ladder."

Then Willy called nostalgically across the dark sea-level yard to his boy, who was now lazing in a hammock: "Hey, Jake, you remember the wreck of the *Sun Chaser*?"

"Oh, yeah," the fifteen-year-old said from beneath the shade trees without moving. "I remember the ladder."

At this late date, though, no one, not even the vaunted crabber and mariner, remembers what ever came of *Sun Chaser*'s fateful, and fatal, jacuzzi.

Only one island other than Durant lay *in* the broad Albemarle Sound: Heriots Ile, identified and named by Jamestown's Captain John Smith on his 1624 map and situated on the northern side of the sound just off the mouth of the Yeopim River, about a mile due east of Drummond's Point. As the seventeenth century progressed and the Carolina fur trade advanced with it, Heriots Ile became the property of a western Albemarle fur-trading-post operator, one Nathaniell Batts, and, by 1672, Heriots bore the trader's name and was now Batts Island. Time moving in only one direction, though, by the 1690s the forty-acre Batts Island had come to be called Batts Grave.

"When the truth becomes legend," advised an old Shakespeare-spouting editor in a John Ford Western, "print the legend." One late-nineteenth-century Albemarle editor did just that, taking the paucity of what is known about Nathaniell Batts—his last name, his doings with the natives, and his island—and ginning them up into a romantic legend of cross-cultural natural love and tragedy.

Richard Benbury Creecy, who edited and published Elizabeth City's *The Economist* for over thirty years, said of this island: "Within living memory no man has dwelt thereon, but, within living memory it was the roost of myriads of migratory gulls, who held undisturbed possession of their island home." Aided by $200 in publication support from the North Carolina State Legislature, Creecy made *his* story of Jesse Batz one of his 1901 *Grandfather's Tales of North Carolina History*, to wit:

The Chowanoke Indians called the small island *Kalola*, and here on their visits they found Jesse Batz, who had made *Kalola* his temporary home, though what his island pursuits were was not clear. Batz joined the Indians in their hunting, and soon met old King Kilkanoo's daughter, the "pretty, nut-brown Kickowanna," who "sometimes looked at Jesse Batz with the love-light in her eye."

So far so good.

Till Chief Pamunkey of the Chasamonpeaks to the north fancied, and was rejected by, Kickowanna. War between Kilkanoo and Pamunkey ensued.

Batz joined the ranks of the Chowanokes, and in battle fought hand-to-hand with Pamunkey, got him down and was prepared to brain him when Pamunkey begged for mercy, and Batz relented and let him live. For both valor and empathy, King Kilkanoo adopted Batz into the Chowanoke

*Near Drummond's Point . . . lies a solitary island, now uninhabited, once the home where the goat browsed, and the gull built its nest and defied the storm with its discordant scream.*
*—Colonel Richard Benbury Creecy,*
Legend of Batz's Grave *(1901)*

tribe, naming him *Secotan* (meaning "The Great White Eagle," according to Editor Creecy, but in topographic fact this was the name of a sixteenth-century Indian village south of the Pamlico River, visited by artist and future Lost Colony Governor John White, the word really denoting a "town at the bend of a river") and smiling upon Jesse and Kickowanna's living and loving together.

Multiform were the modes of passion: she penciled his eyebrows, put golden rings in his nose and ears, festooned his neck with pearls. Batz "made frequent visits to his old island home," to which Kickowanna also came, paddling a light canoe "sometimes in the silent watches of the night, sometimes in the glare of midday." Whenever she came to *Kalola*, "it was love's high pastime."

One hideously stormy night Kickowanna and her craft were lost to the wind and waves, and Batz, broken-hearted and deranged, never left the island again. "He rests there in his final rest," wrote Creecy, "till the resurrection note calls him to meet his loved Kickowanna." Creecy billed the fanciful tale as "a legend of love and sadness."

A tricked-up legend it was nonetheless, and if the story reminds one of more recent twaddle, such as the 1960 popular song "Running Bear and Little White Dove," 'tis small wonder.

———————

Heriot of the island's original name was the great Elizabethan scientist and explorer Thomas Hariot, or Harriot, "the English Galileo," credited along with his contemporary, the Italian Galileo Galilei, as being the inventor of the telescope, as well as discoverer of sunspots. In 1607 Harriot observed the stellar trail that Mark Twain would much later say he came in with and would ride out on—Halley's Comet. By penning and pinning Harriot's name to the little island then in Virginia, Captain Smith was saluting and promoting him not primarily for his algebraic, navigational and astronomical prowess, but for his primacy as an explorer and observer of the New World, for his strong role in the colonial efforts at Roanoke Island in the 1580s sponsored by Ralegh (as Sir Walter consistently spelled his name after 1584).

Harriot had sailed from England as a member of the seven-ship Sir Richard Grenville–Ralph Lane expedition on April 9, 1585—and, though this is only conjecture, he may have even been a member of the Amadas and Barlowe exploratory journey to the New World the previous year. When Grenville departed Roanoke Island and went back to England in late August 1585, he left 107 men at Roanoke Island under the command of soldier Ralph Lane, Harriot among them. In October, some of them headed for

Chesapeake Bay to explore and overwinter, and artist John White—who had already been exploring and mapping the Outer Banks and Sound Country together with surveyor-scientist Harriot—was probably in that lot.

The following spring, in March and April 1586, Lane's men explored the Albemarle Sound further, and went up the Chowan River and the Roanoke River. Biographer John Shirley has written that Harriot was "almost certainly" in this expedition, though whether Harriot or any other of Lane's men then set foot (or had done so the previous year) on what John Smith forty years hence would name Heriots Ile, we will never know. That they might have paid the islet a visit is not at all hard to imagine, for, with two- and three-fathom depths all around it on the soundside, Heriots Ile would have been an easy and natural place for a pinnace to anchor and lay by while still smaller boats went on up the Yeopim River to sound it and take its measure.

Between the time one of Lane's men sighted Francis Drake's fleet off Hatteras on June 8 and Lane's June 16 decision to abandon Roanoke and return to England with Drake, two powerful events occurred. On June 10, Captain Lane made a preemptive attack on an Indian village on the mainland, killing its leader, Wingina. Three days later a hurricane hit the coast. Harriot's instruments and detailed papers were lost in rough, post-hurricane churning waters during the ferrying of men and materiel from Roanoke Island to Drake's ships out in the Atlantic, along with various rocks, minerals, specimens and, possibly, historian William S. Powell has speculated, some of John White's paintings.

Though his field notes were jettisoned and buried in New World waters, back in England Harriot reconstructed, in February 1588, his observations of the plants, crops, beasts, fish, and native people of what was then the "Colonie in Virginia." Harriot's *A briefe and true report of the new found land of Virginia*, "Imprinted at London 1588" in quarto and oft reprinted and cited since, is celebrated by coastal Carolina author David Stick as "the first English book drafted in America" and by Roanoke historian David Beers Quinn as "the most delectable of Americana." *A briefe and true report* is an extraordinary inventory of what Harriot and his colleagues found here, and an equally extraordinary window into this brilliant, liberal English mind's taking stock thereof.

Harriot praised *Uppowoc* ("the Spanyards generally call it Tobacco") for its purgative qualities ("it purgeth superfluous fleame and other gross humors") and counted it among the "commodities for sustenance of life," bringing it back to Sir Walter Ralegh, who then led the Elizabethans in popularizing the practice of smoking. Harriot noted the Sound Country's plenitude of fowl and fish—"in winter great store of Swannes and Geese," he wrote. "Herrings . . . most delicate and pleasant meat." Like countless Carolinians to come, he admired our salty oysters—"those that we had out of salt water are far better then the other as in our countrey."

Harriot continued to study the Indian language he had begun to fathom before this "first colony" trip, for he had learned the speech and habits of Roanoke Islanders Manteo and Wanchese during their sojourn in England in 1584 and 1585. In America he went among the native Algonkians with great interest in them and considerable sympathy for them, judging them poor in material matters but "very ingenious," preaching Christian doctrine to them, and seeking "by all meanes possible to win them by gentlenesse."

He also clearly saw the aftereffects of the pathogens the Englishmen were spreading as they went village to village: "within a fewe dayes after our departure from every such towne, the people began to die very fast." He bore witness to the Indians' confusion over the meaning and cause of these lethal visitations, their wondering if the English were really the walking dead, if they were firing spectral weapons, if the English god were raining death upon them. As to the mysterious ways of the Lord in such matters, Harriot could not help but sympathize, admitting "Wee our selues haue cause in some sorte to thinke no less."

Still, the conclusion to Harriot's *Briefe and true report* as to climate, commodities, and the future of New World settlement by the English was highly optimistic, an unmitigated *aye*, calculated to allay any fears, talk and rumor to the contrary. Near the work's end, he remarked:

"I hope there remaines no cause whereby the action should be misliked."

---

A rather different sort of fellow was the American pioneer whose name succeeded Harriot's on the little Albemarle island and who undertook the very sort of settlement Harriot and his *Briefe and true report* promoted. This was Nathaniell Batts, who lived at Batts House, a two-room cabin twenty feet square built between the Roanoke River's mouth and Salmon Creek "as early as 1655." Historian Powell has identified Batts as the "first known permanent white settler in North Carolina."

Society of Friends founder George Fox met Batts in late 1672, during Fox's proselytizing 1671–73 journey to the West Indies and America, visiting him and, according to Powell, even sleeping "on a mat before the fireplace of his small house," the little domicile that appears clearly and prominently as "Batts House" on Comberford's 1657 map of *Carolana*. Wrote first Friend Fox of his host:

"Amongst others came Nathaniel Batts, who had been governor of Roanoke; he went by the name of Captain Batts, and had been a rude, desperate man. He asked me about a woman in Cumberland, who, he said he had been told, had been healed by our prayers, and by laying on of hands after she had been long sick, and given over by the physicians; and he desired to know the certainty of it. I told him we did not glory in such things, but many such things had been done by the power of Christ."

Just how rude and desperate was this fellow Batts, who by the time Fox spied him had been a resident of Carolina for nearly twenty years?

Born about 1620, Batts was described in 1654 by Virginian Francis Yeardley, a governor's son and sponsor of Carolina exploration, as "a young man, a trader for beavers." Next year Batts was operating his outpost of progress on the western Albemarle, Yeardley having had the house built for Batts (though dying, unfortunately, prior to paying the housejoiner, who then had to go to court to get paid off). The year after that Batts was marrying wealthy widow Mary Woodhouse in lower Norfolk County, pledging in a nuptial agreement *not* to use *her* property to pay off *his* debts to "some men in Virginia." Impecunious he may have been, but still he coined new place names with his own surname: the former Mrs. Woodhouse's plantation "Roede" would come to be known as "Batts Quarters." In 1657, the year after he wed the widow, the Virginia General Court decreed a twelve-month-and-a-day protection for Batts from his creditors, a reward said to be for Batts's discovery of an inlet on the Outer Banks (probably "Musketo," also known as "new" Inlet south of Currituck Inlet, then open) and a balm apparently allowing him time and cover to buy and sell nearly a thousand acres in Nansemond County (where Suffolk, Virginia, is today) and to move *back* into Carolina. Mrs. Batts—rightfully indignant that her ingenious, indigent new husband was seeking to be paid for the board of her children sired by the late Mister Woodhouse and that she was forced into court to get Batts to relinquish property bequeathed to those children by Woodhouse—may well've been what sent him south very much alone.

Where on the twenty-fourth day of September 1660 Batts bought off of Kiscutanewh, King of the Yeopim, the west bank of the Pasquotank River, from its mouth at the Albemarle Sound up to the headwaters of New Begin (now Newbegun) Creek, almost *ten miles* of shoreline—a purchase cited by historians as producing "the oldest known surviving North Carolina land deed."

Though Captain Smith's "Heriots Ile" from 1624 had carried over as "Hariots Island" on Comberford's 1657 chart, the name of Batts, who died in 1679, quickly supplanted that of Harriot, like bad money driving out good, and the appellations of Batts Island and, not much later, Batts Grave were in local-records use and on subsequent charts from the 1670s on. Given the historical importance of Thomas Harriot to England and to North Carolina,

one might think it queer that *his* name now lives here just upon a cross-street signpost in Manteo and, only quite recently, on an academic banner at East Carolina University: The Thomas Harriot College of Arts & Sciences.

Yet Batts spent a lot more time in the Carolina Sound Country than Harriot did, and, despite whatever shell-game shenanigans he may have engaged in up in Virginia, in Carolina he probably acquired a lowland luster, a gone-native mystique, somewhat like Kurtz way up the Congo in Conrad's *Heart of Darkness*. In addition to Batts Island, whether through progeny or admirers unknown, the Batts name has held on elsewhere, migrating and now gracing: a church, Batts Chapel in Edgecombe County; a reservoir, Batts Pond in Wilson County; a stream, Batts Mill Creek in Pender County; and an intersection, Batts Crossroads in Beaufort County.

What did Nathaniell Batts in, finally?

Too much rudeness?

There certainly would have been enough to go around in that country in that era. Did he have dealings with the Durants of Durant's Neck and Durant Island? Why, yes, indeed: George Durant witnessed Batts's Pasquotank land deal with Kiscutanewh. Did he know William Drummond, who came down from Virginia in the mid-1660s as governor of Albemarle? More importantly, did Batts lose his grip on the Albemarle beavers to Drummond, whose payment for gubernatorial service was supposed to have been the Carolina fur trade?

And how much desperation could a debt-ridden old governor like Batts be expected to take? No records apparently exist to show that Mrs. Batts ever wandered down from Virginia to see him and pay him a conjugal call, as the legendary Kickowanna often came to visit Batts's tall-tale *alter ego* Jesse Batz. In blunt fact she is said to have remarried quickly after Batts's demise in 1679. When Jesse Batz died in Creecy's tale, his remains remained on that island, but what of the *real* Nathaniell Batts? Who, if not Batts, is really buried on Batts Grave?

Better to ponder the fate of Batts Grave, the island itself—which thousands of years ago was actually attached to the mainland and was, in fact, land's end as the land reached easterly toward the sea another mile from today's Drummond's Point—and its drowning over two centuries and a half. Historian Powell reported the little Albemarle island's size in 1749 as being forty acres, writing that it "had houses and orchards on it; by 1756 it had been reduced to twenty-seven acres." What event or events happened between 1749 and 1756 causing Batts Grave to lose thirteen acres in a mere

*Batts Island, detail from U.S. Coast Survey, chart 40, Albemarle Sound, 1860*

seven years? Those of us who watched with interest as Hurricane Isabel made landfall over Core Banks and Hog Island in September 2003—that is to say, everyone in North Carolina—and who noted that much of the territory in Carteret County east of the North River bridge lay underwater, and further noted some eighty feet of shoreline recession along the Chowan River, some of its enormous bluffs simply blown away, we might well answer with the name of a song:

"Stormy Weather."

The island's fate is a tale of continuing shrinkage till eventual oblivion, of land subsidence—nowhere in the American east is the land sinking at the rate it is in the Albemarle, which was the most uplifted, or levered, during the most recent Ice Age by the sheer weight of the southbound sheet of ice on lands to our north; of the simple, basic and steady effects of sea level rise; and of the equally steady erosion by nor'easters and sou'westers. By the early twentieth century Batts Grave was a muddy shoal, a forlorn setting of dead trees and occasional fish camps, and the Federal Writers Project's 1939 *WPA Guide to North Carolina* remarked of the fading island: "In Colonial times it was part of the mainland and, not long since, was within wading distance of the shore; but tide erosion has widened the channel and reduced the island's many acres to one."

Powerhouse hurricanes during the 1950s—among them Hazel, Connie, Ione, Diane—sank at last what little was left of the island.

Whatever we may make of the legend of Jesse Batz or the thin history of Nathaniell Batts, the parable of this island, the late Batts Grave, is the very real story of our coastal future.

When I heard about a party from East Carolina having "found" the lost Batts Island in the 1970s, I sought out and asked East Carolina geologist Vince Bellis about that find.

Bellis reported coming upon a lone dead cypress in the Albemarle Sound nearly three-quarters of a mile off Yeopim Creek. His team also "found it on the 1849 smooth sheet used by the Coast and Geodetic Survey to create the navigation charts. Batts Grave (*sic.*) is shown and was used as a triangulation station for the survey. . . . Based on the scale of the smooth sheet," Bellis wrote, "*I estimated the island as being 10 ac in 1849.* The 1915 smooth sheet does not show a land mass, although it was again used as a triangulation station." On an earlier document, the federal navigation chart *Albemarle Sound 1860*, Batts Island is clearly situated approximately a mile and a quarter east of Drummond's Point and just under a mile south of the mainland east of the Yeopim River's mouth, its shape a bit like South America a quarter turn clockwise.

Never mind that the word "grave" is close cousin to "greave," among the meanings of which is *the sandy shore of a river*, or, given the orchard once upon the island, that "grave" might even be a corruption of "grove." A generation and a half after Vince Bellis found that lone cypress, at a spot almost due east of Drummond's Point about three-quarters of a mile off the Chowan and Perquimans mainlands, the charts still show what must pass as the grave of Batts Island, symbolically close by each other as the natural lovers Jesse and his Indian maiden Kickowanna (though, alas, not Nathaniell and the Widow Woodhouse) would naturally have had it:

A pair of *Stumps*.

Wild *rosa Carolina* was in bloom, its pale pink flowers in the old creekside cypress stumps, on the blue-sky June day several years back when Jake Mills and I put in at Conaby Creek and N.C. 45, just east of Plymouth in the three-rivers area of the lower Roanoke River basin. Here the Roanoke and the Middle and the Cashie Rivers drain down and, braiding together, very nearly become one, not unlike the way the South Edisto and Ashepoo and Combahee do in South Carolina's low country. We wound downstream in his fourteen-foot Boston Whaler for the big river itself and the lower Purchace Islands there. At midweek, only one other pickup and boat trailer lay up in the ramp's parking lot, so we knew we would have both creek and river pretty much to ourselves, and that the only noise we'd likely hear other than an osprey's *scree* would be our own.

Out of sight, off in the ripshin-thicket interior of the forest we floated through grew patches of pond pine and juniper, protected by impassable pocosin growth—sweetbay and redbay, pepperbush, ti-ti and dog hobble—from any casual foot traffic. As these woods were timbered for cypress over the century between the 1870s and 1970s, the logging was done by barge, and naturalist Merrill Lynch wrote in 1981 that there were "no roads, tramroads, canals, or other landscape modifications within the tract."

Wild country, even at this late date.

Crossing the bar at the mouth of Conaby Creek, the depthfinder went to work, its reading dropping from five feet quickly to thirty-four feet out in the big Roanoke itself. This quick shift forecast the wide and rapidly varying underwater topography Jake and I would find as we floated and sounded our way all around the Purchace Islands. Though here in the lower river we were sixty miles west of the Atlantic's breakers, as we headed for the embayment that was Albemarle Sound, we threaded through islands that were essentially *at sea level*.

Jake turned the Whaler downriver from Conaby's mouth, Rice Island now to our left. We passed only the long narrow Louse Island, spying a few crabpot floats and just one lone cypress as we boated out into Albemarle Sound between Swan Bay and Batchelor Bay, rounding Rice. The brilliant late-morning sun lit the big broad sound with all the light in the world, an unrelenting sheen, and stirred up enough of a breeze that we were pre-

*He stood for a moment—a child, alien and lost in the green and soaring gloom of the markless wilderness. Then he relinquished completely to it.*
*—William Faulkner, The Bear (1942)*

sented with a light chop at the mouth of Eastmost River, the distributary of Middle River separating Rice from Goodmans Island.

Mullet were jumping as we crossed the three-foot bar and found a twenty-foot bottom just inside the Eastmost. Every now and again we would pass a pale green stretch of freshwater marsh grass, twenty feet here, forty feet there, fringing the river's edge, so much brighter than the darker swamp-island woods behind (maple and cedar and pine mostly) that even in this midsummer noontime each reach of grass seemed to shine like a lamp.

At the head, or top, of Goodmans Island, Jake and I found a surprise, a fascinating geo-feature, an enormous hole that the Middle and Eastmost Rivers had collaborated on corkscrewing and scouring out. Right where the Middle distributes Eastmost to the right while going off itself to the left toward the Cashie River, we were cruising smartly along, the Whaler's gauge showing depths of four feet, eight feet, eleven feet and so on, till suddenly the sounding plummeted and hit *sixty-eight feet*. After running down the Middle along slender, drowned Wood Island to the Cashie and coming about near the mouth of Cashoke Creek and Terrapin Point, we returned to this deep hole, swinging the boat back and forth over it this second time till we now hit a depth of *sixty-nine feet*, reckoning the hole to measure about thirty yards across and about fifty yards long, coming upstream from the head of Goodmans Island. Years hence I would learn that natives of Plymouth referred to it as "the tourist hole," because they liked to ride outlanders over it and amaze them with this local mystery spot— whether or not it rivals Iceland's Snaefellsness Glacier as a journey-to-the-center-of-the-earth cavity, it is a most mesmerizing depth nonetheless.

"Don't you wonder what all's down there?" I asked Jake as I stared over the side of the boat, pondering that submarine shaft.

"Well," he said, head and hatbrim atilt, studying the depthfinder, "I can tell you there're *some* fish sitting way down there, within just a few feet of that deepest depth—looks like a catfish big enough to tow us *away* from here!"

Up Middle River the Whaler now crept, Huff Island below us, Great Island above, keeping company only with herons, crows, and buzzards, the depths beneath us ranging from ten to twenty-two feet. When at the Middle's last upstream bend we found a forty-three-foot hole, Jake pronounced, "Mountainous terrain." He was speaking of the relief of this part of the outer coastal plain before the ocean's rise thousands of years ago flooded the sounds and turned a small simple creek into the Roanoke River, one of eastern America's major drains. "That's what these depths suggest." Great Island, off to our right, seemed none too mountainous, though, being

*Lower Middle River,*
*Albemarle Sound*
*beyond, June 2002*

flat, layered with boggy mucky peat, its forest just as swampy as it ever got anywhere: bald cypress and water tupelo. On that island's far side, black-water creeks named Grennel and Broad lazed into the Cashie River, and sunfish there drew locals with hook and line.

In another mile, where the Middle flows off the Roanoke, we found an osprey on a log, tearing a fish apart for lunch, while a turtle on the log's other end paid neither that proceeding nor our piloting by any mind at all.

A few folks fished languidly from the banks of the Roanoke at the small grassy park that lay between the river and the backs of the short commercial buildings of downtown Plymouth. Time itself seemed becalmed—it might have been 1955, or 1910, 1880 even. As we floated downriver past the historic little port, I warranted that nothing about the riverine face of the town and its extraordinarily quiet, relaxed waterfront suggested that in this very place 20,000 soldiers and sailors once clashed in North Carolina's second largest Civil War engagement, the Battle of Plymouth, a three-day brutality that ran from April 17 to 20, 1864. Hoke's Confederate forces, attacking the occupying Federal garrison from south and east, in league with the Confederate ram *Albemarle* that sank one Union ship and ran off another, for a time retook the port that had served the Union as military chokepoint on the Roanoke. Two weeks later, the *Albemarle* would stand off seven Yankee gunboats at the mouth of the Roanoke, but, before the year was out, under cover of darkness on October 27, a Union lieutenant named Cushing would boat up the river, lay a torpedo up under *Albemarle*'s metal decking, explode it and sink her—losing his own craft and two of his men in the bargain, and then swim safely away.

On Halloween 1864, Union forces retook Plymouth.

A silver-and-black roadside marker might toss you the bare bones of all this, with still more to tell inside the small old brick Atlantic Coast Line station that fronted the river and now found itself being a museum full of maps and flags and ordnance. But from the Roanoke herself, you would get none of it, nor know nor ever guess that the riverside Grace Episcopal Church once gave up her very pews and gallery planking to make coffins for the Civil War dead.

An old mill chimney now rose over the east side of town, and a barge converted with barnboard superstructure, a river rat's paradise, appealed to both Jake and me, drawing our approval and longing gazes, but she already looked quite spoken for. Back at Conaby Creek, we crossed the bar going back in with a reading of two feet. Then something submerged struck the depth-gauge's transponder, and suddenly it was telling us we were in 191 feet of water and we knew it was time, before we got maelstromed to China, to head upstream a bit and find a cypress to tie up to and have lunch.

As we sat there in our shaded craft, a Bayliner slid by us, a middle-aged white man and a black woman out cruising; another of these floating sofas soon roared by, never slowing at all and so setting up huge wake waves against shore, a man at the wheel and his throttle full out and a blonde beside him, her big hair whipping out behind her like a flag in a gale. We had Vienna sausages aplenty and, too, some of the Lone Star beer Jake had brought back from a recent tour of Texas. Now we took on the pose and role of that turtle on the log back up the Roanoke, calmly witnessing an overpowered boat's sound and fury, signifying nothing.

A fine June day indeed: we had had most of six hours in this lowdown territory, the very bottom of the big bottom, encountering only a half a dozen other boats in all. We lazily followed an osprey for a mile or two after lunch, and called it a day. As we took out back at the N.C. 45 ramp, I thought about the nearly-forgotten island above us that Conaby carves off from the south side of the Roanoke River: Guard's Island. According to George Swain, who lived upon it, the story was that a Federal troop payroll, all in gold, got lost on Guard's Island during the Civil War and was never recovered, and now all memory of the long lost gold is *itself* almost forgotten.

Almost.

Several days later, I was back home in the red-clay hills when Jake called, hydrology on his mind. "I told Jack Long about our river excursion," he said. "Since he's an engineer by training and works with the soil and water authority I asked him about that deep hole we found, and he said you were right about the corkscrew effect that probably dug and is still digging the underwater well. Said that happens in a lot of places where two creeks meet, as at a place on Blount's Creek where he lives, where the depth drops from about ten to thirty feet at the conjunction of two tributaries.

"Guess that's where all the lost things go," Jake said, adding:

"I put two new taillights, the whole assembly, on the boat and they work fine now. I won't need em in Hyde County, though. My neighbor from there says nobody gives signals cause everybody knows where everybody else is going anyhow.

"Where I'm going is after a Lone Star. . . ."

―――――――――

Captain John Smith, designator of Heriots Ile, also tagged these lower Roanoke islands as the "Purchace Iles," for they too appear on his 1624 map of Virginia. He did not call them so on account of some Manhattan-style trinkets-for-terrain trade or "purchase," but rather to salute his friend Samuel Purchas (*Pur'kus*) (1575?–1626), the extraordinarily popular, widely read travel writer of early-seventeenth-century England.

Vicar Purchas of Eastwood, Essex, for a decade met mariners dockside at the nearby port of Leigh as they came off their ships, writing down their myriad accounts of sailing all about the globe, adding commentary of his own as bolstered by his reading of printed and manuscript sources—Captain Smith's included. In 1613 Purchas published the first version of the thoroughgoing book King James I would read seven times: *Purchas his Pilgrimage. Or Relations of the World and the Religions Observed in All Ages and Places Discovered into this Present.*

Samuel Purchas himself would never leave England, but Captain Smith would do him the honor and favor of leaving the noted traveloguist's name on, or in, the lower Roanoke River isles. Nine of them figure into this collage: Louse, Rice, Goodmans, Wood, Great, Huff, Conine, Tabor, and one unnamed island. Though not in the Purchace Islands by name, Jamesville Island, created by Cut Cypress Creek, and the massive, 9,000-acre Bull Run

Island are both right in among them, and how Bull Run escaped inclusion might mystify one were there not something bigger to consider: the presence upon it of a huge, abandoned and long-lost logging locomotive.

On Conine Island, uppermost of the Purchace group, in the 1950s I saw my first egret. It stood below the U.S. 17 causeway on the downriver side, one leg up, pausing between moments of fishing or perhaps fishing in that extraordinarily patient way of the big wading birds. And, in the early 1960s, one of the wildest thunder-and-hail storms I ever partook of hit right here, just a little east of Conine Creek, a bottom-fell-out downpour so vicious it shook and frightened me more than all Hurricane Hazel's wind and rain had, a storm so loud with rain so blinding that had my mother not pulled our small Chevrolet Bel Air station wagon carefully off onto the roadshoulder we might well have merged then and there with all this mighty jungle.

In 1977, the Nature Conservancy's Merrill Lynch, a rangy, mustached upriver boy from Roanoke Rapids, threw himself into the cypress and gum flats, the swamp pocosin forests, all of the big Roanoke bottom, and over four years took its measure like few men ever have, emerging with a deeper knowledge of what was growing and living in it than almost anyone since European contact. Maybe the legendary old-time Occoneechee Neck trapper Q. J. Stephenson had once known it better. Maybe. Lynch, though, was the man who in 1981 wrote the plan for how to protect and preserve eastern America's greatest lowland hardwood swamp, and due to this propulsion and guidance there now existed an enormous Roanoke River Conservation Project, 60,000 acres under protection, a figure that may ere long come up to 100,000 acres—a territory very nearly the equal of the nearby Great Dismal Swamp National Wildlife Refuge.

By the summer of 2005 twelve large tent-camping platforms awaited intrepid paddlers, broad wooden floors cantilevered in among cypress and gum, colonizing the floodplain in generally out of the way (what, indeed, in this wild bottom was exactly *in the way*?) crooks with names like Barred Owl Roost, Beaver Tail, Cypress Cathedral, and Bear Run—with Lost Boat and Otter One over on the Cashie River, and Tillery, a high-bluff perch over the Roanoke. When in early spring my old friend and fellow Red Clay Rambler Clay Buckner and his then-bride-to-be Jamie Allison boated in (from Gardner's Creek to Devil's Gut to Lower Deadwater Creek) and spent the night at Barred Owl Roost, they found it true to its name. Clay and Jamie said they bore witness to a constant avian concert through the long swamp night, and slept not.

"Being rather knackered we dozed right off, but not for long," Clay told me. "Within moments the swamp around us was alive with the sounds of,

*Kuralt Trail,*
*Conine Island,*
*September 2004*

as near as I could tell, the Haunted Amazonian Rain Forest. Howler monkeys screamed at each other through the night (all night), ghosts wailed, and, pretty frequently, grown women were murdered in the treetops. I have not been in the presence of such an uproar since the last time I attended a top fuel drag race. Apparently there is more than one kind of owl out there."

On a little islet back in the Sweetwater Creek area just downriver of Williamston, on a Good Friday float a few years back, after paddling into the bottom beneath hanging hanks of Spanish moss and past tarantula-sized spiders suspended over the shallows and cottonmouths in camouflaged coils almost invisible atop tall cypress knees, a bunch of us stood listening to Jeff Horton of Windsor, then the conservancy's Roanoke preserve manager, as he described the disruptive effects of flows out of the upriver dams at Kerr Lake and Lake Gaston. Destructive flows—too much water standing in the floodplain during growing season. How hard the conservancy and others have worked, trying to get the Corps of Engineers, which regulates the Kerr Lake flows, and Dominion Power, which sets the Gaston flows, to allow water flowing into the undammed lower Roanoke below Weldon to mimic the natural flows of years past, and, thereby, to allow the forest and wildlife, the floral and faunal communities within this great refuge, to maintain their character, to sustain themselves and remain something of what they were and had long been.

Not that the natural flows of old hadn't been problematic. Before the dams of the 1950s, heavy spring rains in the upper basin created walls of water—ten or twenty feet high, or greater—and sent them cascading down into the lower river, earning the Roanoke its unsentimental nickname, *River of Death*. An enormous flood poured through the basin in 1940, rerouting streams, inspiring authors (Mebane Burgwyn's 1947 adventure novel *River Treasure*), and cresting at twenty feet, five inches at Williamston—the greatest known flood-crest—on August 22, 1940, flood stage there being ten feet!

The Roanoke had grown that week in almost no time from a hundred yards wide to four miles broad as it submerged its bottomlands in brick-red waters and took whatever it wanted. Hundreds of acres of peas were lost. Between 5,000 and 10,000 acres of cotton, peanuts and corn went under in Bertie County. Watermelons floated, rabbits climbed trees. Three hundred convicts trying with sandbags to keep the flood from overtopping the causeway connecting Williamston and Windsor lost that battle one morning at dawn. The Gardner sisters—Annie Mae and Carrie Dell—of Smithwick Island nearly drowned when the roiling waters flipped them out of their small boat, and they clung to tree limbs till they were rescued. On Moore Island, farmer Frank Barber and a small boy were found trying to save tobacco Barber had already cured—the markets' opening was only days away. "Advised [by the Coast Guard] that the waters would not leave a dry spot on the islands," reported the *Williamston Enterprise*, "the old farmer looked out on a hundred acres of fine crops and turned his head to hide the tears that trickled down his face. . . . A dozen or more hogs and three hound dogs seemed to keep their eye on him as if they were looking to him for safety."

The Coast Guard, many guardsmen having come in from the Outer Banks stations to help, was heroic. The *Raleigh News and Observer* told of a twin-engine Grumman amphibian flying a two-hour aerial survey over the Roanoke's flooded bottom, calling it "the first errand of mercy of the new Coast Guard Air Station of Elizabeth City." And the *Enterprise* saluted them outright: "The Coast Guard forces that morning had risked their equipment and their lives going through treetops, grape vines, and thick trees to make sure that everyone had been removed from the islands."

Even with managed flows in the here and now, the Roanoke's waters could still be highly unpredictable: though 2002 was the driest year ever on record for the Roanoke River, 2003 was the wettest. During the growing season of 2003, 72,500 acres of Roanoke hardwood bottomland lay underwater from March through August, drowning tupelo and cypress seedlings and putting epic stress upon the great forest. Once the basinwide floodwaters fell away back into the river's channel, what they left was a foot or two of sludge, and, when Hurricane Isabel came in at Hog Island later in September and headed for the western Albemarle, Isabel's surge floated this sludge and released it into the lower Roanoke and occasioned one of the biggest fishkills the river has ever known—even doing in eels.

As North Carolina Nature Conservancy's director of science and stewardship Sam Pearsall said, critiquing the noxious water of Isabel's legacy:

"It takes a *lot* to suffocate an *eel*!"

By the middle of 2005, two full years later, satellite eyes had seen for us an awesome truth: photosynthesis in this basin had not yet recovered from that extended flooding of '03. Sam Pearsall said he had come upon beech trees growing on ridge-and-swale terrain in the bottom where they should not, yet he found no regeneration of bottomland hardwood.

"Water impounded on the floodplain wouldn't happen in a naturally fluctuating river," said Pearsall, "but it happens very often on the Roanoke."

What difference did it all make? What did it matter?

*Slough, Roanoke
bottomlands,
September 2004*

When Pearsall came to Carolina from Tennessee in the early 1990s, he had picked up the Roanoke plan and started going after those whose hands were on the levers at the dams, who were treating the lower river and its

islands as a drain of no consequence to them. He worked for many who knew it mattered fundamentally that a natural river would not normally behave like the Roanoke has been made to behave, like one being used for the generation of cheaply made, dearly bought electric power, without regard for the consequences to fish, animal, *or* forest life in the bottom-lands below the last dam and below the falls. Wildlife is only so adaptable, after all.

"Bats roost by entering trees through openings in the bottom," Pearsall said. "They won't go in at the top—so, if flooded, that tree is inaccessible to them as a nesting site."

After years of stakeholder negotiating for *adaptive management* on the lower Roanoke with Dominion Power, the owner and operator of the two dams downriver of the Corps of Engineers' Kerr Dam, Sam Pearsall was finally, in 2005, able to grin and say: "We've got a plan and it's working. We've got a forty-year commitment—we'll monitor these things and get better flows. Ten years ago they said, 'We start measuring flows and next thing they'll want to measure butterflies.' And now we got butterflies." This long-range monitoring would also include tree seedlings, fish, ter-restrial crayfish, aquatic macro-invertebrates, and bank erosion—in short, a good deep look into the river's life and health.

Most of the water in the Albemarle lagoon, the largest enclosed embay-ment in the world, comes from Albemarle Sound, and most of the water in Albemarle Sound comes down out of the Roanoke River valley and through its lowlands and swamps. Pray for this jungle, and the freshwater that flows through it. Pray that a tongue of saltwater, which will intrude into Albemarle Sound as the ocean rises, takes its long slow time getting to and licking away at Swan Bay's deep peatlands at the Roanoke's mouth, for salt will surely melt that peat away faster than methane will rot it.

Anyone wanting a true hold, a powerful purchase on wild territory such as Ike McCaslin learned from Sam Fathers in Faulkner's *The Bear* need look no farther than right here in the lower Roanoke. Going down that river—from its rich blue *camassia* slopes in Occoneechee Neck to its ridge-and-swale territory and its deep and seemingly endless cypress swamps till at last its drowned cypress mouths of Roanoke—is to traverse the massive jungle that met the first Europeans, Ralph Lane and his men in early 1586, when they were pushing on to the brink of starvation, searching for silver as if their souls depended on it. One might well have expected then, thereafter, and even now, only rude and desperate men like the old governor Batts to be living in this territory. Only South Carolina's Santee Swamp—whose ten- and twelve-foot cypress went down before the blade in the early 1940s—ever rivaled it.

The Purchace Islands lie in our last big bottom, last of the eastern South's truly huge hardwood bottomland swamps. The river to which they belong, the Roanoke, is our Amazon.

### KNOTTS ISLAND

When New Currituck Inlet closed in 1828, the waters of long, broad Currituck Sound quickly passed from being salt to fresh, though the powerhouse Atlantic still retained prime rights to make occasional seawater incursions, two notable occasions being in the year 1846.

Knotts Island scribe Henry Beasley Ansell wrote of the effects of the first of these, an early March nor'easter: "The people living on the midland of the Island did not know what had taken place on its waterfronts, but the news flew that the Atlantic was now breaking on the Island shores. I with others went down to the bay side. Such a sight had never been seen before. No marsh, no beach. The tops of a few mountainous sandhills were all that could be seen. The great salt waves were beating, pounding and breaking at our feet."

Note well that Ansell was describing Knotts's eastern shore, a good three miles west of the seabeach at Currituck Banks! Ansell, but a boy of fourteen at the time, observed men boarding a twelve-oared boat, forming a rescue party that would be successful in plucking two families—those of the expert gunners Cooper and Bowden, natives of Knotts Island who had moved out to the Banks to be closer to good waterfowling grounds—from the garret of a house the rescuers found anchored, afloat, and tied to liveoak treetops.

Saltwater from the storm stood six to eight feet deep in the piney woods of western Knotts Island, and few pines survived the spring inundation. Ansell described melodramatically that forest scene in the summer of 1846: "By some freak of nature a lone pine could be seen here and there draped in green, looking like a single sentinel guarding his dead comrades under a flag of truce, waiting for the burial party."

No less weird and intriguing was the dead cedarwood the nor'easter revealed out on the Currituck Banks themselves, by washing away the sand dunes that in migrating westward had buried the forest. Ansell's Uncle Johnny Beasley, having boiled salt forty-odd years earlier in those woods when they were still green—a War of 1812 effort—now after the March 1846 storm led a crowd out to look for his decades-lost salt kettles, huge three-foot by six-foot affairs, ten inches deep. These folks found and dug out two of the three big kettles, then split the dead cedars to use as boat timbers.

*Ille terrarum mihi praeter omnis angulus ridet. [This corner of the earth pleases me more than any other.]*
—The Swan Island Club Motto, from Horace, Odes, Book II (ca. 24 B.C.)

Then came the early September hurricane of 1846, the same storm that to the south opened both Hatteras and Oregon Inlets, the ocean again overwashing the Currituck Banks and flooding the sound, with tides running so high before the storm, Ansell reported, that "schools of porpoises promenaded the [Knotts Island] channel, and all kinds of salt water fish were abundant. . . . I caught with a hook six flying fish, the first I ever saw. . . . The water was so full of fish that we could catch them without bait by drawing the hook swiftly through the water. . . . No one had ever caught a fish with a hook on the Great Shoal. . . . That school of fish presaged the storm which swept through the island that very night."

Ansell's lengthy manuscript lay unpublished in his lifetime, though *Elizabeth City Independent* editor and publisher W. O. Saunders brought it out serially in his newspaper as *Recollections of My Boyhood on Knotts Island* in late 1934 and early '35. In addition to his reportage of Knotts and the natural world, long-lived native Ansell (1832–1920) gave voice to some of the island's superstitions, none quite so arresting as the clear and simple reason why Knotts Island folk refused to scent their lard with rosemary. A witch had once been seen boating through Currituck Inlet at sunrise—she came ashore at Knotts Island and promptly planted a rosemary bush on island soil. Since rosemary had come to America by the agency of a witch, many islanders would not use the herb, as Ansell said, "to this day."

———

When the intrepid Northerner Nathaniel Holmes Bishop boated down Currituck Sound in his lightweight shellacked paper canoe early one December in the 1870s, he was a waterborne witness to the salt-to-freshwater changes that agrarian Edmund Ruffin had reported decades earlier, shortly after Currituck Inlet's closure. Ruffin had observed that "the oysters and other sea shell-fish all died; the water grasses were entirely changed in kinds." Now Bishop wrote that "The sound is filled with sandy shoals, with here and there spots of mud. The shells of the defunct oysters are everywhere found mixed with the debris of the bottom of the sound."

On an epic small-boat traverse from upstate New York to the Gulf of Mexico, Bishop had hereabouts seen "clouds of ducks, and some Canada geese, as well as brant" fluttering continuously as they lifted up and away off the water. "Away to the southeast extended the glimmering bosom of the sound, with a few islands relieving its monotony." After a night boarding in the then-as-now tiny settlement of Currituck Courthouse, which he spent before Mrs. Simmons's "grand old fireplace" talking about Carolina's native viticulture with Doctor Baxter, "the physician of the place," Bishop got a blacksmith to fix the outrigger's juncture with his rowlock—broken as he and his small craft had labored under heavy north wind the day before—and then continued boating, heading down the west side of the sound.

No sooner had he reached Coinjock Bay, only a few miles below Currituck Courthouse, than a big storm blew up from the south. Bishop rowed quickly for cover at Bell Island Point, where Captain Peter Tatum, elder "proprietor of Bell Island," waved the traveler in and gave him shelter at his and his wife's cottage.

The next day, Thursday December 10, 1874, Bishop fought "a swashy beam sea," abandoning his plan to go down the western side of the sound along Church's Island and instead rowing south to the head of Coinjock Bay, portaging eastward back over to the sound from there, and then rowing south to Currituck Narrows for the night. At Van Slyck's Landing (now Poplar Branch) he was pleased to find "a comfortable hotel" that catered to Yankee gunners. On Friday the eleventh, he kept to the sound's west side, passing Rattlesnake Island, Marsh Island and Long Point Island, then at Dew's Quarter Island getting himself advised by another elder to go on and cross Currituck—"Git across the sound afore the wind rises. Sich a boat as that aren't fit for these here waters"—and then hug the back of the Outer Banks on down to Colington Island, which he did, eventually finding a room at dusk in one of the old Nags Head hotels.

All along the Currituckian way, west side and east, Bishop had seen hunters in their pine-boughed blinds, "which looked like little groves of *conifera* growing out of the shoal water." He heard their big guns booming constantly, and saw not carved but *live* "decoy-birds" anchored and floating near the blinds.

"The best 'gunning points,' " Bishop wrote, "are owned by private parties, and cannot be used by the public."

Indeed. The circa 1881 *Prospectus of the Kitty Hawk Bay Sportsman's Club —Property Located in Currituck and Dare Counties, North Carolina, Comprising 40,000 Acres of Land and the Control of Many Square Miles of Water*, put forth by one E. E. Pray, reported Currituck Sound's island geography in detail, as it related to the waterfowling trade's locking-up rights thereto, and the rates therefore, for example: "Grandy's Island—Three hundred acres, more or less, located in Big Narrows, near Van Slyk's Landing, interspersed with numerous fresh ponds. Ten years' lease, privilege of extension, annual rental $225. Due Nov. 1st, each year. All kinds fowl shooting."

A spate of testimonials in Pray's brochure kept telling, and selling, the story. "Sandford Dunton and myself have killed in seven days nine hundred and thirty-six canvass-back and red-head ducks in Big Narrows, in the vicinity of Rattlesnake and Long Point," W. H. Walker reported on May 18, 1881, adding that "the grounds of this immediate locality were selected for

*Children on long
dock, Church's Island,
about 1908*

the shooting of the Grand Duke Alexis and party." (This particular grand duke, fourth son of Tsar Alexander II of Russia, had made a so-called "goodwill visit" to the United States a decade earlier, though the trip was apparently a collage of bon-vivantry and hunting—he had also shot eight buffalo on a hunt with Buffalo Bill Cody.) On that same day in 1881, when Mister Pray was obviously out collecting commentary for his *Prospectus*, Walker's hunting companion Dunton said that he had "killed from a blind on Brant Island last winter over one hundred canvass-back duck in one day with an old-fashioned muzzle-loading gun."

Though the 1870s and 1880s were seeing the divvying up of the Carolina sounds' shooting grounds, it was not quite *all* going to royalty, the quality, and outsiders—the prototypical non-native, wealthy Northern sportsmen. When H. H. Brimley of the State of North Carolina's Museum visited Currituck just a few years after the Pray *Prospectus*, in February 1884, he did so in the company of Uncle Ned Midyette of Church's Island, who used three-log dug-out sailing canoes—each of them big enough, Brimley wrote, to carry a half a dozen cattle—to get his *market*, not *sport*, hunters and his four shooting batteries out to areas of the sound where each battery's two-man team could do its work for pay. Brimley recalled that Canada geese went for half a dollar—four ducks equaled "a pair," and per-pair prices of that day were a dollar for canvasback, fifty cents for redhead, and two bits for teal, ruddy and buffleheads.

Prices rose in the coming years to such an extent that market-gunning was Currituck's big business—during the first decade of the 1900s, 400 Currituck market hunters were doing a volume slaughter with eight-gauge cannons called "punt guns" and sharing a $100,000-a-year income, real money a century ago. One of the best at this prolific wing-shooting was a man named St. Clair Lewark, who during November 1905 with his partners shot and shipped 2,300 ruddy ducks and then split $1,700 cash four ways, Lewark alone having taken nearly 300 ruddy ducks in a single day!

More tension than the surface of Currituck Sound abounded. Once the Audubon bird-protection law was in place, one Currituck game warden going after a firelighter—an illegal night hunter—in early 1908 got himself shot for trying to enforce the law. Warden James Evans took pellets in the face and elsewhere, yet, though he caught up with his assailant and identified him, that was the end of it. For both firelighting *and* assault with a deadly weapon, the night hunter got no conviction in court—the miscreant walked.

Writer Alexander Hunter, touring the South in the twentieth century's first decade, took a good hard look at Currituck, his first observation of the waterfowling situation there none too flattering:

*Huntclub pillar,*
*Knotts Island,*
*September 2004*

"Shooting every day of the week; gunners everywhere, blinds, batteries and sink-boxes sown thick over Currituck Sound; market-gunners, poachers, irresponsible guides, thoughtless, improvident natives, game-hogs who slaughter duck in the nighttime, had, early in the season, either killed, crippled or frightened the ducks away." On this particular trip, Hunter chose instead to try his luck with some clubmen from the Ragged Islands of Virginia's Back Bay.

Yet he later gave Currituck her full due, making in 1908 a survey of the sound's many waterfowling clubs, noting the reason the game was there in the first place: "The bottom is as thickly covered with wild celery as a well-kept lawn with grass." He confirmed the highly proprietary scene in the sound—"There is not a foot of this ground in the whole territory that is not owned, registered by title-deeds, recorded in the archives, and watched over as if it sheltered a gold mine." He visited the fine, now-legendary clubs built by Northern wealth, by publishing and steel monies, among them: the Swan Island Club (where the keeper kept a rooftop rifle-on-pivot ready to fire warning, warding-off shots at would-be poachers); the Currituck Club ("with a fine library and well-stocked wine-cellar"); and the Lighthouse Club ("oldest, most companionable, easy-going, hospitable sporting combination in the locality"). Due to single-gender companionability, though, this club was later, in the 1920s, bought and folded into the enormous, copper-roofed Whalehead Club at Corolla, so that owner Edward Knight of Philadelphia could bring his wife into this formerly-females-proscribed territory and do so without the embarrassment of wild-hog, anything-went partying.

Hunter included in his 1908 survey the native variant, the market hunters' shanty, which he called the "Poor Man's Club": "A bunk with some straw, a little sheet-iron stove, a frying-pan, coffee-pot, and tin plate constitute the commissariat; while the one room answers the purpose of half a dozen. The bar is represented by a stone jug of villainous corn whiskey that would lay out any one but a North Carolina coast-man. This 'club' consists of two market-hunters; and the lank, lean, unshaven pair manage to bag more game than the largest syndicate on the sound."

---

After market-gunning was outlawed in 1918, a powerful demarcation still stood between Currituck County's native gunners, reduced now to pot-hunting, and the county's many clubs and their members from well beyond Currituck's borders.

At two o'clock in the afternoon on Thanksgiving 1920, two young men of Powells Point on mainland or peninsular Currituck County set out in a fourteen-foot rowing skiff "to go goosing" in the soundside marshes of Currituck Banks. James Shannon and Derwood Gallop pulled several miles, crossing Currituck Sound and coming into the marshes of the Pine Island Club at just about sundown. Then came two of Pine Island's "marsh guards," club employees St. Clair Lewark (a former member of the U.S. Life Saving Service as well as successful former market hunter) and John Wicker, approaching in their own skiff, Lewark cursing them, calling them "s.o.b.'s" and telling them if they came ashore he'd show them what he had in store for them.

Shannon and Gallop shoved off and away from the marsh, but when they had gotten only a hundred yards or so distant from the marsh guards, Lewark opened fire on them with a high-powered rifle. Gallop dropped down into the skiff, where Lewark's fifth shot, penetrating the side of the skiff a few inches above the waterline, caught him in the groin and gut. So wounded, Gallop then called out:

"Lewark, don't shoot me no more—you've shot me once!"

Lewark fired eight or ten more shots before he and Wicker went on around the marsh without offering any help to the wounded Gallop and his companion Shannon, who rowed for Sowers' Camp in the sound and, finding no one there and taking a quilt to wrap Gallop in, then made it on back to Betsy's Creek on the mainland about eight o'clock that night, and went for help.

"I didn't see him die," Shannon later said.

Derwood Gallop's father did, though, on Saturday night after Thanksgiving, and he heard his dying son (twenty-three years and eight months old) declare that it was St. Clair Lewark who had shot him. Shortly after young Gallop's death, Shannon's statement of all that had happened in the Pine Island marshes, *the* version thus far, resulted in the arrest of both Lewark and Wicker, who were picked up on Sunday as they left a lawyer's office in Elizabeth City, the Pasquotank riverport two counties west.

Feeling in Currituck ran so high against the marsh guards that they were held in the Elizabeth City jail for their own good and safety from late November until their March 1921 trial at a packed Currituck Courthouse, during the course of which a rather different depiction of the Thanksgiving events was revealed.

Lewark and Wicker said they were nowhere near the scene of the shooting of Derwood Gallop. Rather, they were in their camp, a houseboat tied up several thousand yards south of Ark Cove and Ark Cove Island, where Shannon said the shooting had occurred. Wicker had spent the afternoon working on an engine, and Lewark had gone out for a spell alone to check eelpots. Neither of them had ever laid eyes on Shannon and Gallop that day.

Furthermore, the superintendent of the Pine Island Club—Doctor Julian C. Baum—had been ensconced all afternoon, till after sunset, with club member Charles Ogden of New York City in a duckblind on the east side of The Shoeheel, a spot that lay *between* Lewark's and Wicker's houseboat and Ark Cove. Doctor Baum could see their camp, and *them*, and swore on a *Bible* that they had no high-powered rifles furnished them by the club and that they neither went to nor came from the scene of the shooting.

Congressman Hallet S. Ward joined solicitor (and future North Carolina governor) J. C. B. Ehringhaus and posed, for the state, simply that Lewark had boated to and fired upon Shannon and Gallop after sunset, *after* Baum and Ogden had left their Shoeheel blind. The congressman got the forty-four-year-old Lewark to admit, under cross-examination, that he kept three rifles at camp, one of them a .44 caliber, for protection—*marsh guard* being a dangerous occupation, he allowed, "due to the ill will between the native hunters and the club men."

Prominent Elizabeth City political foes E. F. Aydlett, a Democrat, and Ike Meekins, a Republican (who would become an eastern district federal judge for a generation) teamed up for the defense, and proposed the theory that some other party or parties unknown—*not* Lewark—had shot at Shannon and Gallop, having mistaken the two of them for Lewark and Wicker. The Thanksgiving gunfire, then, by this conjecture had really been an attack upon the marsh guards themselves!

Currituck sentiment had clearly swung way around. After a three-day trial the jury went out for only three hours, one of those hours spent at dinner, and returned with a verdict of *Not Guilty*. The furious judge, terming this one of the plainest cases for the state he had ever seen, gave the jury a tongue lashing before leaving the courtroom. Interpreting the verdict's message editorially, though, W. O. Saunders of the *Elizabeth City Independent* saw the locals as ultimately unwilling to smite the vast wealth arrayed in Currituck's huntclub culture, to which their county found itself in economic dependency. The jury took Doctor Baum's word over James Shannon's. The jury bought the defense's story of alternate attackers, phantoms never brought to justice for the murder of Derwood Gallop. Editor Saunders wrote:

"If the guards of Pine Island Club had been convicted of killing a resident gunner, every Club in Currituck County would have been given a black eye from which recovery would have been difficult."

One Currituck hunter, born the very year of the Lewark murder trial, much later recalled those times and those feelings. "A lot of people used to hate the hunt clubs," Vernon Creekmore, 82, told the *Raleigh News and Observer*'s David Cecelski in 2003. "Back years ago, before the clubs got so much of it, you hunted where you wanted to and nobody cared.... A lot of the local people felt like, you know, they came down here and had a bunch of money and stopped them from going in the marshes. The hunt clubs never bothered me. You knew where their property was and you just didn't go on it. I didn't want to go on it anyway."

### MACKAY ISLAND

Into this Currituck milieu nearly ninety years ago moved one of America's major millionaires, the printing and publishing tycoon Joseph Palmer Knapp of New York, son of a lithographer and a Methodist hymnwriter who had literally taken over his father's business (buying him out at the age of twenty-seven) and made it into an empire, purveying magazines like *Farm and Fireside* and *Women's Home Companion*, and, in time, six million *This Week*s every Sunday.

Knapp took an interest in the hunting lodge at Live Oak Point, the southwesternmost part of Mackay Island, adjacent to Knotts Island, at the north end of Currituck Sound—so far north, in fact, that the top of Knotts Island was a piece of the state of Virginia. Knapp bought the lodge and 7,000 acres off *Clansman* novelist Thomas Dixon, who in turn had gotten it in 1916 (just a year after his novel about the Ku Klux Klan had been made by D. W. Griffith into the now-classic film *Birth of a Nation*) from Norfolk's John L. Roper Lumber Company. Roper—an outfit that had already sawed its way across the Great Dismal Swamp and much of the rest of eastern North Carolina (with mills in Belhaven, New Bern and elsewhere)—had moved in on Mackay Island and built its crew quarters at Live Oak Point.

Dixon may have called the old lumberjack dorm a lodge, and Knapp may well have enjoyed Dixonian hospitality there before he owned it, but once the place was in Knapp's possession he very quickly decided he wanted a place in nature far more presidential. Knapp tore down the Roper building and put up a thirty-seven–room Mount Vernon of his own and kept a staff of sixty working the place. Rusticity, *adieu*! Then, with a powerful sense of *noblesse oblige* and *largesse* to match it, with a liberal baronial hand Knapp funded Currituck schools, libraries, government, and in his own way reigned here until his death in 1951.

With a liberal environmental sensibility to match, as well—for during his thirty Currituckian years, Knapp also had a goal of nothing less than the replenishment of the North American waterfowl population. In 1929 he brought John Huntington to Mackay Island, where he bred for release

*School, Knotts Island,*
*September 2004*

3,000 ducks that spring, a practice Knapp would successfully promote among thousands of farmers. By 1931 Knapp had hired Huntington and started a group called "More Game Birds in America," absorbing the earlier American Wild Fowlers and laying the organizational groundwork for the 1937 founding of Ducks Unlimited—all in all a visionary clutch of hunters who sought and meant to repopulate the flyways by repairing the drought-stricken Canadian breeding grounds for most of this continent's ducks and geese.

In this effort Knapp would enlist his friends, among them the textile chieftain and, by 1945, neighboring Dew's Quarter Island huntclub owner Richard Thurmond Chatham. Joe Knapp knew the way back and forth from Mackay to Dew's Quarter well enough—he and Depression-era Dew's owners George and Ramona Eyer, who held Dew's between 1929 and 1943, were said to have been great friends—before Chatham (of Winston-Salem and Elkin) took the place on during World War II. Referred to as Dew's Quarter Island in wills as antique as 1784 and 1810, the long lean north-south island on Currituck Sound's lower west side also got called, in olden times, Jew's Quarter Island and Deuces Quarter before Dew's Island, its now-popular name. One prior owner, a Doctor York Patchen of Westfield, New York, was still recalled in Jarvisburg just a generation ago for the wonderful roses he grew out on Dew's Island, and was remembered no less for the snakes he caught, smoked, and ate there.

Chatham's efforts at horticulture were even more exotic than Doctor Patchen's, though he may have consumed fewer snakes. In the early 1950s Congressman Thurmond Chatham dredged thousands of cubic yards from the floor of Currituck Sound and built up the land at Dew's Quarter Island, establishing Dew's Island Nurseries as a natural outgrowth of the water-fowling Dew's Island Club. He acquired *pangola* grass from the Cheeha-Combahee Plantation in low-country South Carolina, shipped English walnut and Japanese walnut and Chinese chestnut seedlings to John Wright Jr. of Jarvisburg, his manager at Dew's Island, even "some Tree Peony seeds I bought in Japan." The Chinese ambassador gave him some Chinese grass seeds ("I think it is a type of orchard grass"), which he also forwarded to Wright. Chatham even put a herd of Santa Gertrudis cattle on the island, livestock come all the way to Currituck from Texas's famed King Ranch.

His eye was always on the duck-and-goose sky, though. In October 1953, he wrote Manager Wright, entreating him: "I hope you are getting everything planted that you can heavily so that our friends from Canada will have good grazing." January 1954 saw Chatham well pleased with the shooting over the holidays and remarking to Wright: "I feel we had the best season in our history, due mostly to your supervision."

By June of that year, however, Chatham had to answer a challenge from the natives. A petition to him, the Fifth District's sitting congressman, from *100 fishermen and guides* in Currituck Sound observed that the Dew's Island dredging activity had left the water thick and muddy and caused game and fish to go elsewhere. "We feel that these operations are seriously handicapping our fishing and hunting activities, particularly in the South end of Currituck Sound."

Congressman Chatham, stating that he had "been fishing and shooting in Currituck for more than forty years," suspended the dredging at once, hoping to see an improvement with its cessation and to review it all in time. By February 1955, his attention was strong on trapping and banding ducks on the property's north pond and sending a report to the Wildlife Research Branch at Patuxent, Maryland, saying, "I think we will become an important banding center."

Author and philanthropist Frank Borden Hanes Sr. of Winston-Salem wrote me in 2004 about times he had spent out in Currituck, recalling that "Dew's Island had a separate charm and I had some wondrous times there. . . . The house had its own charm, old country furniture, fine kitchen and comfortable old bedrooms from which you could peruse the sound. . . . The island provided comestibles, and there was a pond adjacent to the

*Soundside lane, Live
Oak Point, Mackay
Island, October 2005*

collards patch where some folks shot wood ducks as they came in for the night. And another called North Pond where we tried to knock down ring necks as they dove like fighter planes.

"In those days (before World War II) you could be back in a float blind and shoot red heads which flew in flocks that are now non-existent."

Nowadays in Currituck, at Pine Island where St. Clair Lewark once guarded the marsh, the name of legendary artist-hunter John James Audubon hangs on, in the form of the Audubon Reserve there. And Knapp's name is everywhere. On the high flyover bridge spanning the Intracoastal Waterway at Coinjock, you will see the name Knapp. On the collection of North Caroliniana at the Currituck County Library, you will see it. On a marble graveslab enclosed by a brick wall, with small boxwoods nearby, in tiny Moyock twenty miles west, beneath the epitaph *Here was surely a masterful generous American*, there you will see it. Even on the School of Government building at the University of North Carolina at Chapel Hill, 200 miles west, will you also see his name.

And at Live Oak Point on Mackay Island, where the lumberjacks once roistered and where Dixon once invested some of his Hollywood money, near the glade where old Mackay, the original settler, is buried you will see upon a trail and upon a black marble monument too the name of this lover of birds in the wild, a name more recent than Audubon but of a man with a love no less strong, a mighty actor in the drama of protection and preservation of species, a man though not native now forever a resident of this place, Joseph Palmer Knapp of Currituck.

### MONKEY ISLAND

In my closet since boyhood has stood an Excel .410, a hardware-store shotgun from the early 1900s that either my grandfather got for himself or, later, got for my father, who gave it to me when I was about eight years old and just large and tough enough to tote and heft such a piece and take its kick. Only recently did I learn that, before my father gave it to me, he had earlier made a long-term loan of it to Travis Morris of Coinjock, son of my grandfather's and father's old friend Judge Chester Morris, and that Travis—sixteen years my senior—had later returned it to my father when Travis figured I was about the right age for it.

Judge Morris represented many of the hunting clubs out yonder on the Currituck islands, and Travis, who knows more about them than most anyone still alive, at one point ran the Monkey Island Club, during the years 1974 to 1978. The very place had once been in Travis's family way back—his great-great-grandfather Samuel McHorney sold it just after the Civil War for fifteen dollars. Travis himself operated Monkey Island for the first and

*Pamunkey Island Clubhouse, early 1900s*

only time as a *public* gunning club, getting out of it after ice killed the hunting season's end two years running—and after he had had, also due to ice in the sound, to airlift the resident caretaker and his mother-in-law off Monkey Island by helicopter. As he observed, much later, to me, "You know, way out there you're four miles from a box of matches."

It was Travis Morris who, during his time managing Monkey, in 1976 took pen in hand and wrote some of its story, from the time his kinsman let it go for a short fistful of dollars, up through the Northern-sportsmen era, till the Penn family of Reidsville came into the picture in the 1920s, with American Tobacco executive Charles Penn ("perfector of *Lucky Strike* cigarettes"—and therefore promoter of the acronym L.S.M.F.T., "Lucky Strike Means Fine Tobacco") joining the Monkey Island Club in 1927, becoming its president in 1930 and then buying out all the other members in 1931. Travis was managing Monkey for the Penns—Ed Penn had died in 1973, but brother Frank (a good friend of my father's) and other family heirs still had the property in 1976.

From Frank Penn, Travis heard more about the visitors, particularly the writers, Monkey Island had drawn over the years, men like: Bob Davis, *New York Sun* columnist whose regular offering was called "Over My Left Shoulder"; Elridge Warren, *Field and Stream* owner and publisher, who got Penn's nod for best shot he had ever seen—Warren would take only twenty-three shells out to the blind with him at a time when the bag limit was twenty-

*On the Currituck to*
*Knotts Island Ferry,*
*October 2005*

two ducks, saying he brought that last, extra shell to give to his hunting mate of the day; humorist Irvin S. Cobb, the famed "Duke of Paducah"; and Rollon Clark, a wildlife artist who carried only sketchpad and pen into the blinds and who kept returning to Monkey Island even after he lost his sight, loving the camaraderie and the very vapors of the place.

One of the individuals Travis Morris identified most strongly with Monkey Island was its fixer, its hands-on handyman for all seasons, Marcus Griggs of Coinjock, who during the thirty years after the end of World War II had "kept the boat running, the generator going before they had electricity, the plumbing fixed and anything else that needed fixing."

Travis recalled one stiff night about 1970, when he and fellow guide Hambone Twiford had some visiting hunters "tied out in Lighthouse Bay [behind Currituck Banks] in a float box. Just as we started to take up, the wind shifted to the northeast, turned cold, and blew a gale. . . . It was dark before we could get all the rig taken in and then we had to cross the sound to Waterlily. It was probably the worst night I have ever crossed the sound and also the darkest. When we tied up at Mr. Casey Jones' dock at Waterlily, I looked down the dock and Mr. Marcus was coming in behind me in the old Monkey Island battery boat (built in 1910). After he secured the boat and was walking up the dock dressed in his foulweather gear, he called to me and said, 'It's a rough night, ain't it, boy?' I assured him it was and asked what he was doing out in weather like this. He replied, 'The old furnace at Monkey Island broke down and I had to go fix it so they wouldn't freeze to death out there.' With those comments he got in his car and went home.

"Incidentally, the two sportsmen we had have never been back. I think they must have gotten scared to death that night."

Well as well do I remember the Monkey Island bulkhead failing twenty years ago, and waterfowl historian Neal Conoley recently told me the little island had eroded considerably and was now infested with cottonmouths. Of the island's demise due to inattention during the years since Fish & Wildlife has owned it, Travis Morris had said to me only: "I'd hate for you to see it like it is now—it'd make you sick."

That may be the truth, yet truth to tell that is not what I think of when I recall Monkey Island. I remember sitting with Ann one still October afternoon, watching a solitary teal swimming lazily along the sound shore near Pine Island, and her telling me about being out on Monkey Island's dock one flat calm summer night during a meteor shower, the stars falling from Perseus toward their own reflections rising from the water and meeting, over and over again, in a glorious, incandescent match. I remember going out to Monkey late one Friday afternoon in June with Jim Seay, the great Mississippi and Carolina poet, in his Boston Whaler, navigating the grass-beds in a chop and pulling into the Monkey Island dock at dusky dark, the lights left on in the clubhouse for us by the late waterman and caretaker Earl Baum, the weathervane with its ducks for compass points on a shaft down into the big clubroom turning in the sweet evening breeze. We sat out late on the long screened porch facing east and drank it all in, the full, red strawberry moon coming up and looming large over Currituck Banks.

And through the gauze of this hot thick night I gauged and saw my father's ghost.

He was lanky enough, a short man of five-foot-ten, a college boy who already had behind him one summer working the United Fruit banana boats and dodging tarantulas between Central America and Hampton Roads, and another summer heading West on a Georgia tour bus and seeing the Big Sky Country as far north as Banff in Alberta, Canada. He had caught the eastern Carolina milk-train home to Elizabeth City from school in Chapel Hill, and then caught a ride from there on down to Currituck.

*Apples, Knotts Island,*
*September 2004*

*Apple orchard,*
*Martin Vineyards,*
*Knotts Island,*
*September 2004*

Now he was stepping from the prow of the juniper skiff that had brought him out from the mainland landing to shoot ducks this wintry weekend about 1940 or '41. They say he was a great wing shot and that he made the trip often, nearly every weekend during hunting season. Frank Penn, who told me not six weeks before my father died that he had carried him out boating in Currituck Sound on what they both knew would be his last trip, said Daddy loved it way out there.

Having swum in the warm summer shallows behind the Banks, having driven the soft marshy soundside road, having pulled milfoil off the prop going up and down the sound, having boated hither and yon with the poet and seen that blood-red moon rise over the Banks and then, by day, seen the sun beat down on the marsh islands and bleach their grasses and then watched a rain curtain move in and lower itself gray and certain over

Currituck Sound and its islands, having fallen under a harvest moon's spell twenty years later with Ann and our daughter Cary as it rose and lit up Live Oak Point before we ferried across for picking apples and plucking scuppernongs on Knotts Island the next day, having seen it all up close and been in it and drunk deeply of it, I believe I know why.

Deep in 1587 I once sat, right on the edge of upper Shallowbag Bay across from Ice Plant Island, pondering the many seasons of loss that have claimed Roanoke Island and do not and will not let go. Not 1587 the year, but rather the half-timbered Manteo waterfront bistro of that name, which, like such other place names about town as Ananias Dare Street, have kept the early though not initial loss of this first English colonial redoubt ever in everyone's mind. I was having a slow ale with the man who was then captain of the *Down East Rover*, a two-masted topsail schooner moored at the Manteo docks just outside the bar doors in his island fiefdom—the *Rover*'s captain was also the dockmaster here at Dough's Creek.

*Nature feels no throb of pity Makes no pause for human heartbreak.*
—Sallie Southall Cotton, The White Doe, *or* The Fate of Virginia Dare: "An Indian Legend" *(1901)*

The spring night was dark and cool, and I stepped outside and stopped for a moment, looking down the street at the old brick 1904 courthouse that my grandfather Page helped build and wherein my grandfather Simpson practiced law. Walking from the waterfront back to a cedar-shingled barracks on Harriot Street, I thought again of the young scientist Thomas Harriot, Sir Walter Ralegh's apprentice and lieutenant, who was with the first colony of English who lingered here on this island, from fall 1585 till summer 1586. When this bunch, Captain Ralph Lane's crowd, scrambled just after a June hurricane to leave Roanoke for Francis Drake's waiting ships, Harriot in a small boat experiencing maritime melee in still-churning seas lost his year's worth of notes and all his scientific instruments.

Those seasons of loss that began so long ago, how were they peopled?

By the three soldiers Lane in his haste could not find and thus abandoned, by the fifteen more left behind soon thereafter by Sir Richard Grenville to guard the abandoned Roanoke outpost in the summer of 1586, men who under apparent attack later took to their lone boat and disappeared. By the John White expedition, the first attempt at implantation of a community of men and women, of real *settlers*, by the English in the New World in 1587, which vanished—and with it Virginia Dare, White's grandchild and first white child born on this continent and namesake for this county—sometime between White's voyage back to England for more support and supplies and his long-delayed return in 1590. By the Confederates nearly three centuries later who, encamped in forts on Roanoke, were totally routed by a Federal force that first shelled them from gunboats on Croatan Sound, then stomped through the Roanoke marshes and swamps

*Old Dare County*
*Courthouse, Manteo,*
*October 2005*

and came upon them and won for the Union its first major victory in February 1862. And by the scores and scores of runaway slaves drawn to this victorious Federal force, who made for themselves a freedmen's colony on the island's north end between Weir's and Pork Points, till they were dispossessed of it and lost it two years after the Civil War's end.

If ever a place in America has claimed loss as its theme, has long had loss playing its bass line, and has held fast to loss whether it wanted to or not, Roanoke Island is it. We are haunted forever by all of it, by all these disappearances, losses and undoings, from the distant past and the not-so-far-off as well: for in our own time, another disappearance still haunts Roanoke Island.

On the night of July the first, 1967, a young woman just shy of twenty named Brenda and a young man named Danny went out after a show to a small plain nightspot on the eastern edge of Roanoke Island, a watering hole on the causeway over to the beach called the Drafty Tavern. She sat and watched while he drank a beer and shot pool with another couple, and then they cruised across the bridge over Roanoke Sound in Danny's Corvair and watched the shark fishermen out on Jennette's Pier near Whalebone Junction, South Nags Head.

Later back at his place, a three-man bachelor pad in Manteo, Danny and Brenda went upstairs, reading a magazine and necking, he would recall, till he fell asleep after another beer. In the morning, so he said, she was gone.

She was thoroughly gone.

Brenda did not appear at her work that next day, nor the next. The Dare County sheriff's department and the State Bureau of Investigation moved in and launched a fullbore search, and Brenda's coworkers—assembled and informed that Brenda had gone missing—joined in. One of them remembered, nearly forty years afterward, being asked "to help search the road where she was last seen. It was a grisly task and I remember well, all of us out on the road poking with sticks in the woods and along the roadside, hoping that we would not find her."

The vanished young woman's purse and pants turned up on one of Manteo's side roads.

She herself was next seen on July the sixth in the cypress shallows of Mashoes, a remote community on mainland Dare County across Croatan Sound from Roanoke Island, spied by a small-plane pilot out searching for her. "An autopsy revealed that Brenda had been strangled," wrote the *Raleigh News and Observer* in 1997, "with a braided rope and dumped in the ocean."

Nothing tied Danny or anyone else to her death. No one was ever charged. No one stood trial for this poor soul's mistreatment and murder. An abusive Manteo dentist, according to the wife whom he abused, confessed to her of killing Brenda, following a drunken row with his wife—but this man did away with himself only four years after Brenda's death, and, whatever he knew, he died with it in him.

The case, though cold, has never been closed. Such was the sad and mysterious death of Brenda Joyce Holland—a native of papermaking Canton, North Carolina, in the great blue hills far from the salt sea where she met her end, a home economics and drama major at Campbell College— who was a makeup artist that summer at Roanoke Island's long-running outdoor drama of the vanished communards of 1587, *The Lost Colony*.

---

Now comes history in black-and-white, in the form of a silent movie.

An old salt sits upon a beach in England, telling two small boys, one of them Walter Ralegh, of a land beyond the sea, a land of liveoaks and sand hills. Next, years later, the men of Ralegh's Amadas and Barlowe expedition to the New World arrive in a pair of small boats, coming ashore with a white flag adorned with horizontal cross, along with a wooden cross, and claiming this land for queen and country before traipsing up a sandy hill. Indians bring the Englishmen fish, for which the English trade with a dipper and a pan, and Arthur Barlowe then goes exploring to the sapling-fenced village of Granganimeo, where he witnesses the cooking of fish and the grinding of corn.

An Indian mother feeds her child, who according to the silent-film dialogue card says the Algonkian equivalent of "Yum Yum."

This expedition returns to England with Manteo and Wanchese, friendly Indians who are not long thereafter repatriated by Grenville's voyagers in 1585. An English visit to the Indian village Secotan ends in violence, when a silver cup dropped by an Englishman winds up in Indian hands, not to be returned. The English burn the village and ruin the corn crop, and Grenville heads back for England, leaving Lane in charge.

Now men in feathered caps build a fort. Indians war-dance about a fire. Lane and the colonists catch a ride home with Francis Drake. Grenville, returning shortly thereafter and finding no one, leaves fifteen men from his party, literally to hold the fort. They enter the stockade with drooping shoulders, the depression of a potential New World doom already settling upon them.

And now a year has passed, and to this place comes another group, men in white collars, bonneted women, children, a Jersey cow. Women wash clothes in the shallows of a Sound-Country beach, and salt shall be their starch. Against this cheerful domesticity, an Indian crawls into the scene and sneaks up on and kills colonist George Howe, whose main sin seems to have been crabbing in this paradisiacal spot. Then a friendly Indian recounts to these colonists the fate of Grenville's lost guards: Indians came to the fort and cut loose with spears, arrows, clubs and slaughtered all the white men in the New World.

Back in the current moment, an Indian teaches an English boy how to use a bow and arrow. A priest in white vestments baptizes Manteo as Lord of Roanoke, and all settlers kneel and bow for this. Virginia Dare is born, and when her father Ananias brings her forth from his home, she is already in her christening gown and, in a scene echoing the baptism of Manteo, a week after her birth the first English child born in America is also baptized.

Winter is a-coming and supplies are a-dwindling—the colonists rightly fear they face famine—Governor John White, grandfather of Virginia Dare, is entreated by the men in feathered hats to return to England and from the Motherland bring more supplies. Receiving their written testimony that this is their wish, not his, the governor gets a hug from his daughter Eleanor, and is away.

Their life, reads the narrative card, "became one long gaze out to sea."

The colonists now go trudging away from their log village, Eleanor carrying baby Virginia and coming last in the walking train, Eleanor turning wistfully to look back one last time.

Three years pass. John White at long last returns to Roanoke Island and is grief-stricken at the ruin and overgrowth he now finds. A chest half-buried in the sand near the sound shore reveals within it John White's own papers and maps, and only when the governor finds upon a tree the vertical sign

C
R
O
A
T
O
A
N

does the governor's sanguinity return, for there is no sign of the cross— an earlier-agreed-upon symbol for danger—there with the word *Croatoan*. The governor reasons that his family, his colony, has gone safely south down the coastline to Manteo's village and people. A mighty storm, though, defeats White's possibility of seeking them out, and he goes back to England where he dies knowing they are lost to him but not knowing they are lost forever.

This black-and-white movie about Ralegh's lost 1587 colony was shot entirely on location on Roanoke Island sixteen long years before Paul Green's stage pageant *The Lost Colony* bowed on July 4, 1937. The movie that predated Green's "symphonic drama" was the brainchild of Mabel Evans Jones, Dare County's superintendent of schools and Roanoke arts-camp operator in the early 1920s. The Atlas Film Company of Chicago shot it during September 1921 for the North Carolina State Board of Education, with help from the Division of Fisheries and with Elizabeth B. Grimball of the New York theater directing. When Mabel Evans Jones sat down in 1920 to draft a screenplay about America's longest lost white men and women, she was working in a theatrical medium scarcely two decades old—D. W.

Shooting a film on
the Lost Colony,
Roanoke Island,
September 1921,
C. A. Rheims and
Red Stephens
of the Atlas
Film Corporation,
Chicago, and
Director Elizabeth
Grimball of
New York

Griffith's *Birth of a Nation* had been released only five years earlier. Most of Jones's thespians were not only *not* professional movie actors—most of them had never once in their lives even *seen* a movie.

In the film's opening frames a small white wooden passenger boat, the *Gretchen*, motors into view, thirty-odd thespians—Dare County locals, as well as citizens from Elizabeth City and Edenton north across Albemarle Sound—waving enthusiastically as they and their craft, towing a skiff, approach the Manteo waterfront of that long-gone day. These men and women would wear the capes, the collars, carry cross and flag, smear the warpaint, and tell us from across eighty-five years their take on a handful of English lost to the American jungle nearly four and a quarter centuries ago, yet storied and storied again.

Did they become Lumbee Indians down in the Scotland County swamps? Or did they create the mestizo population of Chowan and Gates Counties' Scratch Hall? Or were they really settlers down on Cedar Island, at the south end of Pamlico Sound? Or did Powhatan see some of them slaughtered, as he claimed? Or are they buried out in remote Beechland on the Dare County mainland, where logging-road dredgers decades ago were said to have banged into coffins and, fearing they had found the literal remains of the

Lost Colony and wanting none of it, put them back into the wild ground? Read all about it, watch it in the theater, see it on film in black-and-white, and tell me, and tell yourself, just to make sure you are sure of what you said, and tell it again, and again.

And then wonder forever.

Wonder as fiercely as the man playing one of the Indians in Mabel Jones's movie, the man who was so deeply into his latter-day role in the Lost Colony tale that, when a greasepaint shortage occurred during the filming, he solved it for himself by sleeping in his costume and his makeup for a solid week, his family banishing him from bedroom to livingroom and, finally, to barn—an unmistakable sign of devotion to the story of the disappeared that is in and of itself no small cause for wonder.

---

During the weeks leading up to the second-year's reopening of *The Lost Colony* in 1938, Roanoke Islanders planning to offer their domiciles as *tourist homes*, seeking to capitalize on the expected repeat influx of tourists, knew they needed gear sufficiently up to the task. Forty-five thousand people had come to town and seen the "symphonic drama" its first season, theater critic Brooks Atkinson for the *New York Times* and the President among them—and, remembering the typical tourist's battle-cry as being "Where can I get a bath?" Roanokers ordered bathtubs by the score.

On August 18, 1937, the 350th anniversary of Virginia Dare's birth, down from Elizabeth City on a Coast Guard cruiser had come President Franklin Delano Roosevelt, Guardsman and Roanoke Islander Louis Midgette standing beside the President the whole way and describing the landscape to him as they cruised. Wearing a straw hat as he stepped off the boat onto a tumbledown gasoline dock in Manteo, FDR immediately greeted *Lost Colony* producer and local leader D. Bradford Fearing with this jaunty remark: "Well, Mister Fearing, we're on time and things are clicking." In an open touring car Roosevelt was driven to Fort Raleigh, slowing on the way to wave and greet men from the Civilian Conservation Corps camp, and at the fort he harangued his political enemies before a crowd of perhaps 15,000—and then he was off to the Outer Banks to dine at Durham tobaccoman John Buchanan's Nags Head cottage. After dinner the President returned to the Waterside Theater, where he watched *The Lost Colony* from his car atop a specially-built ramp—"He was clearly impressed," the *New York Times* reported. After the show, the performers crowded around the open car and received the accolades of FDR.

During the second-season rehearsals in 1938, director Samuel Selden complained that he could not get playwright Paul Green to quit reworking

*President Franklin Delano Roosevelt, Governor Clyde Hoey, and Congressman Lindsay Warren at Fort Raleigh, Roanoke Island, August 18, 1937*

the script and introducing authorial changes every quarter hour, disconcerting a company anxious to learn the show it would be opening and running with. Perhaps Selden felt relief and took solace when, on June 25, 1938, Green and fellow writers Phillips Russell and Ben Dixon MacNeill quit Manteo for a day and hied themselves to Roanoke Island's "lower end," as Wanchese had been known till the coming of its post office in 1886.

A massive midden a millennium and a half in age drew them there. They wanted to dig into these Indian shellbanks and see what they might see, and so enlisted Harry Hayman of Wanchese, two ccc men named Ralph Tillett and Randolph Berry, as well as actor Donald Rosenberg, an out-of-towner who was playing the Indian Wanchese in Green's show.

These men stumbled and stomped around the yaupon-and-cedar hammock that locals called the "Thicket Lump" and whose oystershells they used freely as a source of lime for their gardens, till they found a spot in which to dig. Green's party did not dig long, hard or deep, for at the depth of a foot one shoveler struck a human backbone. Abandoning the shovel, the men now scooped and sifted by hand, slipping over the vertebrae of the long dead.

At last they grasped some potsherds, felt a piece of thighbone nine inches long.

Found a few fragments of human skull.

Having made this remarkable, sudden discovery, they then backed off, Green and Russell telling the *Dare County Times* that they were "of the belief that this section contains important untouched evidences of Indian life that ought to be competently investigated."

On both counts, they were right.

Forty-one years later, almost to the day and very possibly in this same spot, excavators from East Carolina University disinterred three Indian skeletons, adding them to the one they had already exhumed, for a total of four found on their May–June 1979 dig into what was now called the "Tillett Site," after owner Gilbert R. "Moon" Tillett. The diggers also lifted a pair of ceramic smoking-pipe stem fragments, fifteen projectile points, wood charcoal, all kinds of ceramics fragments, and enough flecks and flakes of shell and bone to tell the tale of who had lived here, and when, and why.

The rising ocean sea that made an island of Roanoke and that cut an inlet due east and seaward of it and that flooded the new sounds with saltwater had made an oysterbed heaven of a home for the Indians. For over half a year every year starting about A.D. 400, from March till October, they were encamped, en*villaged* really, at several key spots on Roanoke: at Northwest Point, just below where the old U.S. 64 bridge lights out across Croatan Sound for the Dare mainland; at the Elizabethan Gardens site near Fort Raleigh and the Waterside Theater; and at the Thicket Lump on the lower end, the Tillett Site south of Wanchese harbor.

And while encamped, Lord, how they ate!

Did they not love their shellfish? Tillett's shellmidden still stretched to nearly three acres—200 by 600 feet—and this was after its reduction by generations of Roanoke settlers who found garden fertilizer here. By the millions, the Indians devoured oysters, clams, three breeds of conch (lightning, knobbed pear, and horse), and conscientiously consumed their cockles too.

Were they not partial to finfish as well? Sheephead, the sweetest fish that swims, found a clientage among the Algonkians, and so did the croaker, the catfish, the red *and* black drum that ranged from one to three feet in size. Speared, netted, bunched up and caught in weirs, then skewered and smoked up for lunch right over open fires—this was good eating, all right, and these natives had known and enjoyed it for sixty generations already before Walter Ralegh ever launched the first English ship toward them.

At the evening meals they ate heavily.

For their first four centuries at the Thicket Lump—the Mount Pleasant portion of the Woodland period—they favored deer, raccoon and rabbit, varying this board with ducks, turkeys and turtles. Merganser also made it into this ongoing menu during the Colington age (A.D. 800–1600), as did at least one black bear—the Native Americans left behind the bear's atlas bone, the top vertebrae, to let us know. And through it all they kept gnawing on all kinds of turtles: snappers, mud turkles, sliders, loggerheads, and diamondbacks.

One forensic analyst stared into the teeth of all four Indian dead found in 1979 and remarked simply that he had seen there proof of "an abrasive diet and powerful mastication."

It would be hard *not* to stare at these long dead, who had lain just a few feet from each other, bathed by the tidal salts that permeated the midden, yet otherwise undisturbed for so many centuries till the investigators' spades quite literally turned them up. Two of the four were women, two men. One of the men showed signs—scrapes on his left parietal bone—of having been stripped of his flesh before burial. One of the women was a good five foot seven—she stood tall.

The one longest dead and buried was the last to be discovered. While the tall woman lay nearby in her opened burial pit, the pit full of saltwater and the woman's legs folded up beneath her, an excavator worked away on this newest find, slowly clearing the mud and sand from his skull. Anyone just happening upon this scene might well have thought the archaeologist, though squatting hard by death, was really sculpting a new human head out of damp sand.

It was the head of an old man, one whose own colony Time had granted more than a millennium of living and loving here at the Thicket Lump, dining right and extravagantly so for centuries before a different people wandered in on them. If he were lost, he never knew it, and if a colony of those different ones were lost somewhere near him, he never knew that either.

What the digger was doing was freeing the ancient one, letting him take the vapors and test the very air of the brave new world, offering him the smell of salt and the green of marsh in the new day, by which his open nostrils breathing and his hollow eyes seeing he could now at long last know, though the names of his people were still writ upon the land, even upon the waters, how much had changed since he had called the day his own.

How very much.

---

Near the corner of crepe-myrtle-lined *old* U.S. 64 and Harriot Street in Manteo sits the Virginia Dare Restaurant, a warm snug spot beside the busy highway, a traveler's friend tucked just off the lobby of the half-timbered Elizabethan Inn. Most of us who have often visited the Dare County seat have found our ways to—and *back* to—the breakfast buffet's warming pans brimming with grits, biscuits and gravy, and other staves of life.

In this agreeable spot I once sat tapping a china coffeecup and trying to enumerate all the places and purposes to which the vanished babe's name has been affixed over time, beyond this eatery and the county itself.

My first awareness of her was as a grand palace, the Virginia Dare Hotel in my old hometown of Elizabeth City, a nine-story, blond-bricked, hundred-room wonder that opened up back in 1927 (charging $2 a room) as the Albemarle's first skyscraper. Nearly eighty years later, it is the Albemarle's *only* skyscraper. The two-story base of our eye-catching hotel had a balustrade with urns, and inside it was a ballroom and a diningroom where we ate fried chicken on Sundays and set linen napkins in our laps, and a passageway to the two-story, skylighted Virginia Dare Arcade, replete with wrought-iron railing and tile floor, swivel-stooled soda fountain and, above its Main Street entryway, a decorative cartouche emblematic of Ralegh's Roanoke voyages.

If living on in memory were ever a goal, here then is one who succeeded and who found by the circumstance of her birth and through the pathos of her disappearance a never-ending *re*appearance of her name. Virginia Dare has also been, and lent her appellation to, variously: the once-most-popular wine in the United States (Paul Garrett's sweet white scuppernong, an early-twentieth-century treat); an extract company (what Garrett turned to after Prohibition took hold); a novel (Miss E. A. B. Shackelford's 1892 *Virginia Dare*, "a romance of the sixteenth century"); a sidewheel tourboat on Smith Mountain Lake, Virginia; a bicycle tour to raise money to fight multiple sclerosis; a Virginia soil-and-water conservation district in Chesapeake and Virginia Beach; a Daughters of the American Revolution chapter in Kill Devil Hills; a highway (Virginia Dare Trail on the Dare County Outer Banks); a red-and-purple-rosed bedchamber at the White Doe Inn in Manteo; a statuesque female sculpted in 1859 and now standing in Roanoke Island's Elizabethan Gardens, not very far at all from Miss Dare's birthplace; a "winery plaza" in San Bernadino County, California; a three-inch-tall shot glass with "Virginia Dare" arched above a frosted field featuring an eagle, five cherries and the further legend "Garrett's" and "American Wines"; and a prized canine offspring, her parents No Time to Lose, sire, and Noel Mama Jama, dam, the bloodhound Virginia Dare.

She has appeared on a commemorative coin—in her mother's arms on the *verso* of the Raleigh silver half-dollar in 1937, and on a 5-cent U.S. postage stamp, again in her mother's arms, first issued at Manteo on August 18, 1937, when and where a half million of them were sold. She has engendered a postmodern folk trio in San Francisco, its lead instrument an autoharp. She occasioned a follow-up, if not sequel, novel to Miss Shackelford's, Mary Virginia Wall's 1908 paean to hope and regeneration called *The Daughter of Virginia Dare*, and she inspired a much later artist, a comicbook author named Harahap, to envision her as a young woman traveling to seek Queen Elizabeth I's aid, only to find "herself as the subject of Count Otto Von Doom's assassination attempts." If one felt no sympathy for Virginia Dare before, surely the story of her surviving being lost in America only to face the maleficent Von Doom in comicbook Renaissance England would penetrate the most ferrous heart.

Virginia Dare's most popular and most sympathetic manifestation may have been as the legendary White Doe, tragic heroine of Sallie Southall Cotton's 1901 epic poem with its *Hiawatha* scansion. In this work Virginia, having been acculturated into the Indian world as Wi—no—na, is transformed into a deer by the covetous medicine man Chico, through the "weird power" of a string of pearls he has given her. The old women of the village figure it all out, though, and then Wi—no—na's true beau, the warrior Okisko, acquires from yet another medicine man, a rival of Chico's, the recipe for a countercharm, to wit:

Make an arrow of witch hazel, use a shark's tooth as arrowhead, one with "three mussel-pearls of purple" inlaid, a heron's feather as tail-end, go hunting for the White Doe, dip the arrowhead into Roanoak's magic spring, shoot her in the heart, and watch her change before your eyes back into Wi—no—na!

Okisko does it all just so, though unbeknownst to him another Indian, Wanchese, is also out hunting the White Doe, and he, too, has a special arrow—his is tipped with silver given him when he made his celebrated trip to England with Manteo. In a moment worthy of literary woodscraftsman James Fenimore Cooper, both Okisko and Wanchese release their arrows *simultaneously*, both arrows piercing the poor White Doe's heart, "charm and countercharm undoing."

In a gleaming mist and with a misty halo above her, Wi—no—na, long-lost Virginia Dare, appears, then vanishes, dead, gone, lost yet again. Yet when Okisko washes her blood from the silver-tipped arrow, Wanchese having run off, a "tiny shoot with leaflets" springs forth from the arrow, "the Vine of Civilization in the wilderness of strife." Since much viticultural comment precedes the epic, Roanoke's celebrated Mother Vineyard and a Virginia Dare Vineyard being portrayed in word and photograph, one might easily infer Cotton's strong support of the scuppernong onrush then pouring over the world.

Cotton's frontispiece shows a mature and comely young Virginia Dare, standing in a forest all decked out in a long deerskin dress. In the Virginia Dare Extract Company's logo-cameo, she appears to be eighteen or twenty years old, long curls down about her cheeks, and wears a tailored vestment with a hood. In Louise Lander's 1859 statue in the Elizabethan Gardens she is a grown woman standing tall, left knee slightly bent, clasping a tunic around her waist, and is otherwise nude.

Babe in film, babe on stage, babe on stamp and coin, we wanted you, though disappeared into the wild, to be taken in by those whose people had awaited you and your coming in that forest fastness for 1,200 years. To be raised by them, foundling, as one of their own, and to grow up strong, gorgeous, magical. To sail the ocean sea and present yourself proudly before Elizabeth I, the Virgin Queen. To have a daughter of your own. And whatever else we wished for you, what everyone was after, what those of us on our third cups of coffee in the little Manteo restaurant carrying your name really wanted above all was never, ever, to let you go.

———————

Coming onto Roanoke Island over the old William B. Umstead Bridge from the north, driving down the lane of crepe myrtles with big pines to the sides, one would not immediately suspect that few places in North America have been as fought over, as crawled and pawed over as much and for as long a time as this island has. Coming east over the new, 2002 Virginia Dare Bridge, one flies above Croatan Sound and the westside marshes, the bridge's long span designed to spare those wetlands and move over Roanoke's midsection like a belt. As the Virginia Dare deposits eastbound travelers most of the way across the island, many a one would hardly suppose he or she had just crossed an island at all.

A few hundred yards east of the U.S. 64–N.C. 345 stoplight, there now sits heavily upon the marsh ridge a gated "fishing" community called Pirates' Cove, several hundred million dollars worth of very precariously perched condos and triple-flying-bridge boats. Yet 'twas not always thus: thirty years ago there was nothing at all along this stretch of causeway but a small plain workingman's bistro, the modest hot spot called the Drafty Tavern.

Back in October of '72, New Hampshireman John Foley and I sat several nights sipping slowly, and slowly sipping, in the Drafty, taking stock of Dare County, testing the measure of ourselves. We were down yonder in

*Post office, Colington Island, 1937*

Dare painting the decks and trim on my grandmother's cottage, a low bungalow over on the Banks, snug against the front dune and dating to the early 1930s, near where the man-of-war steamer USS *Huron* shipwrecked in late 1877 with the loss of 103 men. We were there right at the post-equinoctial point when Indian Summer still lingered, before the balmy golden afternoons we felt would last forever gave way to earnest lashing winds and beating rains. Some evenings we would drive back to the sound-side for the sunsets, past the Wright Brothers monument and over two bridges to the liveoak hills of Big Colington, site of Lord Proprietor Sir John Colleton's 1660s tobacco plantation and horse-and-cattle range and where by the lights of the eminent writer David Stick "undoubtedly the first Banks settlement was founded."

By night we were reclining at the Drafty.

Our favorite number on the joint's jukebox was Ray Charles's cover of "Look What They've Done to My Song," which we played repeatedly. We loved Ray's exhortatory voiceover-fade lines about the song, particularly "They done put it in the bottom of a shake-and-bake bag and mix it all up!"

No pretense could survive the Drafty, it being as down-to-earth as sea level, and we knew this to be the source of the place's seductive allure. Even and perhaps especially here men spoke of loss, and in unexpected ways would the subject come up. One evening when Ray was done singing, without intending to Foley and I overheard an odd self-interrogation going on, a half a dozen local fellows standing at the bar suddenly conducting a sober survey and questioning each one's natural male ability. This progressive confessional continued chromatically on down the line, with insistently stated "Well, *yeahs*" and "*Hell*, yeahs," till it reached a short wizened fellow at the end. An older man than the rest, he had slumped perceptibly as he heard each declaration before him coming toward him until finally, at his turn, he lifted himself up just enough to speak, upon his shoulders the weight of many a millennium's hurricanes and nor'easter smashings and Virginia Dare's turning into a white doe and a Lost Colony and a Lost Cause both, saying at last with a noble honesty:

"Nope."

# Behind Ocracoke

### BIG FOOT ISLAND

After lunch with Jake and Rachel Mills at their riverview home in little Washington, my young daughter Cary and I drove farther on down east, through the big-sky and five-mile-fields country of Hyde County, and caught the four o'clock Swanquarter-to-Ocracoke ferry.

When first under way, we sat on deck beside our little gray station wagon, then moved forward and leaned upon the black, heavy iron bow railing as the *Silver Lake* made her crossing, plowing through Pamlico Sound, a light early-evening chop on the waters and shrimpers all out and about. Presently Ocracoke Light appeared, standing out as a tiny white needle, easy to spy in the late afternoon summerlight from ten miles west.

Next morning dawned clear and bright, and at seven Cary and I met up with veteran birders Micou Browne and John Weske and joined their motley crew at Ocracoke's ferry-landing boat ramp for some feathery purposes out in Pamlico. Goateed Micou from Raleigh and lean John from Patuxent, Maryland, have been banding colonial nesting birds in Carolina's inshore waters for seven decades between them, then loading the band-numbers into a national database, and thereby giving the world an uncommonly fine, elaborate portrait of these populations, their movements and nesting habits. For this work, the reward has been the simple satisfaction of getting it done and down, and the passionate slamming out into a big open-air, open-water life, smack into the middle of it so many scores of days just like this one: a gang of people in an open boat (John's was a twenty-foot Privateer) loaded with rolls of quarter-inch-mesh wire and stakes to hold it in position as a corral. The target we were aiming for today was the huge tern colony on Big Foot Island, a 12$^1/_2$-acre bald sand dome on the north side of the Big Foot Slough ferry channel about three miles out into the Pamlico Sound behind Ocracoke.

Within an hour John Weske had ferried almost a dozen folks (first our boatload, and then a second, including a lifeguard, a turtle man, a piping-plover man, and the burly and bearded Mickey Knight, who worked at the Hatteras Island Fishing Pier and who looked like he could bench-press all the African pompano you could load him up with) out to Big Foot Slough. We uncoiled the wire rolls, staked out a circular corral thirty or forty feet in diameter, and herded a fortune of young terns, which nest on scant scrapes on such open, unvegetated sandy balds, a waddling multitude of them, into the corral.

Cary, then eight, leapt right down into the corral's small holding pen and found herself a task, handing the fluffy birds up to us banders, who kept her busy calling out to her, "I'm ready, Cary" and "Give me a bird, Cary" and "Ready over here." Big Mickey worked quickly, and he was gentle, affectionate even, with the small white birds, holding them as if they were fragile as the eggs from which they so recently hatched. Anyone who dropped a band got John Weske's eagle-eyed admonishment to find it and get it onto a bird's leg—"A lost band is the same as a dead bird."

Clearly enjoying the ritual he has carried out innumerable times, Micou laughed as he told me, "When we take the corral up it leaves a big smoothed-out circle in the sand. I'll be standing at the ferryboat's rail going right past here tomorrow, and I'll hear people say, 'What's that? What's that circle there?' and I'll tell em: 'It's a *devil ring*—devil worshippers made that!'"

By the time we recoiled the corral wire, still well before noon, we had spotted a few pelicans here and there about the island—"Loafing," said Micou—and we had banded every single young and flightless tern on the place. Months hence, Florida birders with fantastically high-end optics would be throwing down their lenses on some of these very birds and at fifty yards reading the tiny numbers on the silver metal encircling their legs.

Cary herself banded half a dozen birds before her work in the pen helped save the backs of the grown-up birders, and she memorized the day's count and later recited it at will and often: "Eight sandwich terns and 1,358 royals." If this were devil worship, she and I were nonetheless very glad to have had a pass to the service.

---

Given a shot at an afternoon trip over to Portsmouth Island on the lower side of Ocracoke Inlet, Cary demurred, and so got left off back at the Ocracoke ferry-landing with Micou's jolly brunette wife Mary Ann. Weske, Micou and a couple others of us then stood for Beacon Island, a low marshland islet to the south, the spot where pelicans were first discovered nesting in North Carolina in 1928 and where we soon beached and walked up on, quickly surveying the pelican young in the grass throughout. To call their aroma pungent would be polite—the small, mud-gray featherless pelicans lay there defenseless in the August coastal heat, not a tree or bush on the island, croaking hoarsely at us even so, *Angk angk angk!* Banding these characters, allowed both John and Micou, was a "smellier, and more physical activity" than tackling terns. Even miles out in the sound, as we were, I sensed their understatement.

Then we were off toward Portsmouth, touring first Shell Castle Island, the former port now mainly a long oyster-shell reef, waters rippling over a shelf on its upper end. Above Shell Castle lay North Rock, as the Occockers called it, though it was known as Long Rock down in Carteret. "I assume you know there is a sort of Malvinas vs. Falklands situation in Ocracoke Inlet," John Weske said drolly, "where Carteret County watermen call an island complex one name and 'cokers call it another. I'm referring to Long Rock vs. North Rock. As far as I'm aware, however, this naming difference has not yet resulted in open warfare." This civil controversy may have cooled, though, as Ocracoke historian and sage Alton Ballance would later advise me that Occockers make use of the name Long Rock, too.

Weske next cruised us on around the end of Casey's Island, a marsh islet with forty crabpots stacked near one lone shanty. Casey's was once home to a menhaden plant in the far-off past, till that plant, seeking to move and being spurned by Ocracokers, headed on into Beaufort faraway to the south. Sailor Jim Cheatham told of an artesian well freely flowing on Casey's, which he and his wife Bren had seen over fifteen years ago, but that well flowed no more.

We ran aground. All out now, and we were walking the boat across shallows. I was stepping on clams right and left, reminded of foot-clamming with Cap'n Jim Rumfelt in the short water south of Harkers Island. When I walked up a foot-and-a-half flounder, startling us both as I nearabout gave him the full force of my foot, he scooted off to deeper water and greater glory.

At Portsmouth Island's soundside, Weske pulled into the Haulover Point dock and tied up, and now we strode the path through the marsh to the ghost village, passing a single white graveslab, a few short cedars, mosquitoes finding us the second we were out of the wind. As we walked, Weske conferred with the Cape Lookout National Seashore volunteer, Emerald Isle novelist B. J. Mountford, who for four years had spent most of her summer time at Portsmouth, here at the seashore's upper end, mowing. She was a bright-spirited, energetic blonde woman whom Weske occasionally enlisted for pelican banding, and she spoke to him that early afternoon of a couple hundred young pelicans that had either blown or been washed over to Portsmouth from Beacon Island—the work of Hurricane Dennis in September of '99—and how they were all here, till the one day when she looked out and they were all gone. None straggled in or out—they moved

as one. The talk proceeded: how the young terns were late this year because a late spring nor'easter had forced a re-nesting.

For an hour or so I stared hard at the spot Mountford kept so well
groomed. I climbed up into the lookout's cupola atop the old Portsmouth
Coast Guard Station and enjoyed the incredible three-sixty panorama this
purchase affords of seemingly boundless sound, frothing inlet, ocean sea to
Africa, sand beach and myrtle jungle running forever to the south down
the banks, now sound again, the blue vault over all, thinking about those
gone pelicans and those gone Gilgos and other former residents for whom
this was long called home.

*Why would you ever leave?* I wondered again and again, beguiled, hypnotized, drunk with love for this sand-filament land of wind and water,
this edge of everything.

Back in Ocracoke that evening, Micou, Mary Ann, Cary and I ate squid
and shrimp at the Jolly Roger café, set right there on Silver Lake harbor,
along with Cap'n Norman Miller of the *Rascal*, an old friend of the Brownes
and a marine habitué of Ocracoke and her inlet since 1973. Lean, bald, flint-
eyed, Norman had first come out here as a night watchman for the Ocracoke ferry, then taken up carpentry and built houses, parlaying his high
energy and canny collection of skills into a business that now included a
motel, as well as the thirty-foot *Rascal* and a second, smaller charter craft, a
Sea Cat. When I got around to asking him about Shell Castle Island, he
laughed and said:

"Lot of folks around here, they call all of those rocks out there Shell
Castle, but that's not right. They've all got names, and there's only one
that's Shell Castle Island and I know which one it is. I know these waters
extremely well, know the wrecks, all of it—I know where the old Shell
Castle Island pilings and foundations are, so you just say when, and I'll take
you out there.

"I'll take you right to it."

---

Upon each of a pair of small ceramic pitchers in North Carolina's state
archives lies the only known illustration of the port-of-entry enterprise
that throve at Shell Castle Island for twenty years two centuries ago.
Though from Weske's Privateer I had seen a mere half-acre shell reef, in the
detailed image on these little celebratory pots an American flag was flying,
single-chimneyed and double-chimneyed clapboard houses stood cheek by
jowl with warehouses, a tavern, a lighthouse (the *first* along Carolina's
coast), even a governor's mansion.

*Ceramic pitcher with*
*an illustration of*
*Shell Castle Island,*
*about 1800*

An energetic and, some might say, visionary inlet pilot named John Wallace in the late 1780s threw his fate in with that of the wealthy Washington, North Carolina, shipper and mercantilist John Gray Blount. In 1789 Wallace represented Carteret County in the state assembly, and attended the state's convention on the federal Constitution with Blount, events overlapping in time and both occurring in Fayetteville. With Blount's social and political support and his periodic investments, Captain John became Governor Wallace, chief executive of Shell Castle Island, and for the next twenty-odd years presided over the nexus of North Carolina's maritime communication with the world. If it were only a short time, what an active and adventurous pair of decades for this remote spot they were, when millions of cypress shingles and thousands of barrels of tar and pitch and salt herring went out into the world through here, to be traded for finished goods.

Wallace quickly took hold of the uninhabited shellbank lying long and low beside one of only three deepwater channels leading in and out of Ocracoke Inlet, built log-cribbing all around it and filled the area behind these bulkheads with turf both to hold it together and enlarge it. Upon his and Blount's shored-up real estate Wallace became master of all he assayed, a tiny maritime transshipment town, the former Old Rock, rechristened Shell Castle. As estimable island historian Philip Horne McGuinn has recounted, the Blount-Wallace partnership eventually engaged in "piloting, lightering, shipbuilding, brokerage, freighting, fishing, porpoise oil fishery, warehousing, coopering, government contracting, servicing of navigation aids, ship's chandlery and tavern, salvage" and so on.

All three deep-draft channels—Teach's Hole Channel, to the east or Ocracoke side of the inlet; the Ship Channel (now Blair) more or less up the middle; and the Portsmouth Channel to the west—ran out of ocean-ships' depth before reaching the deeper waters of Pamlico Sound. A spread-out shoal called the Swash, with varying single-digit depths, stood between the upper ends of the inlet channels and the sound—ships had to have their cargoes sufficiently unloaded onto smaller craft called *lighters* to allow the shallower draft of them to get past this block. Ships that were ocean-goers only would have to warehouse their cargoes at Shell Castle, from whence sound and river boats would carry that cargo on into the Carolina interior. Shell Castle's key advantage lay in having twenty-foot water immediately adjacent to it, whereas the villages of Portsmouth and Ocracoke could not handle craft with depths of more than seven feet.

Another renaming in which Governor Wallace played a part involved the Portsmouth Channel, which soon served Shell Castle far more and better than Portsmouth village, taking on the governor's name—from his day, about 1792, to ours it has been called the Wallace Channel. So an honest merchant claimed the west channel with his surname, while the east channel bore the name of the pirate Blackbeard, Edward Teach, who had been killed and beheaded here by Virginia's Lieutenant Robert Maynard in the Battle of Ocracoke, November 1718.

Presumed honest merchant, that is.

After writing Blount twice in April 1792 that "rum is the only thing that I have made any Progress in Selling" and "Nothing you have Sent Sells So well as Rum," Governor Wallace by mid-October of that year stood accused by his own storekeeper—who also wrote Blount—of never recording sales in the store's ledger and of taking "all the money out of the Store So that I can't make change one half my Time when people wants [.]" Clerk William Smith also observed Shell Castle's capacity for rum—"In the corse of three weeks there was 13½ gallons of rum drank in the house at the castle." And Smith postscripted an oblique accusation toward Governor Wallace, penning "four times week Drunk," below his own signature.

Historian McGuinn reported on *antebellum* maritime race relations: in a 1793 incident four slaves made free with a boat and slipped away down the sound, Wallace himself giving chase and capturing one of the four, his man Pinkham apprehending the rest. Wallace nonetheless employed slaves as watermen and pilots, though not to the approval of all. Many, if not, most of the forty-odd working residents of Shell Castle by 1800 were bondsmen —an 1810 census showed four households here, with nineteen whites and twenty-two black slaves. Due to the vagaries of wind and wave, one of the black pilots unwittingly became a free man—after he had piloted the ship *Betsey* out over the bar into the ocean in 1802, the inlet became far too choppy for this man to be fetched back to Shell Castle. The ship he found himself upon took him north to Alexandria, Virginia, and, as he received a freeman's wages there, he then considered himself a free man, and so sailed on with the *Betsey* to Boston.

After years of planning, squabbling really, over whether a light beacon should be raised at Ocracoke or Shell Castle, a wooden shaft that shook in the wind finally went up on Shell Castle in 1803, its lamp powered by whale or porpoise oil. Yet if this act ushered in a season of light for the busy little port, it would be hard to tell it from a pair of less-than-savory events that soon followed.

A December 1804 nor'easter drove the *Nuestra Señora del Carmine* onto shoals in the Wallace Channel, noted McGuinn, whereupon the governor salvaged her cargo —a couple dozen casks of molasses and nearly 5,000 hides—and stored it. When these goods were sold in February 1805, Wallace's quarter-a-hide warehousing charge added up to a third the value of the cargo, spurring the ship's agents to write John Gray Blount hoping he would reverse Wallace and cut the fee.

In January 1805, McGuinn continued, a Blount expediter named John Mayo auctioned the *Jackal*'s goods on Shell Castle Island for $259, stashed this loot (sixteen $10 gold pieces and "a number of Bank Bills & forty Eight Dollars in silver") in Shell Castle's offices, and then, checking on it after night had fallen, discovered the booty had gone missing. He herded the "great number of Strangers on the Castle at the time" into the Shell Castle tavern, where "a number of them were Stripped & Searched but no discovery made," then locking up for the night a Shell Castle worker named Pidge whom tavern-keeper Nathaniel Pinkham had accused of the theft, and whose letter of complaint about the incident to John Gray Blount tells all. When neither the incarceration of Pidge nor Mayo's next-day rifling of all trunks and chests on the island recovered the lost money, Mayo devised a bribe-and-quiet-closure scheme and posted a notice "which was wrote in a very moveing manner" telling whoever had taken the money to return it and keep $48 in silver as a finder's fee, and that would be that, no questions asked. Lo, the *Jackal* cash soon appeared on the office's porch—and barman Pinkham was the one who found it.

On July 11, 1810, John Gray Blount in Washington drafted a letter to Governor Wallace proposing that, "as we are both advanced in years and have each a Family for which we ought to make some arrangement," the two longtime partners split the island (giving the governor "the choice of ends of the Castle & Rock") and settle their accounts payable and receivable and call it quits. Eighteen days later, on July 28, surveyor and opportunist William Tatham—an 1806 guest of Wallace's when Tatham was taking measure all up and down the Carolina coast and, coincidentally, losing all his instruments in a storm much as Thomas Harriot had over two centuries earlier—wrote a letter of his own from Portsmouth to Blount, proposing a new survey, new design, and new management for Shell Castle— all Tatham's.

What had occurred between the writing of these two letters was John Wallace's death.

Governor Wallace was buried on Sheep Island, just over the creek not far south of Portsmouth village, and his flat graveslab read:

Here is deposited the remains
Of
Captain John Wallace
Governor of Shell Castle
Who departed this life
July 22, 1810
Age 52 years and 6 months

Shell Castle mournes; Your pride is in the dust
Your boast, your glories in the dreary grave.
Your sun is set ne'er to illume again
This sweet asylum from th' Atlantic wave.
He's here beneath this monumental stone
This awful gloom amid the silent dead.
Thy founder lies whose sainted soul we laid
To heaven's high mansion has its journey sped.
Mourn charity, benevolence be wail
Kind hospitality his lot deplore.
And own with one unanimous acclaim
Misfortune's sons will view his like no more.

As historian McGuinn saw it, the end of the governor was the beginning of the end, too, for Shell Castle as the great Carolina port. The Wallace Channel soon shoaled. A British fleet with 2,000 men attacked Ocracoke Inlet in July 1813, tore up Portsmouth, and darkened Shell Castle's light— lightning blasted it for good five years later. Rebecca Wallace followed her husband to the grave in 1822 and was buried near him on Sheep Island. In early 1836, ten sailors with smallpox were banished from Portsmouth village and found themselves exiled in an old dwelling out on Shell Castle where no doctor would attend them—only six of them lived to tell the tale.

A September hurricane—the same storm of 1846 that opened both Hatteras and Oregon Inlets up the Banks and flooded Knotts Island to the north—finished off Shell Castle Island, this port-of-entry once considered so valuable that John Wallace was even said to have spurned an ostensible purchaser's offer to carpet the island with silver dollars. Shell Castle had now been sliced down by storm, time and tides to next to nothing: one-half acre, rating a tax value of a mere ten dollars, its first and only governor long dead and its pride forever buried out in Pamlico Sound, in a small curve of shell chips and oyster dust.

---

Two years after Cap'n Norman Miller promised he would take us to Shell Castle Island, he made good—twice in the same day, the last Friday in June of '02.

Again we met the John Weske–Micou Browne contingent at 7:00 A.M. down by the National Park Service docks. This time both Ann *and* Cary were along, and we clambered into Cap'n Norman's twenty-one-foot Sea Cat with its twin Johnson 70s, Weske also taking a party—two young men, two

*John Weske and Cary Simpson banding pelicans on Beacon Island, June 2002*

young blonde women from the Student Conservation Association, and, again, big bearded Mickey Knight from the Frisco Pier—in his Privateer.

Off to Beacon Island for the smelly and physical work of pelican banding we did go, briefly stopping in fourteen-inch water when Norman ran over a shoal at speed, several of us then going over the side and walking the Sea Cat to freedom.

"What's your boat draw?" I asked.

"More than this," Norman replied.

Once on Beacon, we all dove into the earnest affair of grabbing adolescent pelicans by their beaks and trying not to get scratched by the small sharp downturned tips of those beaks. One held their upperwing bones *above* the joint as they yelped *Angk angk angk* and bit, while one's partner did the banding—the good fortune in all this being the soft, pliable nature of the beaks of the young birds.

"Come on now," Micou pled with them as he pliered the big broad silver bands closed around their legs. "Here's your graduation ring." More seven- and eight-digit numbers for the database, and if the glory and danger of, say, Lord Franklin's quest for the northwest passage around the pole was not immediately apparent in the birdbanding adventure, the spirit of discovery and advancement of science was the same nonetheless. Charles Darwin would've been right at home this morning on Beacon Island, and Rachel Carson would've reveled in the fact that, since the ban on DDT, the pelican comeback has been a powerful change for the good: an ongoing increase from 300 nesting pairs in the state of North Carolina in 1972 up to 4,100 pairs in 2002.

By 10:30 A.M. we were done, having banded 534 young pelicans. Cary acquired a two-inch scratch on her right forearm, and Ann got pecked on her chin just below her lower lip, a bite drawing blood, of which my wounded wife remarked jauntily at the time: "Quite a kiss!"

On we boated, over the shallows to East Ledge, where Cap'n Norman slowed and judged the tide lines on the shore, saying quizzically, "Now, see, this would normally be an extra low tide, but here it is right at high tide time." This boded well for seeing more of these oyster rocks exposed as the tide changed and went out. We cruised on to North Rock and Northwest Rock, getting off the boat again and sloshing along in the waters between the two. Of North Rock's bird population, Micou said that a description from three years ago was just about the same as T. Gilbert Pearson's comments on this spot from a hundred years earlier.

Then, with serious good humor, Cap'n Norman stopped striding and gestured first toward the shells and then the sun and sky and said: "I'm just going to put this theory of mine out into the wind—an idea that a *meteor* blew up in the midst of all these *rocks* and created a circular basin, a *rim* of them, including Shell Castle and Shellbank."

Now we toured on down the rim, gliding in to check the water level at Shell Castle Island itself, where a rectangular series of grassy stones formed into pilings and, just scarcely submerged on the island's western end, very neatly described the outline of an old foundation, and where in the tideline sand and mud wooden frames were still intact. It was high noon—much of what we could now easily see in the clear inlet waters would be out of the water and exposed by the late afternoon low tide yet to come.

Ebb and flow could not have been better. The wind had been blowing out of the southwest for most of a week, and, as the Full Strawberry Moon had just occurred the previous Tuesday, we would be getting the strongest possible advantage of the three-day-post-full lag effect on the tides. This afternoon's low should be *very* low. As we headed down the Wallace Chan-

*Old foundation,*
*Shell Castle Island,*
*June 2002*

nel with the southwest wind abeam, we kept asking, *Where's all the water?*
*Avon? Back Bay?* Though it didn't really matter where it was—only that it
wasn't *here.*

After lunch and some calm out of the heat of the day at Serendipity
Cottage on the west side of Silver Lake, we again boarded Cap'n Norman's
Sea Cat and launched back down the sound, our first goal the recently-
discovered ruin of the Confederacy's Fort Ocracoke, a well-submerged mass
of stone and masonry a good 150 yards off Beacon Island's east side. Norman thought that with this low a tide we'd likely get a better look at it, all
sunlit and us looking through not quite as much water. We came in on it
about half past three, floated over it in only about twelve feet of water,
though I found it hard to make out much more than a dark, grassy lump on
the sound's bottom. Upon Beacon lay no sign at all of the Rebel outpost,
which burned early in the Civil War, or of Ocracoker Gaskill's market and
sport hunting camp—a 26- by 30-foot prefab—that succeeded the fort.

*Ballast stones,*
*Shell Castle Island,*
*June 2002*

Shell Castle Island, North Carolina, five o'clock on this June afternoon, dead low tide! To the west, the endless waters of Pamlico Sound, lit by the sun behind high-piled summer cumulous clouds, were a vast plain of green and gold.

Just three of us were along boating now—Cap'n Norman, Ann, and I. The tops of those underwater foundation stones, submerged earlier that day, stood very much out of the water now. Norman and I did a little tidewater dimensioning, walking it off, my take being that the building once standing here was seventy-five feet square, though Norman had it at a hundred feet a side. Doubtless one of the warehouses.

On the island's western end, timber frames lying down in the ground were oriented to the north-northeast, while in the island's middle, on its south side more or less facing Portsmouth, more such frames lay on a west-southwest bias. Curious, though no less so than the whole epic enterprise these architectural relics represented: the building of an international seaport on a shellbank almost sitting in the sea herself!

"What a tale these rocks could tell!" Cap'n Norman mused, as he stood and stared at the antique evidence all around us.

A collection of tales, really, for the mix we surveyed had been loosely assembled here from all over the world: ballast stones, smoothworn coral, a lava rock, an unusual gray concentric, a thin brick . . . a piece of roofing slate. A chunk of tabby masonry. Wooden posts long ago pounded into place, eaten at by time, tides, and worms, no doubt, but still posts and still there.

In this rich field of debris, potsherds caught my eye. I studied a light brown curved piece of bowl, a fragment about the size of my hand—lowfire, lead-glazed earthenware with coggle-marks decorating its rim and pipeclay slip décor inside the bowl, most likely from Britain or New England. A handle from a jug or pitcher was iron wash, salt-glazed British stoneware. The turn of the eighteenth and nineteenth centuries was all around us. We were standing in it, walking on it, holding it. Who once poured, or guzzled, from the jug whose handle now encircled my index finger like an ungainly brown ring? Governor Wallace, "four times week drunk"?

What does Ocracoke Inlet offer on this point?

What does the deep sea say?

"We've got about fifteen minutes!" Cap'n Norman hollered out. The man who believed a meteor made it all had been mindfully keeping a weather eye, and was now standing in the shallows near the Sea Cat, reading the sky. That little cloud in the west I had noted a while earlier—arising out of the sea like a man's hand, as the Good Book says—had grown larger, darker, and a menacing storm was now blowing our way from western Pamlico Sound.

Ann and I heard him all right, yet we kept prowling for a few minutes more about the old warehouse pilings, Governor Wallace's detritus now our delight. Remote Shell Castle was simply not a spot we happened by on most of the days of our lives.

"Let's go!" the captain called in earnest. "Gettin' *dark*!"

Our time was up—no longer any question. A huge, bruise-black, sky-effacing thunderstorm, its long dark front north-to-south, came moving in quickly upon us. Cap'n Norman gunned the twin Johnsons down the Wallace Channel, and his Sea Cat swam Ocracoke Inlet like a shark, knifing the inlet's big chop as we passed the series of white *pvc* pipes that the old-time Occocker Rudy Austin—a skillful and premier native captain on these waters—tended and moved about to mark the everchanging passage to Portsmouth. If we were cruising at twenty-five knots I could not tell it, so smoothly was the catamaran cutting the waves.

Way to the north the outbound six o'clock ferry to Cedar Island moved beyond Big Foot Island where the devil-rings come and go, just a Dover-white dot against all that dread-dark sky. "It's going to get *hit*!" said Cap'n Norman excitedly, as faraway flashes of lightning clicked on, silver electric jags above and beyond the ferryboat that seemed so inexpressibly vulnerable out there alone in nothing but wet desert and storm.

Then in just a few elevated heartbeats we were at the top of Teach's Hole Channel and Cap'n Norman was throttling back. Into the remarkable haven of Silver Lake harbor from Pamlico Sound we rode, but not before one final over-the-shoulder judgment from the captain as the first big drops of rain started pelting us at last:

"Lord, that *is black*!"

## PAMLICO SOUND AND RIVER

Bearing west by northwest out of Ocracoke, a boatman might stand for the mouth of Pamlico River by crossing Pamlico Sound and slipping between two long submerged ridges, sailing below the Middle Ground and above Brant Island Shoal. While most of the central and lower sound holds depths of fifteen to twenty feet of water, the Middle Ground will sound at less than ten, and the now-drowned Brant Island has long stretches of two-foot water.

Before, during, and after World War II, Brant Island still lay enough out of the water to be a fisherman's outpost, a poundnetter's trove. A couple dozen men or more spent summers fishing out there, living in shanties fifteen feet square and each with nothing but a wood cookstove and a stack of bunks, someone boating down out of the Neuse River and icing down their catch and carrying it back to the docks at Oriental. The fishermen lived free, unfettered and unbothered until navy planes in 1942 started using the place for target practice, coming in at 300 feet and dropping water-filled rubber bombs down on Brant. Then the fishermen would take to their boats and push away from the island till the exercises ended, though a ricocheting five-foot waterbomb once came bounding down upon a tethered netskiff, blew its bottom out and sank it. When the navy went to live ammunition about 1948, the fishermen pushed off for good, and hurricanes and rising seas since then have done the island in. Yet the shoal is still a military target named *BT 9*, offering airmen a sunken freighter and two grounded tugboats, and sailors bound from Neuse River to Ocracoke still note, as they pass it off port, the flashing light at the lower end of Brant Island Shoal and the nearby wreck of the ferryboat *Governor Scott*.

Above the Middle Ground lies another cluster named by Captain John Smith in 1624, though what woman he honored by calling them "Abigails Iles" we will never know. Here are Bell, Judith, Swanquarter, Marsh and Great Islands, and, of these, Great Island, thirty acres of marsh mud, was in past times a favored gathering point for fishing boats wanting to sell to the markets up Pamlico River. Down to meet them came the Washington buyboats, their holds filled with ice, and, barring breakdowns, they would just have time enough to make it back upriver to town before the last ice had melted.

*Doctor Bryan had a big fishery on Castle Island and millions of herrings were caught and processed each year. They would give you all the roe you wanted. They had no way to can or freeze it. The herrings left but some of Dr. Bryan's money is still in evidence.*
—Edmund Hoyt Harding, "The Old Hoss of the Pamlico," Washington, North Carolina

At the lower side of the Pamlico River's mouth sat Goose Creek Island, a huge, five-miles-by-five marshfringed island with the Intracoastal Waterway's big ditch on its western side, featuring five fish houses, several hundred people, and some of the best place names anywhere around the Sound Country: Boar Point, Bull Gut, Maiden Point, Minktrap Point, Mouse Harbor, Oyster Creek, Big (and Little) Porpoise Bay, Ragged Point, and Sow Island Point. Its two tiny towns changed their names in the late nineteenth century, when Goose Creek Island became Lowland and Jones Bay became Hobucken, after the man who would be its first postmaster saw "Hoboken, New Jersey," on a letterhead accompanying some Irish potatoes sent back from up north, and renamed the place. One summer's day several years ago, Ann and I roamed about the island, from the end of Middle Bay Road east of Hobucken up to where the Lowland Road runs out into Goose Creek itself, where we ate pimiento-cheese sandwiches and sardines, and we never saw the first nickel of tourist money rolling down the road anywhere about.

Another ten miles or so to the west lay Indian Island. Whether this was the place of John Lawson's Pamtecough Indian town that he called Island, or the site of the last strategy session before the great region-wide Tuscarora attacks of September 1711, or an internment camp for defeated Tuscaroras bound for execution at Martinborough, more recent matters are better known: a man named Ed Springer once had a forty-acre farm on Indian Island, as only his furrows now attest; an older Rocky Mount native, William Bennett, remembered camping on the island as a boy and getting a first-rate case of poison ivy; he also recalled there being a lodge on the island's north side and an Indian burial ground on the south.

Seen from well out in the Pamlico River, Indian Island's eastern end seems cut loose, though from closer in one can tell that this portion, East Point, is still knitted by marsh to the lean, mile-long (and scant third-of-a-mile wide) forested island. As was the case with Batts Island and Drummond Point in the Albemarle, the whole of Indian Island in ages past was itself tied to mainland nearby, the land reaching back to Hickory Point over what is now a long shallow shoal. So the divide between the Pamlico River and South Creek long ago started nearly two miles soundward from where it does today, beginning in the ancient age at Indian Island's East Point.

"Could we camp there?" I once asked a freewheeling fellow from little Washington, who read the full Right of Free Trespass back to me as he raved:

"You can do whatever the hell you want to on Indian Island!"

## CASTLE ISLAND

The first time I ever saw Castle Island was in the great Caroliniana scholar H. G. Jones's office at the North Carolina Collection in Chapel Hill. An old-time wharf and waterfront scene depicted in a large painting on his wall looked achingly familiar to this former rivertown boy, and, seeing my interested gaze settle on it, the bemused H. G. said encouragingly:

"Little Washington."

Though no two of our interior riverports are alike, a few grand while many are miniscule, sound and river towns such as Hertford, Edenton, Plymouth, Columbia, Bayboro, Bath, Washington, New Bern, even Wilmington do favor each other in some ways. Cypress trees and their short wet knobby diminutive forests of knees fringe the ports' waters, greening them up deliciously each April with the promise of yet another year of lowland fecundity, then going a rusty, melancholy gold each October. Upon the reflective soul who lingers at such dark margins comes a sense that though these places may not be the ends of the earth, one might just embark and get there from right where one happens to be standing.

"When does it date to?" I asked him.

"Civil War."

"Oh," I said, looking closer. Nothing particularly bellicose here, just a few folks sitting on a wharf and, across the Pamlico River, a warehouse with a chimney, a little house nearby. Vermonter Merrill G. Wheelock painted this riverine scene—a Boston portrait painter and architect before the war, he was apparently in the Union-occupied riverport of Washington as a military illustrator in 1863, with enough time on his hands to render this artful, detailed George Caleb Binghamesque watercolor.

There must have been quite a lot of them, Union troops with time on their hands after the coastal-plain ports fell to the Federals one after the other, during the spring of 1862—all but Wilmington. Some of them, true, were all too glad to get out of our lowlands and traipse on home to Ohio or Pennsylvania as soon as they were let, but any number of them married local women and settled down right where they had been stationed as minions of the occupying army. And any number of them saw in the swamps (whose wild fastness came up like beasts to the little ports) a future peacetime fortune to be made in timber, in cedar shakes and juniper shingles, planks, barrelstaves, floors and doors and beams and joists—and they were right. Back up in Elizabeth City, the Foremans of Illinois and the Kramers of Pennsylvania had come south, each family in brotherly force, and made mills that built a city worth its name.

The painting on H. G.'s wall was before all that. And though I never

*Castle Island,*
*Washington, N.C.,*
*1863, in Merrill G.*
*Wheelock's* Little
Washington

forgot this almost dreamy window on little Washington during that war, years later I would realize that I had not studied it quite carefully enough in that initial encounter.

Castle Island rose in the Pamlico, right there before me, and I did not know it.

So my second look at Castle Island I took to be my first.

One mild evening in 1997, after supper at Jake and Rachel's house on East Main in Washington, the three of us went walking down past the old, no-longer-standing Marsh Planing Mill, where now a half-mile boardwalk traverses the former mill site and goes over a manmade marsh, past the site of what is now the Estuarium—museum of the estuaries, holding the high riverside ground and looking like a wild island art gallery—and we leaned against the metal riverside rails and lingered.

"Well, that's Castle Island, right there," Jake said, pointing at the tall vine-tangle hardly 150 yards across the river.

Streetlights from the roadway running along the Pamlico reflected off the river's surface and dully illuminated the island's curtain of green. So dully, in fact, that I had quite a time adjusting my eyes to be able to see where the island ended and where its forest was distinct from that of the mainland that lay far beyond. At first Castle Island looked enormous and forbidding, but before long I could see that it was merely small and forbidding.

"Can you go out on it?" I asked

"You probably can," Jake said.

"Who owns it?"

"That's the thing—I hear that it's got about fifty owners, always fighting amongst themselves, so nobody can do anything with it. Used to have goats on it, but a hurricane blew them off before we moved here. But it's been all kinds of stuff through its history, a lime kiln, a Civil War fort, a fish house, a house of ill repute . . . and it's surrounded by shipwrecks, and submerged pilings: water gets low and you see all these ribs sticking up. So when you *do* go over there, you got to be real careful or else you'll come down on one of those ribs or spikes and put a hole in the bottom of your jonboat and then you'll be a Castle Island shipwreck, too."

I briefly pictured my jonboat sitting on the riverbottom with older, grander craft, myself marooned on Castle Island (which often appears on maps simply as "The Castle"), depending for sustenance on the kindness of Washingtonians with enough empathy and athletic energy to come down to the railing at dinnertime and chuck light rolls and beaten biscuits out to me, across the river at this narrow point. A marooner I might be, but I'd never starve out there.

We wandered back on up to Main Street, past the faint fading alleyway *Shrimp for Fish Bait* sign, past the gray marker with the raised black letters telling all comers that *Raleigh News and Observer* founder Josephus Daniels had been born nearby, and, for a few minutes, we strode about the liveoak and Spanish moss-shrouded cemetery where the DeMille graves were, the artistic family that engendered epic-scale moviemaker Cecil B. DeMille and modern dance's first lady, Agnes DeMille.

Before that grave-traipsing, though, on Water Street Jake and Rachel had pointed out the authentic Civil War cannonball still embedded in the front wall of one of the old frame houses, and, in the front wall of the house next door, an identical orb, ballistic mimickry in the first degree, and, then, in the front wall of the third house in the line, the silver tailfins of a modest missile similarly lodged, an artist's witticism aimed less at his own house than at the copycat cannonball business next door.

"Whose place is that?" I said.

"Whiting Tolar's, the sculptor," Jake replied. "You'll have to catch up with him—he knows all about Castle Island."

---

A good while later, we did meet up with Whiting Tolar, poet Michael McFee and I did, even toured Castle Island with him and got his top-of-the-line signifying on that spot just before Christmas 1998, after Michael and I had already made a couple of exploratory tours of our own.

To embolden ourselves for the first pre-Tolar tour, on a brilliant blue October day that same year we piloted the Boston Whaler from the Washington Park boat launch on downriver to Bath for crabcake sandwiches at Bonner's Point, after which, on the way back up, we drifted at the mouth of Blount's Bay enjoying a little of what made Milwaukee famous, along with some coconut cake my mother had made. We watched a helicopter fly low to the water, chasing a noisy as all get-out, high-speed cigarette boat from nearby Fountain boatworks, filming it we supposed, a pursuit that went on all afternoon. This may not be every man's notion of a bigtime, or how to mark the passing of one's fiftieth birthday, but it was certainly mine.

Then we came on upriver, passing off to starboard the cypress of small, narrow, drowned Grandpap's Island, and boated in close and poled the Whaler all about Castle Island, minding Jake's warning about the rubble in the water and the remains of old pilings and boat ribs. A tall thin magnolia fifty feet or so in from the island's east side cast a narrow shadow as the sun sank into the valley of the river whose name changes—peculiarly, immediately—as it passes beneath the Highway 17 bridge just upriver of Castle: Tar above, Pamlico below.

In mid-December McFee and I were back out on the river again. The day was sunny but clouding up as we put the fourteen-foot jonboat in at the Washington Park landing and moved slowly out to and through the flooded cypress of Grandpap's Island, then on through the railroad trestle and around Castle Island to a little beach on its upriver and town side, where cypress stood sentinel over a small lagoon and where we tied up.

On the island we walked straight to a two-and-a-half-foot sweetgum a beaver had girdled, its twinned upper teeth leaving marks about the barkless part of the trunk. McFee and I thrashed about through the smilax and catbriars, picking up whiskey bottles (federal law prohibited resale or re-use, though it needn't've, as we saw no bottles we considered reusing) and assaying other odd flotsam, the corner panels of an old cooler and such. Tree drama: one of four close-together oaks swooped townward from a point fifteen feet up its trunk, and coming up right through it almost in attack was a slender light-seeking magnolia.

A pair of great blue herons frequented Castle Island. One had sat atop a downriver-end cypress as we approached; the other, our bushwhacking set to flight. A slate-blue kingfisher kept strafing the channel side, breaching the Pamlico peace with a rattling cry as she sought her supper. Gulls were wheeling near a listing boat anchored a hundred yards off to the south, and an enormous flock of them circled and dove over the shallows upriver past the Highway 17 bridge.

*What about that listing cabin cruiser off near the railroad trestle?* I wondered. *Whose was it, why was it left to take on water, eventually to sink?*

Presently McFee and I made our way back to the jonboat with no plunder for the day. The sky by now had quite clouded over and the dark was settling in. We crossed the Pamlico channel, tying up at the downriver end of the town's docking wall and stashing the motor for the night underneath the Estuarium.

A wet and miserable wintry pall fell over little Washington during the night, and the morning was such a misty mess we thought more boating might be out of the question. Yet Sound Country weather is nothing if not changeable, and by noon the front had passed, and we had ourselves a brilliant blue-sky day.

Whiting Tolar came over from his missile-smacked Water Street home and joined us. A sculptor, he had done the enormous two-story Rube-Goldbergian vines-and-wire installation in the Estuarium's lobby that dramatized with a small moving ball a water molecule's transit from river to sky to stormcloud and back once again to river. An enthusiastic, active, bearded man about sixty, Whiting loved the lore of his homeplace, and he seemed to love no less the time he spent afield chasing that lore. Over Curiosity Shop crabcakes the night before, he had held forth about an old gristmill up Durham's Creek on the south side of the Pamlico, bearing witness that the mill wheel was still there, all silted up. He allowed as how there was a fortune of wood ducks up Kennedy's Creek on Washington's west side, and said also that rickysticks from a local lumber yard had been floated, driven and strewn all up the river by Hurricane Fran in '96, whereupon beavers had fetched them from up in the trees and woven the rickysticks into their dams and lodges, thank you very much.

Now, with lanky Estuarium director Blount Rumley, we made a foursome and jonboated back across the Pamlico. Blount's name in full was Henry Blount Rumley Jr., and he figured his kinship to merchant John Gray Blount of the Shell Castle–Governor John Wallace partnership to be "either my second cousin six times removed or my first cousin seven times removed."

Whatever Blount's kinship to the old import-export tycoon might have been, the river was low. Over near the railroad trestle, the listing boat from the day before now had her pump going, blowing a heavy stream of water out her port side. We pulled in to the sandy beach on the southeast side of Castle Island, lugged the jonboat up out of the river and tied her up.

Then we walked slowly in the sandy shallows, following the old tide-level wharf frames—the same sort of structures Ann and I would see years later way across Pamlico Sound at Shell Castle Island, Whiting telling us how the shippers filled in, inside those frames, with ballast rock and broken china, discarding a shipment's breakage before they ever took any goods over to town for sale. Lo, we found plate edges and shards here, there, everywhere—Whiting said he once found a handblown glass wine-bottle, *intact*, in one of the wharf frames. The colonial docks were here on the island's south side, Whiting said, with later development being on the town side. The frames were just relics in the sand now, yet even as they lay there they were testaments to real industry: these were enormous timbers, notched and fit together and held fast by iron spikes.

I climbed over the vine-covered brick walls of an old, now caved-in building. Perhaps this was part of the island's lime kiln, or perhaps all this brick was the remnant of the Union's cannon emplacement during the Civil War. Even from the ruin, all fallen down nowhere near as high above the river as the structure had originally been, I had an extremely good view down the Pamlico—I could see Maules Point on the lower side of Blount's Bay eleven miles distant.

"See that sandy beach down there on Queen's Island?" Whiting called out. He gestured toward one of the two spoil islands downriver of Castle, formed by Corps of Engineers dredge work on the river channel in 1938.

"That's where old Coconut Jones hung out," Whiting went on. "Coconut was a shellshocked World War II soldier who was always paddling around the river in a flatbottomed boat, paddling with a board. He'd come out here, mess around, paddle on over to that beach, set him up a hammock and lay up in it reading magazines all day, all summer long."

"Did he sleep out here?" I asked.

"Depends," Whiting said. "If he was drunk enough he did."

Now Blount started hacking us a path through the briars over toward the town side, and he got going on how much deeper than the current controlled depth of nine feet the river's channel had been just a century ago. He recalled a Washington-to-Ocracoke boat named the *Bessie Virginia* coming up one time with a load of crabs in the hold. Finding that the local market for crabs was flooded, the captain went all through the town of Washington begging people to come take these crabs.

"My father got three pickup truck loads," Blount said. "Spread them all over the backyard for fertilizer. Mama was *so mad*! She was furious at him about that. Course it *did* smell right much." Blount laughed, adding, "Neighbors didn't like it too much either."

Whiting then said *his* mother told him how there was, back at the turn of the twentieth century, a family living in a shanty out here on Castle Island and steaming crabs for a living. "The daughter went to school with

*Castle Island,*
*Pamlico River at*
*Washington, 1890s*

my mother," Whiting said, "the man taking her over every morning in a skiff to the town side. But none of the town girls would walk with her—they ostracized her, on account of they thought she was dirty and disheveled, unkempt and always smelling of steamed crabs."

By the time we got back to it, our jonboat sat high and dry. The Pamlico had fallen, the work of the wind, between half a foot and a foot during the short two and a half hours we were out there. And we still hadn't seen any goats.

The island's goats, seven of them bought at auction, were the Chamber of Commerce's idea—Jerry Allegood, longtime Eastern-beat man for the *News and Observer*, called them "four-footed defoliators." They were the first line of attack toward reclaiming the old focal point for use by Washington's townspeople. This was a plan back in 1990: Castle Island would be fitted out with piers and wooden plankways and, in time, maybe a bulkhead and a sandy beach. This plan was picking up from where the last unexecuted scheme had left off, the American Bicentennial notion to make Castle a city park with a lighted fountain.

"We are the first generation that hasn't used it," businessman Artie Rawls told the newspaper at the time, allowing that he had camped on Castle Island as a teenager but figured there had been no commercial use of Castle since about 1930—"Although a couple had lived there in a fish camp in the 1950s."

People say sawmilling on the island dated to 1818, and that an island sawmill came up for sale in 1860. In their book *Washington on the Pamlico*, Ursula F. Loy and Pauline M. Worthy declared that an oyster-shell lime kiln gave the little island its name: "The chimneys of the kiln looked so much like turrets on a castle that the island was nicknamed 'the Castle.'" Some say that in the days of a wilder Washingtonian waterfront, when mystic knights of sound and sea cavorted here and if members of royalty joined them they did so with tarnished crowns, a brothel boomed over on the Castle. "I can't verify that bawdy-house tale," Whiting Tolar had told us.

Even with the vines gnawed away by those heroic goats, separating the island's exact truth from its brickbats and old bottles and broken pottery may be a pursuit long in the accomplishing, and the goats—now long gone—produced some unintended consequences on Castle. When I asked Whiting and Blount about those goats, their version had it that to help clean up the island the Chamber put six or seven goats out there about 1988. The goats ate up the vines from '88 on, but the big trees (all bigger than the crop current in 1998, which still included an enormous townside sycamore toward the downriver end) had very shallow root systems and were in fact being held up by the strong, interwoven vines and vine mats. So after the goats over time had eaten up most of the vines, here came Hurricane Bertha in July '96 and Hurricane Fran in September '96, and the biggest trees went down, and their rootballs, massed still, were out there to this day.

"And the goats, during the hurricane, they were out here drowning, you know," said Whiting, "and it got to be a big TV thing, TV people getting folks all upset about the poor goats, so the Chamber of Commerce was catching a lot about it, so they real quick up and said: 'Oh, those aren't *our* goats, we got *our* goats off the island when we knew the hurricane was coming. Those must be *somebody else's goats*!'"

## CEDAR ISLAND

The Cedar Island National Wildlife Refuge—10,000 of whose nearly 15,000 acres are the largest unchanged salt marsh in our state—takes in all of Down East Carteret County between the fishing village of Atlantic and the high grounds of upper Cedar Island fronting upon Pamlico Sound, including the last mile or two of barrier strand west of the Cedar Island ferryslip out to Point of Grass.

A map of refuge holdings looks like a crab-gnawed *N* tipped over to the left. Tens of thousands of people visit the refuge yearly as they motor along N.C. 12 to or from the Cedar Island ferry, and there is an undeniable simple grandeur to the vast, five-mile prairie of marsh they traverse. Shank's mare and a boat of shallow draft afford one even more of this paradise, though, and the sheer size of the Cedar Island refuge lands, in conjunction with the national seashore of Core Banks and the big waters of Core Sound in between them, make it a wilderness well worth note and more exploration—public landings are at the N.C. 12 Monroe Gaskill Bridge over the Thorofare and where the Lola Road runs out into Lewis Creek.

The grassy wildlife road just south of the Thorofare is tabletop flat and seems nearly shot straight. It is an easy lowland walk, not quite three miles from the highway, N.C. 12, to the lane's terminus in a little creek and cove opening onto West Thorofare and West Bays, with Pamlico Sound off in the far distance beyond Point of Grass. Along this outback path just below the Thorofare channel that separates mainland Carteret County from the vast Cedar Island marshes, there is no shortage of variety or reward.

At Old Christmastime in early January of '96, doves and sparrows flushed before the walking party in halfdozens and dozens, rising and flying up into the brilliant red-berried yaupon along the roadside. Blue gentian grew in the pine barrens off to the side, the little flower with five lavender blue petals and the green-gold interior, and cohosh too with its own black berries. Bracken fern flourished everywhere, and nearly a dozen varieties of blueberry called this place home. In the pine savannah near N.C. 12, at the start of the walk, skeletal trees from a fire ten years ago stood stark against the winter sky, but healthy longleafs on the road's north side more than compensated. The cedars in here were soft, not prickly, with berries. A mile or more and the pocosin started closing in, earthbound clouds of wax myrtle

*Tell me, then, and tell me truly, what land and country is this? Who are its inhabitants? Am I on an island, or is this the sea board of some continent?*
—Homer, The Odyssey, XIII (ca. 850 B.C.)

hereabouts called *myrkle*. Mosses carpeted ditch bottoms where no water had lately stood, till a very small and teacolored pond announced a gum and poplar stand, a Dismal Swamp–style landscape so different from the savannah just passed through.

We had eaten Down East hearty the evening before—goose and pastry and rutabaga stew, sweet potatoes and collards—and I was glad of it. An easy walk, yes, yet even at low altitude and no topographical relief, keeping pace and staying warm on a six-mile round-trip at Twelfth Night was, though not the strenuous life, still a task of modest stoutness. The more we kept at it, hoofing down the lane, the more robins we saw, an abundant crowd, and we were reminded that this blackbird once made up as much a part of the Down East diet as the goose.

At Cadduggen Creek lay an old log bridge, a remnant rather, its planking now down to one two-by-twelve, but river otters slid nearby with no concern for the roadway's fate. After the miles of field and forest, our longer view over the bays toward the marshes and the sound was spectacular, the way it opened out. There was no question *whether* about coming back, only *when*.

Nearly three months later, we were drawn here again, and pine pollen like golddust covered everything. Mosquitoes were plentiful. The word from Ann's father, Doctor John Kindell of Sea Level, who walked the wildlife road daily, was that they had been evident all winter, for the first time ever. And these were "high-wind mosquitoes," said to be undaunted and unmoved by stiff breezes. This spring morning's wind, presaging afternoon and evening gales and rains, proved out the word—mosquitoes hung in it, seeming to wait a turn to light and feed as if they were endowed with patience as well as hunger. Nothing to be done about them but slap and spray and marvel. But there was something far more promising and pleasing in the wind than the voracious insect: there was the scent of another abundance, more yellow jessamine twining and blooming this year than anyone could ever recall, and in this corner of the wildlife refuge, at least, the lowlands were redolent of lemon.

Late one summer morning, Ann and I lit out with her father from Don and Katie Morris's marina in Atlantic—one of eastern Carolina's great ports and points of embarkation—in a twenty-one-foot fishing boat for a circumnavigation of the old Hunting Quarters—the land mass so-named by Indians and early settlers that includes present-day Sea Level and Atlantic as well as the southern part of the refuge. Down Core Sound we boated, past Styron's Bay and then up into Nelson's Bay, under the Dan Taylor Bridge and into Salter's Creek. As we cruised slowly through the cut carrying us north again toward Long Bay, I heard from Ann's father, Doctor John, a thing or two about Sea Level's Dan Taylor, who had remembered his roots and raising and underwritten the Sea Level Hospital. Taylor long ago formed up with his brother as the West Indies Fruit and Steamship Company and made a fortune in shipping, starting with Dan Taylor's buying up and warehousing near-worthless ballast salt in the Virginia Tidewater and then being lucky enough to be the one holding salt in quantity at the outbreak of World War I when governments wanted it, lots of it, and quickly.

Out the creek at the upper end of the cut, in ten or twelve feet of water in Long Bay we tried to beat the still and near-suffocating July heat with a swim, but a gracious plenty of jellyfish drove us without delay straight back into the boat. Under way again, we rounded Long Bay Point and came down West Thorofare Bay, within a mile of the otterslide on Cadduggen Creek that we had hiked to.

Three dozen porpoises fell in with us, escorting us down West Thorofare Bay. Porpoise pods of no small size abounded in these waters, and in other reaches nearby—our friend Peter Riggs of Lenox Point has while kayaking come upon a hundred up in North River, and Ann and I happened last summer upon a well-known commune of several dozen that had taken up residence around the mouth of Core Creek in the upper Newport. Hard to imagine it nowadays, but, in addition to the whaling that once went on along the central coast, from Diamond City on Shackleford Banks, porpoise too was a commercial catch. Memoirist Clarence Robinson (Atlantic High School, Class of 1911) recalled: "There was a little porpoise fishing on Core Sound in 1880. Someone said it took five or six porpoises to produce a barrel of oil. Before the turn of the century I saw a porpoise seine, about ten-inch mesh, stored in an old house." And coastal historian David Stick has written that in the late nineteenth century there was a porpoise *factory* down the sound at Lookout Woods just west of the cape.

Where the Thorofare cinched up, the porpoises started dropping away from us, turning and cavorting back toward West Bay and Pamlico Sound. Under the N.C. 12 bridge we went, then across Thorofare and Barry Bays, around Hall Point and back to Don and Katie's little marina, the whole roundabout taking some three or four hours.

Other summer times, and these were the children's favorites, we would stop in at Don and Katie's and from there, armed with a sack of cheeseburgers and chili dogs, French fries and onion rings so big that three filled one of those small red-and-white paper boats and constituted a full order, we would come out the marina channel into Core Sound and bound, usually with the wind, northeast up the sound and straight across Thorofare Bay.

It was the Hammock, Rumley's Hammock, we were boating for, there to set the small anchor somewhere along the pine island's halfmile south-

*Harbor, Cedar Island,*
*July 2005*

facing sand beach that runs between salt marsh on the west and Lookout Point in the sound on the east, to picnic and swim and swat at greenheads for an hour or two. Maybe walk down to the point and watch the waves cutting away at the corner where the Hammock turns north for Fish Hawk Point and Rumley's Bay. Such stormtide flotsam as old net floats and crabpot buoys—broken and blown loose from their charges—that we have regularly fished out of the shallows near the Hammock's beach have since made their way into our coastal Carolina chowderhouse musical, *King Mackerel*, and onto faraway stages in Wilmington; Washington, D.C.; and New York City—so it was that Cedar Island went with us not only in our hearts, but in our touring trunk as well.

At the head of Rumley's Bay there was one more thoroughfare through these otherwise marshes primeval, John Day's Ditch running from Rumley's to West Bay, hired dug in 1927 by Day (a cabin-boy become seacaptain, whom the East Coast and West Indies trade made wealthy) to serve mainly as a *fence* to hold in the hundreds of head of cattle Captain Day was trying to graze free-range on Rumley's Hammock but that kept wandering up toward Cedar Island's high ground to the north and feeding on Captain Day's neighbors' gardens. Island historian Jean Day wrote that, in addition to his livestock operation, the captain had the first car on Cedar

*Harbor, Cedar Island,*
*July 2005*

Island and also had himself a clubhouse out on Rumley's Hammock. With a caretaker. And the caretaker had *him*self a still there on the Hammock and a ready market for his goods down in Atlantic and beyond. When hogs high on mash and staggering back for more led the law right to the unbonded distillery, though, the caretaker went off to stir elsewhere for a spell in a state-owned club called the Big House.

The bootlegger and his works are long gone, and Captain Day's efforts at establishing productive oyster beds up his waterway came to naught as well. Maybe there are mullet to be had up John Day's Ditch, but Ann's best recollections of fishing down this way are of going to the Thorofare bridge with her father when she was a little girl. "That's when I really started to like trout," she said, "catching those Thorofare trout."

Ann also recalled a rather different sport: war games originating at the Marines' Atlantic Outlying Field, adjacent to the refuge at its southern-most. She remembered how during the games airplanes dropped flares by parachute out above the Cedar Island marshes, and how a couple of times those military nightlights torched the whole wet prairie. "You could drive out to the Thorofare, out on Cedar Island Road," she said, "and see a line of fire burning across the marsh at night."

The great marsh has long since renewed itself, and a large part of the pleasure of that renewal is in its wealth of birdlife—from the resident herons, rails, egrets, fish crows and marsh hawks and kingfishers to pilgrims like the warblers coming up from lower latitudes in springtime and the thousands of redheads and scaup and black ducks moving south to Cedar Island in late fall, waterfowl populations peaking here in December and January. A belted kingfisher, like one of those awaiting dinner who sit so nobly and patiently on canalside powerlines flanking U.S. 70 and N.C. 12, has taken up residence with us in the red-clay country far from his, and Ann's, Carteret County home—he feeds mostly off admiration, though, for he is a creation of Atlantic woodcarver Lionel Gilgo.

Cedar Island is way down yonder, at one edge of the world. It may not be the place where the Lost Colony *really* settled and lived on, as some have suggested, but it is and in perpetuity will be a colony of the wild, flooded at times unpredictable by tides of the wind and not the moon, less known and perhaps less appreciated than others in the great chain of refuge that includes Mackay Island, Pea Island, Alligator River, Pocosin Lakes, Swanquarter, and Mattamuskeet. By foot and boat, by parked car along the roadshoulders of the causeway transecting the marsh, it is ours to share with the deer and the rare bear, with many thousands of birds and millions of insects; so along with a pair of binoculars we bring a pair of canisters filled with something to ward off the biting flies and the mosquitoes, even if they once warded do not go away but just hang there in the high winds and regard us hungrily.

"Those mosquitoes are the best thing we got going for us on Cedar Island," Mister Worth Harris, a survivor of the Great Hurricane of '33, once (according to Jean Day) told the water-softener man, adding a barb at outlanders: "Well, you see, it keeps the Ding-Batters out."

*Not all of them, Mister Worth. Not quite all.*

### HOG ISLAND

Those who ply the waters from Ocracoke down to Cedar Island in small craft, once they have crossed the inlet, run down behind Core Banks eight miles or so, then cut over and course down the channel between Harbor and Wainwright Islands, then past Hog Island Point and Hog Island (a group of small islands, really, clustered around Back Bay) to the right, and on into Cedar Island Bay.

Along about 1900, a sailor from this place once beat up the Pamlico River from down Cedar Island way, tacking as best he could. His course was west-northwest, and the wind out of the north hit him abeam. All this way—he had passed Durham's Creek, where the gristmill was, and he could see the mouth of Bath Creek, his quarry, up across the Pamlico River.

*Beach at Lola, Cedar
Island; Hog Island in
distance, July 2005*

Yet he could make no headway straight into the wind. *She's going to be
blowing a gale*, he thought. The sailor would have to head downwind and
give it up for the day. A couple hundred yards from the Pamlico's south
shore he swung her back into the wind, took his canvas down, and hove his
anchors out and waited for them to catch, so they would not drag. Then he
lowered his skiff, and himself into her, and pulled for shore, where his life
was forever changed.

In 1999 at the Ol' Store in Oriental, Lucille Truitt, who ran it then with
her husband Billy, told me about this moment:

"My grandfather lived on Hog Island. He was delivering a boat of salt
mullet up to Bath, and he came ashore because of bad weather at Core Point.
And he saw this beautiful woman on horseback, bringing corn to the mill.

"That was my grandmother, and he brought her back to Hog Island to
live."

*Lupton, Hog Island,*
*painting by Lucille*
*Truitt, about 2002,*
*from a sketch by*
*Callie Lupton,*
*about 1920*

*Back to Hog Island*—what did that mean, though? Most folks nowadays hearing the name Hog Island might think of the huntclub that throve out there during the twentieth century, or the more recent summer camp at the same spot. But Salt-mullet Styron must have been offering his beautiful woman on horseback more of a home than a huntclub, must have known she would want for more society than the rowdy camaraderie of a bunch of wingshooters away from their own families and their two good addresses.

So he did.

The community on the southernmost island in the Hog Island group bore the name *Lupton,* after a Carteret County family of long standing, dating back to when Christopher Lupton shipwrecked near Cedar Island sometime in about the 1760s, married Elizabeth Robinson, and began the begets and begats. From a 1921 sketch of the place made by Callie Lupton, Lucille Truitt drafted and painted several studies of the coastal village, a dot of a place that, though diminutive, was still vivid enough in the eye of the federal government to merit, between July 21, 1892, and May 15, 1920, a U.S. Post Office.

Lupton lay facing Cedar Island Bay, and its residents looked west-southwest across the bay at big Cedar Island itself. Callie's sketch as translated by Lucille took stock of Lupton's architectural inventory: twenty houses, one store, two graveyards, a pond, a ball field, several docks along the bayshore and some fish houses on stilts on the Core Sound shore around the Point ("Cedar Hill"), with an Indian shell mound right there on the Point. Outside the homes gardens grew, all fenced in, and those tending them, their names tied to these homesteads and small plots, were Styron, Lupton, Gaskill, Emory, Spencer, and Downing, the latter a black man who had been shipwrecked and saved.

What remains?

James Barrie Gaskill of Beaufort and Ocracoke, a big, jolly mustachioed fisherman and owner of the Fat Boy Fish Company, once told me—concerning Albert Styron's General Store, which he as a Styron descendant owned and which his daughter Candy ran in Ocracoke near the lighthouse—that the front part of the building, its cedar walls, had been floated across the sound from Lupton about 1920. So an old store continued to invite people in out of the heat and out of the rain, receiving in an Ocracoke summertime half-day more visitors, perhaps, than it likely ever saw in a month early last century back down at Lupton. For want of opportunity, if not society, during the 1920s others tore down their homes there, and now, like the port at Shell Castle Island and the vanished village of Lukens Island east of South River, Lupton lives on only in memory and art.

In the world as Lucille Truitt fancied it and painted it, men and women were laying nets out to dry, ponies enjoyed free range, men worked at their skiffs, children played upon the ball field, while someone tilled one of the gardens with an old self-propelled rig, and a two-masted gaff-rigged fishing boat—jib set—sailed in from Core Sound: all in all, an idyll.

Yet in this island paradise deep trouble lived, too, and, as we looked over her Luptonian artwork one golden August afternoon several years ago, Lucille tapped the post office on her painting and spoke of it simply and directly. "It's a sad story," she said to me.

"Really sad."

## LUPTON—ODE FOR NEVA MAY

On Old Christmas 1912, Neva May Gaskill of Lupton and Eldred Spencer, an Ocracoke fisherman—island natives, both—got themselves a marriage license in Carteret County on the Carolina coast. Neva Gaskill would become a very young bride—on the license she declared she was eighteen, though she was two years shy of that lawful age; for his part, Eldred said he was twenty-three, though he was four years older. No matter to Justice of the Peace Thomas Lupton Goodwin, the local marrying man everyone honorifically called "Squire John"—he married them six days later at Lupton, the tiny upper Core Sound village, just seventy or eighty souls living a scant thirty miles northeast of port towns Morehead City and Beaufort. The Spencers made her home theirs.

On March 18, 1919, the U.S. Post Office appointed pretty young Neva Gaskill Spencer to be Lupton's postmistress. At the time of her postal appointment, though, she was still in grief over Eldred's untimely death in October 1918. The Great War's influenza pandemic had carried him off, and Eldred's passing was not the first time since their wedding that death had struck her closely. This pair had had a boy, Edward, in their first year of marriage, and then twin girls in the summer of 1916. The one named Mildred had lived on, but Metta, the other, had survived only fourteen days.

On April 18, 1919, Neva Spencer's appointment was confirmed. Yet exactly *when*, following her confirmation, her precursor in office turned over the cashbox and stamps and the small frame Lupton Post Office is hard to say—it might have been as late as March 1920 before she actually took charge. Whenever she started and handstamped her first postcard or letter, her tenure would not be long.

For in the late spring of 1920 Neva Spencer lay dying in the old Morehead City Hospital on Shepard Street between Eighth and Ninth, and there on April 23, 1920, she passed away. The Lupton Post Office closed almost immediately, in the middle of May 1920, and Lupton's mail thenceforth went to Lola on nearby and much larger Cedar Island.

The second postmistress to serve Lupton had also been its last.

---

When the federal census was taken early in the year 1920, Neva May Gaskill Spencer was a twenty-four-year-old widow, an unintentional head-of-household with a brood that included her own children Edward, now seven, and Mildred, three and a half, as well as her eighteen-year-old sister Lucie Gaskill and her sixteen-year-old brother Luther Gaskill, Neva's mail-carrier about the island community.

Before Neva Spencer, only five people had served and been in charge of Hog Island's post office at Lupton. They were, by dates of appointment: John W. Lupton, July 21, 1892; Willie C. Manson, September 28, 1892; William W. Styron, May 11, 1893; Ida Lee Lupton, June 8, 1895; and William R. Styron, February 13, 1900.

Something went wrong at the Lupton Post Office either just before Neva Spencer took over, or not long after. Perhaps there had been a robbery—one press account said so—along about November 1918, during which a few hundred dollars in stamps and cash were taken, leaving that loss to stand as a charge against Lupton's account, and a heavy one at that. Or perhaps the truth was simpler and less dramatic: just a $27 shortage on the books by April 1920.

The *Raleigh News and Observer* would report that Mrs. Spencer had received a letter—from whom or what agency, though?—telling of this $27 shortage and stating "that unless the amount was forthcoming she would be sent to prison." This all shocked Neva Spencer who, so it would be told in the *Beaufort News*, "had been very despondent since the death of her husband" and "had shown signs of mental aberration."

To whom could she talk about trouble? In whom might she confide? In a town that was not even a town, in a village that was a huddle of a dozen families no more than a few feet above the level of the sea, telling one would be the same as telling all. The very shame of *talking* about the shame of such an accusation (had it come from some postal inspector or auditor faraway in the national capital?) or of her feeling an overbearing sense of financial responsibility despite her innocence in this matter would be too much. The charge, whatever its source, stood in and of itself as a black mark and a letter of disgrace, and disgrace in such an isolated place as Lupton could shift its shape ever so quickly, and directly, into despair.

Why not sit her younger sister and brother before her and tell them what was dragging her down and weighing so upon her?

Perhaps they were still babies, no more than children in her mind . . . when she was seventeen and bearing Edward, Lucie was but eleven and Luther nine. They were children then and maybe now, at eighteen and sixteen, they were children to her yet—leaving Neva, widowed and twenty-four, the might-as-well-be mother of four, with only her small post-office paycheck and Luther's even smaller mailman pay to support the five of them.

Where but in the ground was her helpmeet when she needed him most? Would she ever have another? What new man could she ever attract? What man would take on this beleaguered quintet? Indeed, what man ever even happened by Lupton, who was not already married, affianced, or spoken for?

Not to be hauled off and imprisoned for something she did not do, Neva Spencer at last wrote her relatives in April 1920, that she would take action to protect herself and her children, so that they would neither go homeless nor live the rest of their lives in shame. Though she had no power to correct or fix what was wrong at the post office, she had come to know that she need not live with a hideous judgment—a *mis*judgment—against her.

Perhaps the heat of the shame inflaming her fired her imagination and granted her the awesome right for a few moments to peer into the future of her family. Perhaps Neva was so prescient she could foresee that if her offspring survived her—her son Edward, say—he would be raised by strangers way down Core Sound, have his last name changed, and, when he was old enough to have his own home, he would then out of the unending shame literally efface his mother by building a false wall over the wall upon which her portrait hung. And foresee further that his son, Neva's grandson, would only learn of all this at his father's death, when his mother would tear that false wall down and let the boy gaze at the grandmother he never knew nor even knew *of* and at long last tell him the whole story.

Had Neva seen what could—and *did*—come to pass?

Yes. If not in such detail, she saw it whole. There were worse things in this world than death, she figured, and she wrote as much in the letters to relatives she penned just before she acted, looking harshly at the life she foresaw for Edward and Mildred and herself, assaying a life of poverty and loneliness and being pitied or, worse, scorned, and decades that would crawl by with little to do but struggle and reflect bitterly on the fates that had brought her to this. Before she would be shunned by her neighbors she herself would shun that very future; before she would see her children treated like dirt and then, further, see them turn upon her and hate her for visiting shame and brutish life upon them, she would shun that too. And before she, feeling entrapped and old before her time and one husband and one infant in the grave and she not yet twenty-five, would watch herself stare down-the-bay hoping for the tops of schooners' masts to come into view, hoping for just one of the sailors on just one of those fishing boats to be in his heart of hearts seeking her, just her and what she Neva Spencer née Gaskill had to offer just to him, before she would see herself glancing from the horizon and the morning sun reflecting off Core Sound to the smaller mirror indoors, which would tell her daily that her looks were going away from her, before any of this, she thought, she would decide for herself what justice and mercy really were, and *where* they were, and if the grace that surpasseth all understanding were accessible to her only in the undiscovered country, there she would go. Those she had borne once already, she would bear again. In the land that knows no parting her children would thank her and her husband would greet them all with the open arms she could no longer know on this earth any more than know peace and dignity, or even a simple calm in her heart. Given the great choice that a later bard than the Bard would pose as being "between grief and nothing," she would choose the nothingness of death; choose *not* to be.

Not to be.

On Wednesday morning, April 21, 1920, Neva rose from her bed upstairs in her island home and stepped down into her kitchen to feed her two hungry children. While others in Lupton broke their fasts with light rolls and salt mullet and smoked ham, Neva prepared for Edward and Mildred a simple concoction in a cup they were to share; and, in a second cup, she mixed the same caustic potion for herself:

Coca-Cola and Red Devil lye.

She told them to drink it and then to lie down on the kitchen floor, and Mildred did as her mother asked. Edward, trying just a little of it, but finding it distasteful and painful and shying away from the drink, quickly ran outdoors to play with some other children on the sandy street. His mouth was badly burned, but otherwise the boy was all right.

Edward said nothing to his playmates of what had just occurred in his home.

Within a quarter of an hour Luther Gaskill, Neva's younger brother, came into the Spencer home and found his little niece on the floor, his sister staggering on the stairs, crying, wailing, and blood everywhere. Having drunk her own deadly brew, she had then taken a butcher knife and, attempting to hurry her own end, slashed her neck to the bone.

The sixteen-year-old mail-carrier fled the house in horror and sought help, but no medic in this tiny soundside hamlet could treat such ghastly wounds as this mother had inflicted upon herself and her child. They would all of them, the boy too, have to journey to the nearest hospital, the one in Morehead City just across the Newport River from Beaufort. No road then ran through the labyrinth of salt marshes, mud, and swamp forest lying between Lupton and that hospital, no road but Core Sound. Set sail they must, and set sail they did.

By Wednesday night, these damaged people were brought to the Morehead City Hospital on Shepard Street, where Mildred anxiously drank a cup of milk after she refused to take it in a glass. A little after dawn she wanted more milk, but she no longer was able to swallow.

At ten o'clock on Thursday morning, April 22, the four-year-old girl died, too badly burned internally to live.

Neva Spencer came to about midday Thursday. She could not speak, though she was able to draft notes:

> When is the doctor going to fix my throat?
> Am I going to die?
> Is Mildred dead?
> I wish I was home with a barrel of water like I was last week this time.

An operation restored her vocal organs, and when she came back to she found a voice somewhere in her burned, gashed throat and now she spoke, first asking for water, which the nurse gave her, and then asking if Mildred were still alive. They told Mrs. Spencer yes, though Mildred had passed away some hours before. None of this occurred in calm, or peace—so great was Neva Spencer's own pain from the lye she had ingested, and so agitated was she from it, the hospital attendants had to strap her to her bed.

On Friday, April 23, at quarter past noon, Neva Gaskill Spencer died.

The family would take the mother and daughter back to Lupton for burial. The surviving son, Edward, seeing in his island home only emptiness and horror behind it, would refuse to return with his uncle and the dead. A. H. Outlaw, the county's welfare superintendent, took a strong interest in the Spencer affair, and reports were that he would seek to place his new ward in the Free Will Baptist Orphanage at Middlesex. In truth, Edward would in time be taken in and raised by a couple in Gloucester, on the mainland across the Straits from Harkers Island, and would eventually spend his life as an electrician in Beaufort.

The *Beaufort News*, telling this grim story the week after it occurred, surveyed three centuries of coastal life, all the decades of shipwrecks, nor'easters and hurricanes, piracy, Revolution, pestilence and Civil War, and then declared the case of Neva Spencer and her children to be "the most pitiful tragedy ever enacted in Carteret County."

---

Now, eighty-six years later, no record of robbery or shortage exists in the archives of the U.S. Post Office that Neva Spencer served for barely a year. The *Fayetteville Observer* had it that she was "believed to have become demented when she found her accounts did not balance at the end of the month. So far as known no charge of a shortage had been made against her." The same relatives to whom Neva wrote before attacking her children and herself and who were never named in the press, even as Neva was being taken by boat to the Morehead City Hospital, apparently seized the Lupton Post Office's records and placed them in a trunk, there to await a postal inspector and an official investigation. Yet no record of any Post Office investigation exists, either, nor is there one from before or after her death in the annals of the Department of Justice. Nothing about this woman lives on in the National Personnel Records in St. Louis, Missouri. Only the news reports are left, dispatches of her distraction, despair, anguish, mental aberration and rash acts, along with the widespread talk.

Some said Neva's end was all too eerily reminiscent of the death of another postmistress, nearby Atlantic's, who had gone out in Core Sound in a boat after similar talk about account shortages and slashed her own throat with a straight razor—only eleven months earlier! Some believed and others claimed to know that another hand—not Neva's—did the thievery and misappropriation that engendered the awful killing to which Neva felt driven.

In one of the small, now-overgrown cemeteries of lower Hog Island, where the myrtle and yaupon hold sway, Neva May Gaskill Spencer abides in the undiscovered country of death. There, her daughter Mildred is always four, and Neva herself is always twenty-four and innocent. She cannot know, as do we, that in the Post Office files in Washington, D.C., there lies but one brief, wholly honorable note beside her name: the second and last postmistress of Lupton, North Carolina, it says, *died in office.*

## HARBOR ISLAND

Harbor Island is a scant half-acre of bone-white shellbank curving away to east and west, with a tabby-walled huntclub ruin at the western side of what little landmass it has. This island stands small—it does not loom—a diminutive ghostly ruin that conjures images of lochside castles in Ireland, of old stone barns and roofless farmsteads glimpsed by travelers from far across the endless barrens of Iceland, perhaps even the fabled house of Roan Innish, or, down Beaufort way, the old fish plant's brick chimney on Phillips Island beside the channel of the Newport River. I first saw Harbor Island and its ruin on a clear, near-still August evening just after sunset nearly ten years ago, from the hurricane deck of Wilbur's Camp on soundside Core Banks. It lay about three miles distant from the camp, but scarcely seemed in that brilliant clarity more than one mile away, and my small binoculars brought the ruin right in close for inspection.

Why, I wondered, was this tumbled-in lodge more intriguing to me than if it had been whole and still functioning at its early-twentieth-century level, when tycoons and mere mortals alike showed up out here for some of the best gunning in the Carolina east? That was the real story, wasn't it? What *Ozymandian* intrigue could there be in two-and-a-half tabby walls, all that remained on Harbor Island? Unroofed and with vacant, eye-like windows, the stranded ruin stood guard over the two sounds' boundary, staring at but passing no judgment upon all comers, human and avian, fishermen and crabbers, plovers and pelicans, upon the long broad waters of Core Sound below it and the vast inland sea of Pamlico Sound above.

"We used to come up here to picnic," Ann said the next morning, as we guided our Boston Whaler north, following the boat-width channel from the creek at Wilbur's, bound for Core's meandering channel, and boating along, around occasionally, when there were no nets or lines, through the pound-net stakes set out in the sound. "And Mom and Dad would send us kids running over to find wild parsley behind the old clubhouse, to put on our sandwiches."

*Harbor Island, 1998*

With us was our own boatload of children, Cary, then four, the twins Hunter and Susannah, then twelve, and their friend Miriam Stone, all bathing-suited and all interested in any island outing that would involve swimming, whether or not it had a pile of historic stones. There was little wind this summer morning, so the sound waters were slack, and we eased on in close to the goal. The nearer we came to Harbor, the smaller the little shellbank now appeared, much smaller, somehow, than it had from back on the topdeck at Wilbur's Camp.

Top of Core, shank of Pamlico, here was Harbor in its full and current glory, though, sitting as delicate as a crescent moon upon the division, nay, *being* the division between the sounds, as if the great waters knew their names, or ever even stayed put. The bow of the boat we nosed into the shelly beach, which dropped off quickly, the stern being in a good four and a half feet of water. We loaded the children off the Whaler with boat cushions, tossed a hook under the bowrail, and watched Cary who was already run-

*Tabby wall, Harbor Island Club, 1998*

ning along the beach for Harbor's eastern tip, shrieking with delight over the bright white narrow trail through these broad, docile summer waters.

The older children skipped shells and flopped in the shallows just clear of the boat, while Ann and Cary—once she boomeranged back—and I strode over toward the huntclub ruin. Near our home back upstate in the red-clay country was a big cistern that once powered a small turn-of-the-last-century gold mine, and the cistern walls were a rough conglomerate—but they were *nothing* like this, for Harbor Island's was the coarsest conglomeration I think I had yet seen that bore the name tabby. The concrete looked as though it were being held together by the shells, rather than the other way around. Perhaps this was why the south wall of the structure now lay in large, chunky pieces in Core Sound, supporting nothing but salt air and blue sky. Or perhaps the waves and the wind that drives them would have knocked over anything so exposed, given enough time and tide and rising sea.

An exposed spot this is, too, just a dot in big, wide open water. One wintry Sunday over half a century ago, the legendary decoy carver Julian Hamilton Jr. made a stormy dash from the Banks across this portion of Core. Hamilton was in a twenty-foot skiff he had borrowed from a cousin, and almost everything went wrong. Following seas came over his stern, his steering cable broke, and the wind blew him sideways into Wainwright Island, where he changed clothes and repaired the cable. He then braced himself and took cold comfort running the lee of Harbor Island as he made for Cedar Island Bay, there encountering six-foot seas and a loon sleeping through the storm.

The waves lapping Harbor this August, though, might not have topped six inches, so still was the air, and so calm was the inside surf. Cary came back from the island's seaward end loaded down with special shells, then dropped them unceremoniously near the boat and made for the ruin, which Ann was just stepping into as if she were walking through time.

And so she was. Ann had not been on Harbor Island in perhaps twenty years, and we both sensed this keenly when I called and pointed out to her the deep green herbs growing with literal abandon just above the hunt-club's north wall, and she exclaimed:

"The wild parsley! It's still here!"

Whereupon we picked and ate a couple of handfuls of the saltiest parsley we were ever likely to find in the state of nature, North Carolina. *Rock celery*, the Greeks called parsley, and the Harbor Island variety was exotic and undeniably delicious, though decades of merging with its environment seemed to have mutated it and rendered it fit for only the most rigorous of high-sodium diets. What a kick it was to see the parsley plants not merely growing or hanging on, but absolutely flourishing out here, as much a monument to the hunters and their small, isolated order as the tabby ruin nearby.

The small lodge went up in the late nineteenth century, when, according to waterfowling historian Jack Dudley, a New Yorker named Lawrence Pike bought the property and with a group of Yankee cronies formed the Harbor Island Club. Before the turn of the century a second group, New Jerseyites, bought the place and renamed it the Harbor Island Shooting Club. Not till its third incarnation in the early 1910s did the place go native, when Carteret County's own Will Webb took over and sold shares in what was now the Harbor Island Hunting Lodge. Inside, the tabby-walled structure held heart-pine timbers, brick-lined fireplaces, and a little something more, as Dudley wrote in *Carteret Waterfowl Heritage*, "Folk tales prevail with occasional rumors of a haunted clubhouse, and a twenty-dollar gold piece placed in the walls when the club was built."

Harbor Island, *haunted?*

"Boy, a lot of the locals, they won't even set foot on it," Doctor John, Ann's father, once said to me at his Sea Level home.

"Why's that?" I asked him.

"And the ones that do, they'll not be on it after dark. Cedar Islanders won't even go by it in their boats after dark."

"But why?"

"I don't know," he said. "You can't get em to talk about it."

One who did talk was Royce Emory, an unsuperstitious fisherman who was born on Cedar Island and has lived there all his life, excepting time spent in the navy during World War II. "Fellow from New York—Pike—was the one who owned it. Monroe [Gaskill] claimed they had a black cook there who disappeared one night, and no one knew what happened to him.

"Ever since then folks have seen a light. Edwin Daniels said he saw a light. Atlantic fishermen going back and forth have said they've seen lights."

Emory was out shrimping once years ago, working on a thirty-five-foot boat, and his craft anchored for the night along with a bunch of others there at Harbor Island. This was after the lodge had been abandoned but was still standing. "About one in the morning, someone woke Captain Goodwin up and said there was a woman hollerin' in that house!"

"Was there?" I asked him.

"No-o-o," he said quickly. But he recalled another unsettling incident about the place.

"Will Webb from Morehead, his wife was in the big room down below, said there was a man lookin' in the window. They looked all over the island, couldn't find anyone, but she never would go down there after that—happened in the '40s." Emory remarked that Hurricanes Dennis and Floyd had taken a toll on what was left of Harbor, judging "That island's about gone now."

Sportsman Rex Beach—the writer who gave the world *The Spoilers*, a novel whose film version featured John Wayne and Marlene Dietrich—at least once came out thisaway to hunt geese, and he wandered right by Harbor Island in a fifty-five-foot shallow-draft floating hotel he had engaged in Beaufort to take him up to Ocracoke eighty-odd years ago, where Grantland Rice, then the grandmaster of American sportswriters, would join him. Beach humorously wrote up the trek in *Oh, Shoot!* in 1921, declaring that "this stormy Hatteras region is the Palm Beach of the Canada goose and his little cousin the brant."

Maybe that is what the haunting is really all about, some gone-are-the-days realization and resonance of feeling, some Shakespearean sense of

*Harbor Island Club,*
*1998*

"bare ruin'd choirs, where late the sweet birds sang" and those birds that come here now are natives, gulls and pelicans, or, if geese and ducks and brant, are mere tokens, one to a thousand, say, of the millions that once were. Nor does this line of thought end with waterfowl alone: what of the ghosts of our fisheries? of our oysterbeds, our very shallows and lowlying shorelines that may see a one-foot rise in sea level not over the next century but over the next thirty or forty years? Shores that faced the ruin of the autumn floods of Floyd in 1999, or of Hurricane Isabel, whose eye surged ashore *right here* at Harbor Island in September 2003, and must try and stand up to other, similar cascades that will surely come.

Brant Island in the Pamlico has already gone under, become shoal, and Batts Grave in the Albemarle, forty acres of farm and orchard only 250 years ago, is now all underwater at the mouth of Yeopim River. Harbor Island was reckoned at five acres when the New Yorker Pike got ahold of it in 1886, and now 120 years later it sizes out at no more than a half-acre.

The other year, after a couple hours with Ann and the children on Harbor Island, our inspection over, we embarked for Wilbur's Camp, and the shellbank fell away behind us, went back to being a floating, haunted ruin. When, later that week, I came back and brought our friends Jake and Rachel Mills from little Washington, they regarded Harbor with a sense of odd wonder similar to my own. In the winter of 1998–99, with Doctor John and his twenty-one-foot fishing boat, *The Other Woman*, Ann and Cary and I were back again, on another day just as bright and calm as the others. With a winter's breeze blowing only lightly from the south, the waters in the upper side of the island's reef of shells were flat calm indeed, and the walls of the ruin were mirrored in them, like Poe's storied House of Usher reflected, "remodelled and inverted" in its little lake.

Davey Jones's locker is roomy indeed—most of the shellbank that got named and known as Harbor Island is already in it. For a spell yet, though, enough of it remains for watermen to mark passage by it as they cruise from Core to Pamlico, enough of it, too, to count in the line of four small islands—Chain Shot, Harbor, Wainwright, and Shell—strung across the sound between Hog Island and the Pilentary Islands, at whose club FDR hunted when he was assistant secretary of the navy, behind North Core Banks. Enough to seek out, to stalk about, to sit upon and eat salt-parsley and ruminate over the fate of man and birds and lands so low, as the tides keep on rolling in, rising higher and higher all the time.

### DAVIS ISLAND

One good hot late June Sunday, our family drove from Beaufort down east to Smyrna, following a sign in the sky: an enormous, pyramidal cumulus dominating the northeastern heavens on the way out, a colossal billowing piling high above the beautiful line of summer clouds stacked up over the Gulf Stream.

Down a lane that led to the water, we piled into Mark Hooper's twenty-two-foot workboat, the *Lucky Penny Too*, a slow-moving chugger with a flat canopy and a double muffler, pushed along by a nice big eight out of a '79 Cadillac El Dorado. Coming ahead on through the shallow channel we went, out from Mark and his wife Penny's seafood operation—crabs and clams, mostly—and into Midden's Creek, while Mark and Penny's collie mix Rusty vigorously chased horseflies and yellow flies, diving and racing about the deck.

Several egrets went flying off before us, stark white and low to the water, vividly flapping their wings as they sought to find the easiest air, a cushion just a foot or two above its surface. Mark, slender and keen at the wheel, rounded the point on the east side of Midden's mouth, where an osprey had nested in a dead tree, and then he steered us almost due east toward the long narrow beach at Davis Island about a mile across the way.

A mansard-roofed huntclub house sat at the bottom end of Davis Island, looking out on Core Sound, and the long strand ran up the island's western or Jarrett Bay side. A runabout was beached, an older couple sitting in folding chairs and taking the shade up under the cedars—they were not people from the clubhouse, who would have walked a short way rather than boated to this remote beach. When the clubhouse was built by a Brooklynite over a century ago, he had the island's cemetery plowed up, the gravemarkers thrown out into the sound. Such was the ire and lingering animosity caused by this desecration that one word had it that the beach on Davis Island's west side was gradually given over to locals' use, a peace-making gesture—not that anyone from the Davis Island Club actually ever stated such a thing, simply that custom developed and an accommodation between locals and outsiders came to pass.

We swam awhile in the shallows, only two or three feet deep well off the beach, and then Ann and I walked hand-in-hand up to the island's top end, past short cedars and myrtle bushes to a small marsh spread out beside the narrow waters separating Davis Ridge and Davis Island, a cut made by the Great Hurricane of '33. Well before then, a strong African American boatbuilding community once lived and worked along Davis Ridge—Sutton or "Sut" Davis's people—though the sounds of their hammers, planes and saws have long since left this place, soughing away on the salt marsh winds.

When we returned to the group and lay out once again in all this wet, wide-open balminess, I asked Penny how she and Mark had happened to come down here to live.

"Well," she laughed and said, "we'd done a lot of diving down in the Bahamas. And there came a point we had to decide: we were either going to be treasure divers or start a family. I made the decision, and we moved here." Now they were so ingrained in the waterman's life of Jarrett Bay and Core Sound, and it in them, one would have thought their ensconcing upon Midden's Creek had been fated. Perhaps they even thought that themselves, now.

The afternoon passed lazily, and, as we lolled unhurriedly in the water, tales of Davis Island came forth in languor. Ann's mother Pat Kindell recalled coming down Core Sound by boat not long after she moved to Sea Level in the early 1960s, docking at the Davis Island clubhouse pier, climbing out onto the land and then, beset at once by an unrelenting swarm of yellow flies, diving right back into her boat and shoving off immediately for the relative safety of open water. I remembered and told David Cecelski's story about his once heading back from here in a kayak, racing a thunderstorm to the mainland, and, looking around, seeing the Davis Island caretaker following him in a skiff, the old-timer concerned for the well-being of a young man in a small craft on open waters with a summer thunderboomer brewing and not turning back for the island till he had seen David safely across.

One tale had it that a group from the Wilsonian era came down and stayed at the Davis Island Club and drafted the charter for the League of Nations, a story that upon inspection seemed to have been an extrapolation of Greenville state senator—and North Carolina Museum of Art champion—Robert Lee Humber Jr.'s having tried out his resolution for a world federation on his relations, friends, and neighbors in the open air of Davis Island's soundside liveoak grove in the early 1940s. Humber, whose family had fled France only hours ahead of the Nazis, gave yearly progress reports on his efforts for world peace, held an oak-grove session out here every twenty-seventh of December. He eventually became vice president of the United World Federalists, a group formed in Asheville in Febru-

*Robert Lee Humber*
*Jr. speaking on*
*Davis Island,*
*December 27, 1941*

ary 1947 and said to have claimed among its membership such men as Supreme Court Justice William O. Douglas, novelist-socialist Upton Sinclair author of *The Jungle*), journalist and labor leader A. Philip Randolph (who directed the 1963 March on Washington for Jobs and Freedom), and President-to-be Ronald Reagan. Nineteen of the forty-one state legislatures Humber lobbied over the years passed his brief resolve—North Carolina was the first, and the Humber resolution, having gotten its first public reading on this Core Sound shore, is still on our state's books sixty-five years later.

Along the Jarrett Bay beach, closer to the clubhouse than to the Davis Ridge cut, an Indian shell midden lay open to view, in vertical cross-section so exposed by time and tides and southwest winds, all sorts of fragments and potsherds among the mud and shells. All about in the shallows of the beach just below, too, lay more potsherds, and the Hoopers allowed as how they had once found there in the midden's face a set of three nesting bowls, set properly together generations ago each in its next larger companion, cut in half as if sliced that way by the waves. Penny said they had called East Carolina University, but by the time somebody got down to check it out a month had gone by, and the elements had done the nesting bowls in, had reclaimed their clay.

Cary did *Lucky Penny Too*'s piloting much of the way back, while Mark talked of being out on the water at night and giving up on both compass and *GPS*—"Too hard to see," smiled the middle-aged waterman—and resorting to just plain old-time steering by the stars. Of being abroad on these waters in mists, in fog, he said, "It's amazing how hard the mind works to figure out the map of where you are when you see just a glimpse of a point, a wood, a piece of land."

Up Midden's Creek Mark took the wheel again, stopping and pulling two or three crabpots and getting about a dozen jimmies. By the side of their channel, in shallows that the Hoopers leased from the state, grew half a million clams, and after we'd docked we went forth with baskets and took about 150 for that evening's Beaufort pot. Mark cleaned the jimmies and the Hoopers then sent us on our way well set for a feast. Within a couple of hours we were steaming it all, intermittently regarding shells and potsherds from many lifetimes ago out on Davis Island, having a simple enormous *fruits-de-mer* feast straight out of paradise.

## BROWNS ISLAND

From the air Browns Island looks like a green bison, a specimen increasingly lean as its legs, flanks and underbelly are taken over by steadily encroaching marshes and rising waters. With shoals and islets all around it, the mile-long island lies across the Straits from Gloucester and Marshallberg, just above the eastern end of Harkers Island.

In early June 1920, a party of summer visitors from Beaufort boated out to Browns Island in the company of its owner, Julian Brown of Marshallberg. Within the 700-acre island's liveoak and pine, myrtle and bay, one of Carteret County's largest heron rookeries lay, and tourists from Goldsboro and Wilson, as well as a Professor Hyman from the Biological Station on Pivers Island, all wanted to get a good glimpse of the big birds. The little blue heron and the snowy egret, so recently threatened with extinction by millinery fashion, now seemed "to be most plentiful," wrote the *Beaufort News* man, who also observed of owner Brown: "He guards with the greatest care his feathered tenants."

Julian Brown had ridden into this section of Carteret on horseback from Hyde County in 1904, and over the next dozen years or so he had assembled Browns Island as one holding all his own. He kept livestock—horses, cattle, sheep, pigs—on Browns Island. His stockman son Claude, known locally as

*North shore,
Browns Island,
July 2005*

the "last pioneer," carried on that tradition in spades into the twenty-first century, and his grandson J. M. Brown of Gloucester remembers there being 40 cattle, 40 horses, 100 sheep, and as many as 150 hogs out on Browns Island in the 1950s—making this one of the largest, and *last*, free-range livestock operations in coastal Carolina.

As for the avian tenants of Browns, that big birdwatchers' outing took place quite a while ago. Veteran colonial-waterbird observer Walker Golder confirmed that Browns Island "has not had a heron colony in at least forty years," and J. M. Brown observed that Hurricane Hazel blew that rookery apart in October 1954, adding that whatever might have been left of it was done in by a 1960 storm.

Beneath the enormous liveoak and large cedar at the Pigott house on Gloucester shore, I sat not long ago at one of three picnic tables looking across the Straits at Browns Island, poring over maps and genealogical charts and listening to the reminiscences of two men who knew that spot well—the big, genial fishdealer, former teacher, and Carteret Tech administrator J. M. Brown and the equally genial, stocky, ruddy and bearded Dennis Chadwick, "Cap'n Chad," retired captain of the ferryboat *Pamlico* who made the Cedar Island–to–Ocracoke run for years and who now lived in nearby Straits. "There're a hundred people in Straits," he said, "half of them Chadwicks and the other half related to Chadwicks." It was the fifth of July 2005, a bright blue-sky day, with a fresh breeze and shade keeping the fierce early-afternoon heat down—"I'd rather be out *here* than in a *house*," J. M. Brown said as he walked up and joined Dennis and me and spoke of older doings and former inhabitants.

Once a Confederate fort stood on the eastern end of Browns Island, armed with two cannon, one set toward Core Sound, the other aimed to cover the Straits, and J. M. Brown recalled the Civil War embankments as still being extant in his boyhood. The Browns had sheep pennings there, and J. M.'s father, Julian Jr., would dig for water for the stock there at the edge of the woods—"Called it soldier's well," he said. "Yellow flies so thick you'd be spitting em out—they'd be coming out your ears."

Dennis Chadwick said he had been camping out over that way with a friend when he was twelve or thirteen and Julian Brown Jr. boated over to see who was encamped on the northeast portion of his island. Finding the visitors just to be a pair of local boys he knew well, he then asked Dennis, "You know where your grandmother's house is?" Dennis said yes, he did—it was right there in Marshallberg. To which Brown replied, "No, I mean the house she was *born in*, here on Browns Island." Brown then led the boys back into the woods a good ways and showed them the blond foundation bricks for the old Maley Nelson homeplace, where Dennis's grandmother Callie Nelson, newborn, first saw the light of day.

The old fort and most traces of that homeplace are gone, for the bleached-dead-tree-littered east side and the northeast point of Browns Island have eroded and retreated to the west considerably in living memory. "It's washed a hundred yards in my lifetime," said J. M. Brown, adding an easily-grasped visual cue: "When you went out to the end of the road at Marshallberg, you could not see the lighthouse."

When you go to the road's-end at Marshallberg today, you most assuredly *do* see Cape Lookout Light past the reigning northeast point of Browns Island and past the comparatively small, lightly-forested island—Batchelors—just above Browns. "My grandfather, Old Man Julian, had a ballfield on Batchelors Island," J. M. Brown recalled. "Beaufort folk used to come over and play ball."

J. M.'s uncle Claude Brown, who had a house and a stockpen just a little ways into the woods from Browns Island's north beach and who only died several years ago and fished his nets till the day he drew his last breath, was remembered hereabouts as being a terrific ballplayer, as being wiry, tough, afraid of no animal, and fast as a deer. Folks said he could run down a Core Banks pony and lasso him and wrestle him to the ground. He did so once in the company of a copter from Cherry Point Marine Corps Air Station, the copter's purpose being to ferry Claude Brown and his new horse back over Core Sound to Marshallberg. As nearly always happens in such affairs, things took a little longer than expected, and the chopper pilot, worried, said he didn't think he had enough fuel to make it back up to Cherry Point. "That's all right," said Claude. "Just jump on over to Fort Macon and gas up—I know the Chief—I'll call him!"

On another occasion, renowned boatbuilder and button-accordionist Bryan Blake, who lived in the next house up Shore Lane from the Pigott house, joined Claude Brown and several others in getting a bull off Browns Island to sell. His technique: Claude would put feed in his pen he had there, leaving the gate open, luring stock in—once he had the bull he wanted in there, he got several folks to come out and help, Bryan Blake included. First Claude lassoed the bull and let him chase him around a huge oak tree—"Big as this one," Bryan said, motioning to the one we sat under at the Pigott place, till he wound himself up. Then Claude freed the bull from the tree, tied his rope-leash to a beach buggy, pulled him out to a waiting barge at the shore, and pinned him down upon it. "That bull's eyes were blood red, he was so angry," Bryan said, pointing to a shave of carrot in his martini and adding, "Redder than that!" The men then pulled the bull (fully grown but not too tall, being an island bull, after all) with main strength onto the barge and tied him down, just as the Lilliputians once tangled and tied Gulliver. As this party barged back on over to the Marshallberg mainland, the bull recovered his steam and wanted to kill them all, but somehow they got him into a trailer, whereupon Claude Brown drove him up to the Kinston Livestock Market.

"By the time he got there," Bryan told me, "that bull was about ready to explode." Claude made the sale and drove off, and the bull—at last out of Claude Brown's control—mortally tore up the Kinston corral to which he'd been assigned, leading the authorities at the market to request of the stockman:

"For God's sake, Claude, don't *ever* be bringing us any more Browns Island bulls!"

What settlement Browns Island has seen over time, never more than a few houses, has always been on the north side. Reviewing the map with J. M. Brown and Dennis Chadwick that July day and moving west along the beach from the northeast point, where the Nelsons (Dennis's people) had lived, J. M., whose memory and sense-of-place accuracy is phenomenal, located these other dwellings: "the Matthew Gooding house" about one-half mile from the point; "the Claude Brown house" a couple hundred yards west of the Gooding position; "the Micajah Nelson house" past Gut Marsh (where livestock often got mired to their bellies) and at the head of Sheep Pen Creek; and, upon the last pine-tree hammock on the west end, or "to the west'ard," of Browns Island, "the Molly Bell house." Of these structures, only the late Claude Brown's cinderblock house still stands.

Yet other things sometimes take hold upon such landscapes better than bricks and mortar and timbers can. Molly Bell was the nickname for Marcy Gooding, the much older sister of Civil War blockade-runner Matthew Gooding, and, though most charts and maps identify the northwest point of Browns Island as "Wading Point," that feature is known to everyone locally as one and one thing only:

"Molly Bell's Point."

We had passed Molly Bell's on a cloudy late June day, after Dennis Chadwick had loaded his nine-year-old grandson Kelly, Lida Pigott Burney, Ann and me into his white twenty-three-foot Brady Lewis skiff, launched from the small ramp and boat cut at Lida's on the mainland shore, and begun piloting a counterclockwise circumnavigation of Browns Island. Once around that northwest point, we could see the enormous Browns Island marshes stretching out for a mile and a half on the long island's south side. Little blue and tricolor herons dabbled in the marsh, and Dennis remarked on the great numbers of willets and oystercatchers he saw out here.

Half a dozen dark horses grazed on the south side, and egrets stood out against the deep green marsh grass like slender little pillars of chalk. Here and there were small liveoaks, few and far between, making these broad marshes appear, at least in this muted light, like an African veldt. Dennis guided us through the narrow thoroughfare connecting Westmouth and Eastmouth Bays between Harkers and Browns Islands, then came into a smaller piece of water the captain referred to as Lugan Bay—a good place, he said, to set a mullet net. A white cow came lumbering through liveoaks at the edge of the marsh off to our left, and Dennis, steadily and almost intuitively calculating wind and water, turned to me and said soberly:

"Always run aground on the windward side of the channel on a rising tide."

Then he laughed lustily and added, "We got a million of those in the ferry business."

A dozen dolphins, including one calf, played about near a pound net on the east side of Browns Island, and Dennis recalled for me, nodding at Lida as he did: "This is where her brother and I caught a lot of mullet—we'd get some beer and a net and come on out!"

The Core Sounder who as captain safely ferried so many tens of thousands of visitors to and from Ocracoke Island on the *Pamlico* now guided his big Brady Lewis skiff through the shallows between the northeast point of Browns and Batchelors Islands, then in an easy *S*-curve skirting a pair of oyster rocks. He pointed out an osprey nest on Batchelors Island off to our right, and One Tree Island that lay before us, and he speculated about the renowned Confederate blockade-runners Matthew Gooding, who grew up here, and John N. Maffitt of Wilmington, the "Prince of Privateers" who as a U.S. Navy lieutenant before the Civil War had commanded much of the coastwise charting between the Outer Banks and Savannah, and who spent time in and around Beaufort—Maffitt's name appeared authoritatively on the 1851 chart of Beaufort Inlet and the channels in and around Bird Shoal and Carrot Island.

"You've got to wonder," said Dennis. "Did they meet each other, when Maffitt was here in the 1850s? Seems like they must have."

We glided along Browns Island's north shore just 100, 150 feet out, looking into the dark pine and liveoak woods and musing on other matters beyond Maffitt and Gooding. What secrets did Browns Island hold? And what would become of it? We passed a duck blind at the north point of Gut Marsh, Pigott's Island also on our left, and crossed the Straits back to the Pigott house, now Lida's place.

A few days later, on the bright and sunny afternoon of Sunday, July 3, 2005, Dennis Chadwick met us again at Lida's boat basin and under his and his wife's leadership—he and blonde, sassy Robin ran Core Sound Kayak Adventures—a flotilla formed up for another go at Browns Island. Dennis again took the helm of the Brady Lewis, this time towing Lida's smaller poling skiff ("I don't want any boat," Lida declared, "that I can't paddle or pole") behind him. He had a boatload to ferry close in to shore in Lida's craft once he had anchored the big skiff well out. Five others of us kayaked across, and we all met ashore on Browns Island.

Into the woods we walked, into high pines and shorter, gnarled liveoaks, a fair bit of holly too. The understory was long and open, a lean sand ridge five feet in elevation and carpeted by pine needles, pine cones, and liveoak leaves. Here and there were cattle skulls, and tiny dark frogs hopped about. A wrinkled hog's hide lay on the ground, well-weathered, cured. Later, Ann would confess to me of feeling a strong sense of creepiness in this place, as if behind its open, white-sand beach lay all grades of predators using the island's beauty to invite you to come on in and be eaten alive. Stopping in

*Liveoak woods,*
*Browns Island,*
*July 2005*

the woods to speak with Dennis for just a moment or two, she had felt four or five ticks on her ankle, just come up out of the pine needles and leaves after her.

We strode about the late Claude Brown's old cinderblock house, around his thick-slatted stockpen, some of its slats falling and angling down from inattention since his death. In a small garage behind the pen I spied a big-tired buggy with a huge old rope dangling off its end, and I wondered if that had been the very hawser that hauled Claude's furious bull those fifty or seventy-five yards down to the waiting barge.

A couple of large fuel tanks cut in half created four watering troughs in the old pen. Dennis's grandson Kelly took a sheetrock-mud bucket at my suggestion and filled it with water from one of those troughs, with which to prime the pump of Claude Brown's sixty-eight-foot-deep well. I pumped, Lida pumped, and once the prime caught—"In the spirit of Claude Brown!" we cheered—little Kelly pumped, excited now that something was happening and not wanting to give up the handle.

What, indeed, would happen out here? After two years of trying, the North Carolina Coastal Land Trust, a top-drawer natural-heritage preservation group based in Wilmington, found itself unable to purchase a pair of the seven separate family ownerships on the island, outbid by a speculator.

*Claude Brown's stockpen, Browns Island, July 2005*

What development could occur here, though? As yet there was no bridge to this island and no official plans for one, not that anyone knew of, though folks in Gloucester had already heard talk that the new owners would want a bridge from Harkers Island over Eastmouth Bay out to Browns Island. One grim local story about Browns proved true: in the late spring of 2005 someone came upon the island and for no reason other than malice afore-thought shot dead five head of horses and eight head of cattle.

As we came out of the woods the northeast breeze was freshening, and in another half an hour I would be cutting diagonally across the Straits, the wind almost abeam to my red kayak, past the duck blind at the point of Gut Marsh where a brown willet fished, probing and stabbing in the shal-lows. But first we drifted to the east'ard along the beach, walked scuffing along between the scurf and the frill of foam at water's edge, until at last we reached Browns Island's retreating northeast point, where Dennis and Robin reached into the shallows and withdrew a pair of tawny bricks from a trove of them there.

"These are the foundation bricks from my grandmother Callie's house, the Maley Nelson homeplace I told you about," Dennis said, before he and his wife threw them back. And then the man who has a thousand times

*Dennis Chadwick piloting Brady Lewis skiff, with Bland Simpson and Lida Pigott Burney, near Harkers and Browns Islands, July 2005*

floated the waters from Molly Bell's Point to the northeast point where his kinfolk once throve said simply: "I've collected a few, eight maybe.

"Might ought to come out and get a few more."

### HARKERS ISLAND

Shell Point to Red Hill long, Back Sound to the Straits wide, at five miles by one Harkers Island is among the largest of North Carolina's inner islands, in company with Roanoke, Knotts, Mackay, and Goose Creek. Captain John Smith named it Davers Island on his 1624 map, and, when *the* Benjamin Franklin's first cousin Ebenezer Harker acquired it in 1730, it was called Craney Island. Not till the 1780s when Harker's three sons divvied it up among themselves did it become known as Harkers Island.

Many of Harkers Island's fishermen, rack-of-eye flarebow boatbuilders, and first-order carvers of duck and goose decoys are descended from the Cape or Ca'e Banker men and women who left Diamond City, the fishing and whaling community on nineteenth-century Shackleford Banks, after a series of pounding 1890s storms climaxed with the devastating San Ciriaco hurricane of August 1899. Puerto Ricans had named the storm for the saint whose day it was when San Ciriaco roared by them, after which it blasted the Carolina coast and killed the Ca'e Bankers' poultry and stock, salted and sanded their gardens, and unearthed and uncoffined their dead. About the Harkers Islanders is an extraordinary practicality, a sense of work to be done in this world, a determination, humor, and a more-than-occasional skeptical disdain for people they deem less-tested, which are those from most anywhere else but Harkers Island and Down East Carteret County, those who come *from off*. In moments of extreme resentment, a true xenophobia here has flamed forth as arson: in 1906, the burnings of a new Mormon church and then schoolhouse; and, much more recently, the torching of the National Park Service headquarters not long after Cape Lookout National Seashore came into being. Not for nothing is native Joel Hancock's excellent study of the coming of the Mormons to Harkers Island entitled *Strengthened by the Storm*.

In the summer of 2004, while Harkers Islanders worked at building a sailing skiff on the Mall in Washington, D.C., as part of the Smithsonian's Folklife Festival, a constant stream of naysayers flowed by, visitors telling some of the nation's best boatbuilders over and over, "Oh, you'll never finish *that* while you're here—you'll never have *that* in the water within a week." Yet before the week's end, there the small craft was, catching the wind out on the Potomac River.

Earlier that year, these craftsmen had built another skiff just off the lobby of Asheville's Grove Park Inn, the mountainside castle where writer F. Scott Fitzgerald once lit and lounged, and even in their native state came more comments of the same style. Here, though, they had put the boat together over one long weekend. As the skiff was loaded onto a trailer to get it to its new owner's piedmont home, someone walking by asked almost incredulously,

"Will that thing *float*?"

Short, strong Karen Willis Amspacher, who ran the Core Sound Waterfowl Museum and Heritage Center at the Shell Point end of Harkers Island Road and whose husband Jimmy had led the boatbuilding, said swiftly, with a scoffing laugh and an adze-like edge:

"Yes, she will, darlin', and she'll come ahead *on*, too."

Harkers Island humor long ago married a Prohibition-era accident—the grounding of the rumrunner *Adventure* out on the Banks in 1923—and produced a song now widely appreciated as the Carteret County National Anthem. "The Booze Yacht," a ballad of the whiskey-boat's jettisoning its illegal cargo and the subsequent local results, was set to the melody of an earlier song, "The Sidewalks of New York," and lyricized by New Yorker Ralph Sanders, who lived on Harkers Island at the time—and then popularized far and wide by a local fiddler named Ivey Scott. The Beehive, Karen

Amspacher has told me, was Cleveland Davis's General Store, once located about the middle of the south shore, just west of where the Island Fishing Center is now.

"The Booze Yacht"
Down around the "Beehive," Harkers Island retreat,
Every night and morning the fishermen would meet.
One day there came a rounder; came running by the door,
Said, "Boys, let's go to Cape Lookout;
There's a Booze Yacht run ashore."

This way, that way, to the Cape they'd run.
The coming of the Booze Yacht, put fishing on the bum.
Some lost their religion and back-slid by the score,
And "King Lock" stoppers were stacked ace high
When the Booze Yacht run ashore.

Things have changed since those times.
Some folks are up in "G."
Others, they are down and out, but most feel just like me.
Some would part with all they've got, and some a little more,
To see another time like that
When the Booze Yacht run ashore.

To see another time like that!

Not likely. Waves now breaking over Harkers Island are coming from landward, waves of money with waveriders on them who are buying out the locals and bidding up the price of land to where only people like themselves and a precious few holdouts can afford it. One Down Easter remarked fatalistically of an enormous marina project that recently surfaced and that was being talked about for the north side of Harkers Island, a proposal that, in order to serve deeper draft vessels, would require the dredging of a channel through the fishing grounds of Eastmouth Bay, out to the existing channel to the east of Harkers and Browns Islands. "What they'll try to do," he said, "is get those waters declared *closed to shellfishing* and then they can do anything they want."

"Meanwhile," author-musician Barbara Garrity-Blake wrote me in the summer of 2005, "two sizeable trailer parks were just sold on Harkers Island, so a pile of low-income folks will have to move off island. . . . There's no doubt that the tipping point for these communities is just about at hand." Indeed. Everywhere one heard word of the strong feelings many natives had about the pummeling they felt the community was taking as real-estate prosperity rapidly changed familial and social equations throughout Harkers Island. One islander told me that realty agents were going door-to-door baldly asking natives to sell out and leave land and homes often held by the same families for generations.

Just a few months later, a number of large-scale condominium projects moving toward county approval sparked a grassroots uprising. Hundreds of locals pulled together as "Down East Tomorrow," jammed meeting halls, and forced a public hearing on a building moratorium. The prescient Garrity-Blake, writing in the *Raleigh News and Observer* in early 2006 to urge "bold initiatives that would protect public access and working waterfronts," mourned over what was happening so rapidly on Harkers Island: "Humble cottages floated over from Diamond City after the storms of 1899 are being replaced by towering beach homes. . . . Descendants of the 'Cay bankers' . . . are compelled to move off-island as the storm of a real estate frenzy washes over them."

Amid the *sturm und drang* of this battle being joined, one legendary Harkers Islander passed away. David Yeomans—storyteller, singer, fisherman and fish-house operator, civic and church leader ("I held every office except president of the Methodist Women")—was a man who moved back and forth between his island home and his camp in the old Cape Lookout Village on the Banks and who for many was the embodiment of both places. When Yeomans died on the first of March 2006, a slick ca'm day in Carteret County, more than a few doubtless felt doubly sad over the whole waterman's way of life that seemed to be leaving with him as he crossed the bar.

---

Red Hill on the island's southwest side was a high sandy bluff looking out toward Middle Marsh and Lenoxville Point across North River near Beaufort. The bluff brightened and lit up red in sunset light, giving the spot its name. Under the island oaks, shaped and twisted by the salt-shearing sou'westerlies, in a small cemetery enclosed by a white fence next to a large condominium, much of Karen Willis Amspacher's family lay interred. Ikie William Willis, her father (1925–2000), was here, buried in the same place, the same spot of ground where he was born. Her grandparents too: Joseph "Blind Joe" and Addie Guthrie Willis were, she said, "born on Shackleford Banks and moved to Harkers Island where they settled in the early years of the 1900s."

"Blind Joe" Willis died when Ikie was nine years old, leaving Karen's grandmother Addie Guthrie Willis to raise the children—she "ironed for the Coast Guard at Cape Lookout, worked at the W.P.A. sewing room," said Karen. In 1943 Ikie became the "first in his family to graduate from Harkers

Island High School," later serving in the army and then pulling thirty-two years of work at the Marine Corps Air Station up at Cherry Point on the Neuse River. He and Wanda Hill of Marshallberg, across the Straits, married in April 1954, and Karen Willis was born to them a little over a year later.

Now fifty, Karen had raised children of her own, taught school, and spearheaded the fundraising and building of the Core Sound Waterfowl Museum, the dramatic, towered archive and social center "at the end of the Harkers Island road," next to the Park Service's Visitor Center for Cape Lookout National Seashore at Shell Point. When she spoke of Red Hill ("My granny's house," she called it, though that house is gone and only the tiny Willis graveyard still remained in her family), and certainly when she stood out there and reflected, she got tearful in a trice. Even so, when she pointed at the markers, "Blind Joe," "the twins," she spoke of the dead as if they were still alive, immortal even, and if full-hearted memory and un-diluted love poured forth at a Southern burying ground could make it so, then they were.

"Although considered blind, 'Blind Joe' would sail by sharpie everyday to Bell's Island to fish, clam, oyster or scallop," she said. "He knew the way and could set sail from the shore behind his house and fish along with the sighted men to feed his family."

She recalled other Harkers Islanders, too, other kin such as Uncle Stacy Guthrie, born Christmas Day 1882. He was "one of the patriarchs of Red Hill . . . [he had] a mind that could 'lay out' a boat on a piece of scrap wood, order the juniper, and estimate the cost within inches and pennies." He was among those who came over from Shackleford Banks—he had whaled in his younger days, and he lived to be nearly a hundred.

Powerful recollections, yet Karen Willis Amspacher has seen the island's future writ large in its recent past, as the coastal real-estate bonanza inex-orably shifted the nature of the place from isolated island to retirement-and-vacation hotspot. Unlike her Uncle Stacy, she has lived to see a realty company sign go up in his yard, in late August 2005, where once she played in juniper shavings from the boats he was building, toted water from a hand-pump back to her family's place across the road, and shot mistletoe from the liveoaks at Christmas. In the introduction she wrote for the popu-lar cook-and-history book *Island Born and Bred*, she observed: "We realize that many of these changes have brought opportunities to the people of the Island, and for that we are grateful. Yet, we have paid, and are paying, a price. We cannot help but begin to savor and cherish the vanishing close-ness and seclusion we once shared."

Prior to those Smithsonian maritime-heritage events on the Washing-ton Mall back in 2004, she had journeyed up the coast to Smith Island, a crabbing place in the Chesapeake Bay off Crisfield, Maryland, reachable only by boat, with a history markedly, understandably similar to that of Harkers Island. Karen once rhapsodized to me about Smith Island, its 300 souls, watermen or watermen's wives all, its bicycling and its slow-moving ways, yet she concluded that rhapsody with a brisk comparison and a deep sigh.

"It's what we'd've been like on Harkers Island," Karen Willis Amspacher allowed, "if we hadn't gotten the bridge."

### PHILLIPS ISLAND

Fifty years ago, many thousands of egrets and herons called Lenoxville Point their home—this was the site of the town of Lenoxville, chartered and laid out in 1816 on the west bank of North River's mouth, just east of Beaufort, but never built. Since the mid-1950s this Lenoxville Rookery split, many of the Audubon protectorate moving south from there and setting up on Middle Marsh Island, behind Shackleford Banks, the rest heading several miles west and finding solace in the myrtle and liveoak and yaupon thicket on the north end of little Phillips Island, in Newport River near the Haystacks, the marshes that border Morehead City.

In the 1990s much of the Phillips colony moved to one of the Bogue Sound islands—Wood Island, a quarter mile long, nearly fifteen miles west in Bogue Sound, about halfway between Rock Point at Salter Path and Archer Point at Emerald Isle—but the egrets have been returning to Phillips, one of the most visible and viewed of all Carolina's inner isles, with its redbrick chimney standing out against the green thicket nearby. People in cars driving across the high span of the Newport River bridge cannot help but have their eyes drawn to this spot of color to the north, and to the bright white egrets circling it or enfolding themselves with their young in the scrub. Those who view Phillips from Town Creek on the Beaufort side may see it of a morning across the emerald-green marsh and, as the sun cuts through a slow-moving scud silvergray as smoke and suddenly lights up the old chimney like an obelisk of red clay, gasp.

Long ago the lone chimney served a fish plant, Melt Lee's Newport Fisheries, one of Carteret County's menhaden cookers, and now near the brick tower's base has sprouted an old gear, its long shaft sprung and bent over like some enormous Picassoan daisy. In the salt grass beyond the chimney thicket stood a clutch of metal plates, rusty brown boxes wherein the menhaden were once boiled down, reduced to fishmeal for feed or fertilizer before the business soured and failed after World War I. Local folks approaching seventy cannot recall the factory as a working place, and believed it went out of business in the 1930s or '40s. Yet Corinne Webb Geer remembered all too well that her grandfather, Irving Davis, had fallen from a scaffold while working at the Phillips Island plant and died from his injuries. In its time a man named Ed Corham ran the plant, and then

*On any low tide of the month, in calm weather, one is able to wade from the sand-dune rim over immense areas of the shoal, in water so shallow and glassy clear that every detail of the bottom lies revealed.*
*—Rachel Carson,*
*The Edge of the Sea (1955)*

*Menhaden plant*
*chimney, Phillips*
*Island, July 2004*

*Old gear, Phillips Island, July 2004*

Llewellen Phillips—whose family owns the island yet and whence it takes its name—took it over, buying firm, factory and gear for $2,701 in 1932. When the old fish plant finally burned one late September night in 1953, hundreds of people drove out and parked on the Beaufort-to-Morehead causeway to watch the great blaze.

One July day in the summer of 2003 a late-morning thunderstorm spawned at least one waterspout, a tall dark spinner that roared up Bogue Sound from west to east toward Phillips Island. Children at the Maritime Museum's Gallants Channel sailing school saw the waterspout's erratic ambling over the way across the marshes after they had tied up their Optimist prams and, as they sought shelter in a cinderblock storage building, saw it come their way and then spin off again. If it did any more than shiver the yaupon or shake the myrtles of Phillips Island, Ann and I couldn't tell it when we cruised out there and circled the spot a few afternoons later.

*Inside the chimney,*
*Phillips Island,*
*July 2004*

Egrets bunched into the branches, and several ibis flew off to the north. Wake-waves from trawlers, shrimpers, and pushboats with barges splash this island's eastern shore as the workboats ply the Intracoastal Waterway, and the snowbirds, the East's recreational fleet, glide by here twice a year. Whatever the mariners do, the real birds will colonize and crowd this miniature jungle just as long as they care to.

## RADIO AND PIVERS

Between Phillips Island and Beaufort lay large Radio Island, traversed constantly by car, truck and the Beaufort-to-Morehead railroad train, and a second, much smaller one, Pivers, easily gained by a little arched concrete bridge from the Radio Island causeway, the fourlane lined with oleander, crepe myrtle and yellow daylilies and running along the marshes between the Newport River bridge and the Grayden Paul bridge over Gallants Channel. I remember fondly one night sitting on the ground by the Pivers Island bridge with Don Dixon and Jim Wann and others after singing *King Mackerel* in Carteret for the very first time, some Southern elixir being passed around as we were hearing newsman Bill Smith's tale about a possum running wild in the lobby of the late Jefferson Motel back over the river in Morehead, laughing and loving it all as always there beside the lapping of the water.

Reports on the rich natural world hereabouts, filed by Fort Macon physicians after the Civil War, bore fruit—Pivers has since 1902 been home to a federal marine biological station. A weather station, too: the National Oceanic and Atmospheric Agency (NOAA) came here decades ago. In 1938 Duke University set up a marine lab on Pivers Island, and nowadays its 57' research vessel *Susan Hudson* and its bold green-and-white 135-foot ship *Cape Hatteras* (a joint holding with the University of North Carolina at Chapel Hill) are moored, prominently, on the Beaufort side of the island. Carolina has run *its* marine sciences institute since 1947 across the Newport River at old Camp Glenn on Bogue Sound, and is homeport of the R/V *Watts Hill Jr.* and other small craft. The little island took its name from early Beaufort settler and landowner Peter Piver, who served under Colonel Thomas Lovick when Spanish pirates attacked the town in 1747, and whose small, late-eighteenth-century house stands yet at 131 Ann Street in Beaufort.

Far larger Radio Island is a real utility spot between the working port of Morehead City and the increasingly dressy Beaufort-by-the-Sea. Its enterprises include a drystack boat hotel, a marina, a few fish-camp cottages, the Beaufort-to-Morehead railroad, a field of jet-fuel tanks (which are occasionally victimized by lightning strikes), the shell of Sonny Lane's discount

*U.S. Bureau of
Fisheries and
Biological Station,
Pivers Island,
about 1907*

marine, a seven-story condominium tower, and the radio tower of the late AM station WMBL, from which the island got its name. One September night in 1961, the lantern of a fisherman on the Newport River bridge fell into the water, igniting gas on the river's surface, and fire then sped like a fuse back to the navy tanker *Potomac*, which was unloading fuel at the Radio Island depot, and set off a chain of explosions—the ship burned for six days, killing two sailors. Bob Simpson, watching the blaze from a boat the first night of the fire, told the *Raleigh News and Observer* that "the whole east sky is aglow."

People with odd visions grapple with Radio Island's future, and cannot leave it alone—in recent years business leaders have proposed first an ethanol plant and then a liquid natural gas facility. Public *sturm und drang* helped ensure that neither notion made it, but the state port in 2005 launched a massive expansion, with 45-foot depth and a 2,000-foot-long wharf in store for Radio's Newport River side, the port's chairman trumpeting: "There is no economic gem on the Atlantic seaboard more attractive than Radio Island." On the island's Gallants Channel side, marine railways and drydocks sprawl along the small waterway known locally as Nasty Harbor, and a fellow relaxing nicely with his gin-and-tonic out on Front

*Rope, Pivers Island,*
*November 2004*

Street in Beaufort during the summer of '05 warned me to expect a hotshot
marina and condo tower ere long in that very funky place.

Down the two-lane blacktop that runs beside the Radio Island boatel, a
small county park beckons swimmers with a sandy beach on the channel
between Beaufort Inlet and Beaufort town. Just a few years ago too much
broken glass lay beneath the shorewaters—left by revelers of earlier times
—for folks to walk out in the water without tennis shoes or sandals. Before
there was an official park here, there was an unofficial one, and those
revelers were out many a weekend night—I used to sit out back of the
west Front Street cottage on the Beaufort waterfront where we were lucky
enough to stay in the early '90s when Cary was a baby, looking past Cape
Carrot down the channel at the faraway lights of Fort Macon Coast Guard
Station, and I could see the Radio Island beach fires a half-mile or more
away. I watched with no small interest as their motorcycles and ATVs tore
up and down the little strand and more than occasionally spun out, head-
lamps beaming crazily up into the coastal night and flipping all around
from the dervish driving they were doing. From that distance, even across
water, the buzz of the high-rpm spinners was muted, and as the evenings deepened those rituals assumed a tribal, road-warrior air, the noise-

making and half-random motion mildly menacing, yet too far off to be much more than a curiosity.

Twenty years before that, in the early 1970s, this spot meant *park* of another sort: boys and girls together in dark parked cars, cheek to cheek and hand on thigh, way down in the delta of love seeking ever seeking and perhaps more often than not finding an easy realization of romance, on deep dreamy nights that are remembered yet, nights with more heat than stillness and without any disparity of desire.

### BIRD SHOAL

"She's blowin'."

"Yeah, she's blowin', all right."

Hurricane Edouard, still far out at sea at the end of August of '96, was moving north-northwest right toward the central Carolina coast, and the steady talk in the waterfront shebangs of Beaufort was of wind speeds and storm surges and wishful thinking about harbors of refuge.

"She comes in here blowin' a hundred on a full-moon hightide, I'm sunk."

"You ain't alone."

"Sure wish I knew somebody up in New Bern that had room for my boat."

"You ain't alone on that one, either."

"Man, if the harbormaster orders these slips *cleared* . . ."

The Friday night breezes grew gusty, and, though the winds weren't yet blowing a gale by Saturday morning, they were sure enough on the way there. We didn't have a big boat on hand to worry about, and so left that uneasy task to the sailors and the fishermen and the cruiser-captains all watching the weather channel at Clawson's, the Back Bar, and the Royal James as if the very Fates were in the boxes before them.

Before noon Saturday—while we still could—we went out in our jon-boat, up Taylor's Creek toward Beaufort Fisheries and into the breach of Carrot Island called Deep Creek, just to spend an hour staring into the rising weather while the storm was still cutting its teeth, just to take the view from Bird Shoal.

There was a ton of water in the slough, way more than usual, because of both the approaching hurricane and the nearness of the full moon, so at high tide—which normally put only a foot or so of water back in these flats—we were able to putter along on the little motor in a half-fathom or better and get right up into the now-drowned marshy backside of Bird Shoal's sandy strand. No one else was out there, and even the wild ponies had made themselves scarce. The real danger of the storm lay many hours away, though, and we enjoyed taking in the full anticipatory moment. We looked upon the bright white egrets stalking fish in the flooded grass, at ibis in there too, and marveled at how snails by the millioncount had slid right up the grass-shafts all about and gotten themselves out of the water and into the wind, grouping up before the blow.

Ann and then-four-year-old Cary and I were awed, too, by the show the lusty breezes made as they tore the tops off waves breaking over a big new sandbar in the bay between Bird Shoal and Shackleford Banks. In Beaufort Inlet, just beyond which Blackbeard's sunken ship would be found only three months hence, Edouard's advance winds were ripping the inlet breakers in half.

Cary ran to the end of a sandspit, and we trailed her, turning up along the way a couple of crabs, a large hermit and a four-inch horseshoe. I studied the slough's low green liveoak and myrtle fringe, the rooftops and chimneys and fishplant smokestacks of the town beyond, mused upon our family's small place in this enormous maritime world and felt thoroughly *at home*. For a moment I reckoned that, if asked, I'd give Bird Shoal as a forwarding address, but then I thought: we've got a big blow coming, and, besides, who on earth other than the Carteret County woman I'm already here with do I need to hear from just now?

If it turns out that all our trips out to Bird Shoal have been good ones, then it is just the plainest of old-fashioned affection that I feel for this patch of islands and shoals, this collection of sandy beach, tidal flats, and shrubby hammocks just over Taylor's Creek from town. Horse, Carrot (or Cart, its antique appellation), the shallows of Town Marsh and Bird Shoal, these were the long-ago haunts of Rachel Louise Carson, who once in bare feet and rolled-up pants stalked the large wading birds and shorebirds alike and who found nothing she observed too small to note: the young horseshoe crab making its way seaward across the sand, schools of minnows in the shallows, the toad fish croaking at her, a black-spiraled snail tracking by, sea anemones, sand dollars, the twin chimneys of the parchment worm, razor clams, whelks laying their sand collars of eggs. She noted such wonders as the thousands of fiddler crabs moving about the mud in droves, the sound of their shuffling "like the crackling of paper."

"Crossing the ridge of sand," she wrote in *The Edge of the Sea*, "one looks out over the shoal. If the tide still has an hour or two to fall to its ebb, one sees only a sheet of water shimmering in the sun." She threw herself into the life of what she called "this great sprawling shoal," and now the three-mile, 2,025-acre estuarine reserve comprising Town Marsh, Carrot Island, Horse Island, and Bird Shoal forever bears her name.

Well Carson knew that no fixed line existed between sea and land,

and that all this intertidal activity and life—big fish, fingerlings, mollusks, worms—was the very voice of the sea, if one would but listen. She heard that voice, and its many volumes and moods, and that she took exquisite delight in slowly strolling through the tidal flats is clear in the affection her own words carry for all creatures here, great and small.

Bird Shoal is an astonishingly easy place to turn one's mind loose, like those twenty-odd wild ponies on the run hereabouts, which slow to a walk, kicking up veils of sand behind every hoof before disappearing into the labyrinth of blackbird-haunted myrtles like Bedouins into an oasis. It is a spot to shake off the jangled onrush and overload of everyday images and to encounter as unencumbered as possible this one sublime, elemental edge of the sea. Those who can envision the entire universe by looking into a single seashell will find here all the universes they'll ever need; what I have found in nearly twenty years of roaming this marge is that I can see the world well enough when looking out from Carrot Island and Bird Shoal.

I can see all the way up the coast to the blackriver Narrows on the Pasquotank at Elizabeth City, where I lived as a boy and learned to love the water around Machelhe Island, and out from there over the potato-fields of Camden and the orchards and produce stands of Currituck and across the big long bridge (named for our near-mythical first fliers, the Wrights) that leads over to Kitty Hawk, where I learned to love the sea. And I can see another spot, a mite closer, where my grandparents met, courted and married, the tiny riverport where the Scuppernong slims down—Columbia, next to which Elizabeth City is Gotham.

What else can one glimpse from this vantage-point? Why, Winky and Nancy Wood's ship's-timber house way up in Wanchese; Commander Hollowell's Owl's Roost where Newbegun Creek hits the Pasquotank; the Cypress Grill when it's open in the herring-run spring on Roanoke River at Jamesville; Jake and Rachel's big 1890 house and backyard oyster midden near the Pamlico River at little Washington; Feather and Willy's blue heaven on the cove at Fort Landing; Linwood and Cynthia's creekside fish-camp palace at Hampstead far to the south; the doublebay-windowed house my mother was born in on Sixth Street in Wilmington just around the corner from the big fountain and just a short, unbrisk walk from the swift-flowing Cape Fear; and then Southport downriver of that and, across the bay, Oak Island where my grandfather spent World War I and where the light that now shines upon the big sea waters is among the brightest in the world. From Knotts Island in upper Currituck way on down to Battery Island in the lower Cape Fear, I swear on a stack of Luther Lewis's Down East crabcakes that you can see the whole Sound Country from a seat in the sand on the long, curving south side of Bird Shoal.

The shoal is a progger's paradise, an unpopulated place to wander around and through. Shorebirds are its leading citizens—plovers, oyster-catchers, willets, sandpipers, dowitchers and more. Pelicans fly low to the water, and porpoises cavort near the sandbank shallows seaward of the shoal. Whales do appear: one Doctor True came upon a very rare whale out here on Bird Shoal back in 1912, and got to name it: True's Beaked Whale.

On the east end of Bird Shoal, Charles L. Ives in the mid-1870s stood with his father and watched a sailing race that changed boatbuilding in Carolina. The Ives family, come south from Connecticut to wholesale fish and oysters in Beaufort and Morehead City, had imported a pair of sharpies from New Haven. Daniel Bell of Morehead challenged the Ives boat *Lucia* to race the Bell schooner *Sunny South*, and when the two boats had it out, the course being Harkers Island to Beaufort Inlet, the Ives men saw their New England craft beat out the local boat, and the boatbuilders of Carteret saw the future, and for them it was the round-sterned Core Sound Sharpie from then on.

In the summertime, when we swim here, this is where we find live sand dollars, furry on the bottom and the color of dried blood. Even late winter is sublime—like the seventy-degree sunny afternoon one March when Cary was two and filled with delight at the sight of a heavy mare and four other ponies grazing mid-island and was still carrying on about them during a scallops-and-oysters dinner back in town. We told our daughter that the largest of the ponies would soon be a mother, and when we saw that mare and her foal walking along Taylor's Creek the next August, Cary remembered.

This sort of carryover, and the comprehension that comes with it, this sort of all's-right-with-the-world feeling, I have begun to come across as well just around the watery corner from Bird Shoal, on up in Core Sound, at Willis's and Morris's fish camps on the banks there, at Wilbur's camp to the north of them, and, more north'ard still, at Harbor Island, the diminutive new-moon sliver of shells separating Core Sound from Pamlico.

But those are places I am still only beginning to get to know; I have yet to crawl over them dozens of times, as I have Bird Shoal. We all of us have such places, and we all know that the steady accretion of meaning— through repeated visits, sojourns, stops, landings, ambles—downright takes a while. In the human world, such things as violence and unkindness *do* reveal themselves all at once; but in the natural realm, woods and fields and waters, however they appear at the moment, are always suggesting what they will be next, once the moment or the day or the season or the wind or the light changes, and suggesting further that one must return to the same place again and again if one would see into the heart of its matter, or even come close.

Now, I admit not everything that happens out here on Carrot Island and Bird Shoal is as well-organized as Hurricane Edouard—who after all the local bluster and talk gave our coast only a pawstroke, a brush, a glancing blow—was the other year. Such misadventures as we have do, though, seem to err on the innocent side.

Once we nearly kidnapped the peddler's cat—by accident, ignorant of its provenance—when it came aboard our jonboat beached near Cape Carrot on the Pivers Island end of things and seemed to want to return to mainland Beaufort. Thinking it a stray, I would've taken it on into the local animal shelter but for the good advice of a Jacksonville lawyer who solved the mystery *and* forestalled all possible litigation with one jaunty declaration: "Well, I see you've made friends with Clam Bob's cat!" whereupon we repatriated the untagged feline to the peddler's live-aboard scow that for years had lain at anchor nearby.

Another time we had a runabout full of family, which is to say many *children*, anchored by the beach at Bird Shoal, everyone picnicking, swimming, having a big summer time of it. When I checked the boat's fuel, I found that we had just about enough left to get us from Bird Shoal back to the main channel into Beaufort where we would run out and doubtless achieve derelict status. The only solution was for Ann's sister Carolyn and me to leave the rest of the party intact and at leisure there on Bird Shoal and to walk back across the flats and the island, swim Taylor's Creek, raid the garage in town for a small gas tank, recross the creek by jonboat, and return afoot with fuel sufficient to get us back around to homeport. Done.

Yet others have swum Taylor's Creek for the islands with darker purpose. One summer morning in Beaufort a man named Pynkham and his confederate crouched down behind the bullpen door at the Carteret County jail, and when the guard looked in and saw no one, she was unnerved and believed for an instant the pair of murderers had somehow escaped, whereupon she threw open the door and the two men succeeded in startling and overpowering her, and the guard had unwittingly set them free. Straight down Craven Street they ran for the water and dove in and swam for it—Pynkham's confederate nearly drowned before he was saved, fished out, caught and reshackled, but Pynkham himself got away to Carrot Island, and, once there, eluded a manhunt all day long.

Copters could not spot him, dogs could not sniff him out.

How did he do that all day? Did he make himself so small up inside the boughs of some Carrot Island cedar that no one could see him cringing there? Or did he bury himself deep enough in the hot sand and breathe through a reed, or was he off doing that somewhere in the waters of Taylor's Creek, or in the channel between Carrot and Pivers Islands, while men in blue and tan searched the sandy swales of Carrot, the long, narrow island that could scarcely support a couple dozen salt ponies now proving quite big enough to hide a killer.

The day advanced, and an off-duty deputy acting as security guard for NOAA figured that Pynkham would make his move in the dark that first night, and that the shortest distance for the escapee from Carrot Island to the trains that run across Radio Island and off into the world was by way of Pivers Island. So the deputy kept a vigil on the channelside bank of Pivers with a walky-talky and a nightscope.

Presently there came a splashing at the Pivers bulkhead not far from where the deputy sat, and the deputy radioed the sheriff and said we've got our man!

But Pynkham, exhausted from his day hiding in the heat and now waterlogged from fighting the channel's swift and conflicting currents, would not come out, and was still splashing about the bulkhead when the sheriff raced in a few minutes later. The sheriff, embarrassed over the jail-break, had long since lost patience with the escapee and his enterprise, so now jumped down into the water with Pynkham and thrashed him, then hauled him out, threw him in a squad car, and drove him without so much as stopping straight up to Raleigh and Central Pen.

Once, in the summer of '94, my Red Clay Rambler partner Jack Herrick and I sat on the porch of writer Max Steele's former Front Street cottage, a comfortable old place with a rope for a railing along the stairs to the second floor. Across Taylor's Creek several ponies grazed in the salt grass uncovered by the ebb. One of them, a mare, was being followed closely by a spindly foal. We sat there in rockers, in an equine reverie, the ponies slowly nibbling their way along and coming up the creek in our direction, till cartoonist Doug Marlette burst out the front door and, hearing no talk, said "What is it? What are you doing?" We pointed to the ponies, he joined us, sat quietly for all of sixty seconds, then leapt to his feet and comically announced that he was going downtown for a newspaper, because:

"This is *too peaceful*—there's nothing here for my free-ranging paranoia and hostility to light on!"

The winter before, Cary and I had seen that mare, gravid, late one afternoon when we made a quick sunset trip over to Carrot Island, and had just come upon her suddenly, she by herself at the top of one of the island's sand hills. Now here she was, along with several other adult ponies, teaching her foal with its spindly shanks—it couldn't have been three weeks old—to stroll slowly and graze with patience in the shallows of Taylor's Creek. On a still, blue-sky summer's day such as this was, when they are grazing right down beside the creek at the edge of the marsh, one can see them reflected, inverted, in those waters, and take no small pleasure in that.

These ferals have been padding and prowling the Carrot Island chain (there are four islands here, after all: Carrot, Horse, Town Marsh and Bird Shoal) since someone no longer remembered put a small clutch of their forebears out there to graze free. This was an antique and much-honored practice, for both Outer Banks and inner islands were long considered and used as open range for all sorts and grades of stock, till a third the way into the twentieth century, and there are more goat islands than appear so, properly named, in any gazetteer. The ponies must literally fend for themselves, as the estuarine reserve brings them neither food nor freshwater. If they find no freshwater pooled anywhere on the islands, they must paw and dig down with their hooves till they come upon it as groundwater.

How would I measure, or take stock of, the pull of the place? Perhaps it started when Ann first brought me here to Carteret County many years ago, with the old familiar feel of Beaufort, its flat sidewalks and streets so reminiscent of Elizabeth City's, and its basic port smells, of fish and fuel from the churning of the fleet, and of the sound of gulls and redwings and the sight of night herons coming in at dusk and taking their appointed positions atop the dockpilings. And the bright waxen look of the red yaupon berries; the good pungency of Carrot Island's myrtle thickets in the heat; the huge three-sixty, big-sky, all-around view; and, too, the sight of children small and large padding across the shoal's broad mud flat; and now and again the heightened sense of being abroad on the water and boating by night.

One summer evening, several of us were in the jonboat drifting down Taylor's Creek, the creekwaters nearly glass and the town's neon lights shimmering on the dark mirror, and music came sliding over the water, some old lovesong from a lone guitarist. We cruised past the short dark cedars of Town Marsh and on around Pivers Island, skylighting channel markers and catching the light from some streetlamp or another and following the reflected streams of light so as to see and avoid anything that might lie in our way. The night sky that evening was murky, except to the south where on the horizon above Carrot Island sat Scorpio clear and bright as a silver fishhook.

So we were caught, and are hooked yet.

One afternoon years later, in the summer of '03, we had been cleaning clams for chowder, cutting them out of their shells right on the Taylor's Creek dock at the foot of Gordon Street. Cary and Cap'n Jim Rumfelt were sailing empty clamshells trying to hit a piling just down the creek, stirring up the seagulls considerably every time they did. That evening, once the

*Carrot Island,*
*November 2005*

chowder had cooked and simmered a while, we suddenly made ready to go kayaking in the gloaming over into the Carrot Island marshes. The idea came up quick as a squall, and quickly we decided *Go* and put in three boats on the narrow beach, and, as we paddled east toward the Deep Creek opening, Beaufort was briefly silhouetted beside and behind us by a rim of red, the vivid end of a flaming sunset sky.

The tide was in flood, nearly full high, and we left Taylor's Creek and cut down into the marsh through a half-acre pool and opening a couple hundred yards or so before Deep Creek. Cap'n Jim led, got out of his kayak and pulled Cary across a few yards of four-inch water and then we were into plenty of water and bound for Horse Island—*not*, incidentally, the infamous Horse Island well east of us down in Core Sound, where two people may have been murdered long ago, and only their ghosts, which fishermen have reported seeing, can tell the tale.

Stars popped out in the darkening sky, and soon we steered by starlight alone. As we rounded the end of Horse Island, the lights of boats out on the sound greeted us and the miles-away beam of Cape Lookout Light flashed low on the horizon. Cary exclaimed "Look, look!"—thrilled by it all, enchanted and also emboldened forever by this first time being in her own craft under her own power out on the water on a warm dark night.

Paddling back on Taylor's Creek—Cap'n Jim first, Cary second, I at the rear—we passed an anchored sailboat, where a couple sat talking in the dark. The onboard sailor spoke as we passed his craft: "Another half hour, and you'd a had the tide running *with* you."

"Yeah," said Cap'n Jim, never slowing, "but we got clam chowder waiting *for* us!"

———————

When our twins were much younger, I used to tell them a story on the way to school, a tale in which they were a pair of heroic travelers who on their own had gone to England, stayed a spell, and even visited the queen at Buckingham Palace prior to coming back to America—all told matter-of-fact, as if it might have really happened.

The sailing ship that brought them home came back into North Carolina by way of Beaufort Inlet, and, once through it, in the tale the children would rush to the ship's rail and see their kin gathered together and waving to them, all of us welcoming them from the shoal's outer beach, and their mythical return to the heart of our coast, as viewed from Bird Shoal, was then and is now altogether meet and wholesome and right.

In January 1862, just shy of seventy Confederate soldiers under Captain Daniel Munn manned an island fort on the central Carolina coast that, though small, had six thirty-two-pound cannon at its sand-and-earth walls and owned a full and commanding view of Bogue Inlet two miles to the south and of the port of Swansboro a mile north.

The company was the Bladen Stars, and theirs was the Southern garrison at Huggins Island, a backward lazy-L of 115 acres, with that much and more in adjacent tidal marsh, a little low land with three miles of shoreline set right where the White Oak River comes down from out of its mossy swamps, serpentines through West Channel in its lower reaches, and here meets the sea.

Months later, a Union flotilla steaming south from Beaufort—some boats through Bogue Sound and some outside the banks to Bogue Inlet—in mid-August 1862, approached Swansboro. The U.S. Navy gunboat *Ellis*, along with the troop transports *Pilot Boy*, *Ocean Queen*, and *Massasoit*, on Friday, August 15, 1862, pushed out through Beaufort Inlet, went down the sea along Bogue Banks and, against hard afternoon wind "with some difficulty . . . passed through the narrow, winding inlet, among the breakers." These vessels anchored in the still water inside Bogue Inlet and awaited two other light-draft steamers, the *Union* and the *Wilson*, which had stayed inside the banks and stood for Swansboro by way of Bogue Sound.

The *Wilson* arrived at dark, with the reconnaissance commander Brigadier General Thomas Stevenson and his staff aboard. As the seagoing craft had been greeted soon after their earlier arrival by the appearance of a lone, large white flag flying atop a high brick building, General Stevenson and the *Wilson* now went straightaway into Swansboro and claimed it.

Next morning the *Union* appeared and joined the rest of the force. The same high winds that made passage through Bogue Inlet a tough game had hindered the *Union*, too, as she steamed down Bogue Sound, encountering water depths of one to three feet. *Union* went coursing past Dog Island, Wood Island, threading her way through Bean Island, Long Marsh and Piney Island, south of Lovett Island, thence past Hunting Island, with little to report upon her late arrival except that she had often run aground.

The fleet then steamed into Swansboro unchallenged—for the Confederate force had moved out in early March, never having fired a martial shot,

*Common prudence dictates the erection of a battery on Huggins Island. . . . Besides its importance in defending the town of Swansborough against marauding parties it would add much to the security of New Berne, as an enemy landing on the White Oak would have his choice of two or more practicable roads to that city.*
*—General Richard C. Gatlin, commander, Department of North Carolina, November 9, 1861*

*Sandbagged parapet,
Huggins Island
Battery, early 1862*

taking the cannon and all their arms and ammunition up to New Bern following newer orders to defend that old town. That lone white flag was all the greeting the Federals would get.

Before returning to Beaufort on Tuesday, August 19, the Federal troops captured one solitary Confederate cavalryman, tore up several large salt-works (the primary mission of this expedition), and the gunboat *Ellis* put in at Huggins Island for an hour or so, just long enough for men under Acting Master Benjamin Porter to torch the vacant barracks and blow up the empty underground bunker—the magazine bombproof—that had protected Huggins Island's munitions.

Archaeologists searching the site a full century later, in May 1962, found the bombproof's collapsed roof and floor timbers, but a half a dozen foot soldiers in this latterday campaign, armed with metal detectors, marched methodically over the old fort and turned up not nail nor hinge nor any metalscrap whatsoever.

The embankments, though, still stood, as sound as the day they were finished in late 1861, and Fort Macon's manager Paul Branch has called them "the only unspoiled example of Confederate earthwork fortifications surviving on the North Carolina coast." And so they stand yet, old parapets overgrown with and protected by small trees and vines on Huggins Island's southwest point, the only pounding they will ever take coming from summer hurricanes and winter nor'easters.

I first boated out to Huggins Island in a twenty-one-foot bateau in April 2001, along with other board members of the North Carolina Coastal Federation. On that outing we were hosting the board of the North Carolina Clean Water Management Trust Fund, which had joined monies with the state's Natural Heritage Trust Fund and Division of State Parks to buy the island in June 1999 for $1.3 million from a couple who had had a change of heart about retiring to a home on Huggins and boating back and forth to the mainland. Instead, Huggins Island would now join its much larger neighbor Bear Island as a part of Hammocks Beach State Park.

That spring day in '01, Ranger Kevin Bleck, a big, friendly, sturdy man who had taken the park's lead in learning the lay of the place, spoke to the assembled on one of the island's upperside beaches and thanked all comers for adding Huggins to the Hammocks system. He acknowledged that there had been some upset on the part of people long used to camping and hunting on the forested, unpopulated island ("This is the third sign we've had to put up," he said, alluding to earlier state-park signs having been shot up, or used for firewood by trespassers), but hoped earnestly that, given time, the park's holding of Huggins would find favor generally, and allow any hard feelings to give way.

Which seems to have come to pass, at least on the part of those close at hand. "I get frequent calls from concerned local citizens," he later said, "reporting fires or lights on the island. Most of the local community realize that we are trying to protect and preserve Huggins Island. Most of the trouble I deal with isn't caused by locals."

Though the park's management plan is not yet set, with primitive and group camping readily available on nearby Bear Island, public activity encouraged on Huggins for the foreseeable future will likely continue to be day-use only.

Mostly, Kevin Bleck sang of Huggins's incredible natural diversity. Pileated woodpeckers and downies were at home here, as were painted buntings and yellow-rumped warblers. Ranger Bleck crawled all over the island, so he said, enjoying becoming one with it till he learned about its plenitude of rattlesnakes. Its varied plant communities ran from salt marsh, brackish marsh, dune grass, maritime shrub, maritime evergreen forest, and, in one small area of the island's northwest lobe, a parcel of globally-rare maritime swamp forest. The small-flowered buckthorn, at the northern limit of its range, turned up here, one of only five sites in North Carolina where it shows its face.

Five Native American shell middens on Huggins attested to its long settlement and use by humankind, the eras ranging from Middle to Late Woodland (200 B.C.–A.D. 1500), with both Siouian and Algonkian peoples represented here by clam, oyster, and conch shells, ceramic sherds, stone tools, projectile points and debris. Protection of archaeological resources was a matter of no small concern to state park planners, for, though the Native American sites are as yet unexcavated, they are thought to be substantial in what they may reveal.

Some colonists once had a peach orchard out here, according to remarks in old deeds, from about 1722 till 1745, when George II of England granted the unnamed island to North Carolina Chief Justice Christopher Gale. Since then, whether for use as seaside farm or haven, this island has had nearly twenty owners, and Carolinians have called it variously: Stones Island, possibly for eighteenth-century surveyor William Stone; Weeks Island, after the man whose spot it was when Confederates and Federals did business here; and Russell's Island, after Daniel Heady Russell, who fashioned the first train trestle over Wrightsville Sound far to the south, and who owned the island from 1888 till 1917 and put three houses on it, none of which survives today.

Huggins, though, was the name that stuck, the honor going to former Onslow County Sheriff Luke Huggins, the island's titleholder from 1822 until his death in 1829.

The last folks known to have lived here were the Leo Maness family, which in the 1920s raised melons, poultry and pork, the latter on a large scale. A 150-pound feral pig, seen cavorting in Huggins's marshes several summers ago, might well have had a lean and nervous look as park personnel considered rounding it up, some atavistic porcine sense of the old days. For a mighty down-home moment people still talk about was the occasion when the Manesses set water to boiling and whetstone to blades and slaughtered sixty hogs at one time on Huggins Island.

---

In January 2002, 140 years after Munn's Bladen Stars garrisoned the Confederate fort, I stood in the jungled overgrowth of its seaward wall and there atop it pondered the modern-day defense of Huggins Island.

Three of us—Ranger Sean McElhone, Beaufort photographer Scott Taylor, and I—had come out by park bateau in the middle of one unseasonably warm Saturday afternoon for a more thorough look around and walkabout than that earlier meeting of the boards allowed for, and as soon as we beached at the easternmost spread of sand on the island's north side and stepped into the liveoak and cedar and yaupon jungle, I thought:

*What an agreeably lonesome spot, yet so readily accessible.*

*Yaupon,*
*November 2005*

A woodcock busted at our approach along the scant trail that ran a short ways through the undergrowth of short yaupon, all spriggy and springy. A few hundred feet away to the northwest, a large, high beechtree shone gold against the winterbrown vines and the evergreens.

As ever, the yearning contortions of liveoaks gained my easy, instant fascination. A pair of huge dead pines—twelve-inch and eighteen-inch—had sloughed off all their bark, which now lay in piles like the scales of great reptiles at the foot of each. One debarked pine lying over on the ground was slick to step upon, as if it had just been greased. Hurricanes from Bertha to Floyd, blowing in here over the three-year period from '96 to '99, had left big blowdowns all over Huggins. A fifty-foot cedar spread out, lower limbs bare, and in the low island earth some cedars slanted against the sky in tower-of-Pisa tilt. There were red berries on much of the yaupon, and sign of gray fox around.

Much more open, and easier to walk, was the forest to seaward, and, when we reached the oyster waters, I strode fifteen feet out to get a look around. The Emerald Isle bridge spanned Bogue Sound a ways off to the east; the crescent of marshy Dudley's Island lay out halfway to the inlet beyond us. Making its way across the waterscape from sea to safe harbor, the Corps of Engineers Bogue Inlet channel dredger went dieseling up toward the Intracoastal Waterway, its low thrumming for a few moments underscoring the wintry afternoon, fifty degrees at half past three and nearly flat calm.

I walked on, my boot treads mingling with tracks of deer in the dark mud, till my boot came down hard on an old treetrunk embedded in the marsh. On a beach of nothing but broken shells, a single lamb's ear grew, its pastel green shimmering with promise against all the bleached-bone oyster white. Shell fragments speckled the roots of fallen-over liveoak trees, and a few young palmettos stood in a slough behind the beach itself.

A couple hundred steps more along the island's marge, Ranger McElhone gestured at a catbriered rise in the woods and said,

"Well, there's the old fort."

The waters this old redoubt looked out upon were still some of the best and cleanest in the Carolina realm. With the island's having been claimed by the state for conservation, and with other upstream (Queen's Creek) and upriver (upper White Oak) properties also in conservation reserve thanks to the Clean Water Management Trust Fund, which since 1997 has put $29.5 million into protecting the White Oak basin, the Confederate fort on Huggins Island now stood as emblem of a deeper defense than that for which it was originally built.

With its jungle of fox and coon and deer runs and its old angled fort, this little island offered as important a lesson as there could be about our goodliest land. Schoolchildren learn it readily, and can come to Hammocks Beach and Huggins Island and learn it anew, and so, too, can the rest of us. Our coastal rivers and estuaries are the real treasures that Sir Walter Ralegh sent us here for, though he may have had other matters and metals in mind. One great test of our collective mettle is the strength of our resolve in the protection and restoration of these waters, to see if together we can make them living models to the world.

On the last day of January 2004, I looked out at the world from Morris Landing, a popular smallboat-launching spot along the Intracoastal Waterway in Onslow County. The North Carolina Coastal Federation was buying it from the Boy Scouts in order to set up a Division of Marine Fisheries oyster-shell dump, and almost two dozen of us from the federation had cruised out from Betty's Smokehouse, the prime Holly Ridge barbeque spot where we had just met, to study up on our new acquisition and to talk about its promise in the broadening campaign to protect and replenish North Carolina's native oyster population. Shells collected from oyster bars all over eastern North Carolina would get trucked in and piled here, and barges could then slide into shore, pick them up, and take them out and spill them over into the prime shellfishing waters around Permuda Island and Stump Sound, where the shells would give the miniscule oyster spat something to cling to and grow upon.

Lena Ritter, an oyster-tonger from way back and one of the federation's early presidents, and I walked down along the edge of the marsh. She pointed out King's Creek to the east, then Permuda Island off in the sound, long and low and cedar-and-yaupon green in midwinter.

"I know all this like the back of my hand," she said. "The school bus I rode used to come down here to this landing to turn around—sometimes the water'd be so high it'd just go through the water. And if the bus broke down, wasn't any cell phone or radio to call for help—we'd just get off and walk home!"

Permuda, a mile long and toothpick lean in the middle of shellfish heaven, was on the very real verge of having condominiums slapped upon its fifty acres twenty years ago, till salty and vivacious Lena Ritter led the Stump Sound Shellfishermen into pitched battle, enlisting the Coastal Federation for advocacy and the North Carolina Nature Conservancy for realty expertise. Lena's efforts resulted in Permuda Island's successfully becoming part of the North Carolina Coastal Reserve, a ten-site program of mostly barrier-island preserves, whose inner holdings now included the 18,000-acre Emily and Richardson Preyer Buckridge tract on Alligator River several miles south of Durant Island, as well as marshy Zeke's Island in the lower Cape Fear River.

Up the waterway just a mile or so east of Morris Landing lay Rice Farm,

*In those days we talked about oysters with scarcely less seriousness or exactitude than I have heard that Inuit people discuss the fine points of ice and snow.*
*—David Cecelski,*
*The Oyster Shucker's Song (2005)*

where Bernice and the late Bill Rice raised a family of oyster gardeners, some of whom are still at it, for this is the site of their son-in-law Jim and daughter Bonnie's J&B shellfish aquaculture operation. Over land, the ride up to the farm from Morris Landing was six or seven miles—"We'll go right by one of the oldest houses in Onslow County," Lena said. "When we turn right up from the landing, it'll be on the left in some big magnolias. So old it was put together with *pegs*!"

Once we were there at Rice Farm, avuncular and grinning Jim Swartzenberg showed the group around the oyster operation—he and Bonnie grew an acre of cultured oysters, some in bags, some in cages, and the rest of their hundred acres worth of shellfish leases were wild. We assayed all their big, tabled boxes, where bags of young bivalves got going, their boats and docks, and their almost brand-new $65-a-foot living shoreline, marsh grass planted behind a low rock sill intended to break the force of the waterway's boat swash and southwesterly storm waves and slow the inexorable erosion. After the tour I lingered on, and Jim and I talked a bit there by the waterway about the vagaries of being a shellfisher in the modern age.

"I've had to chase all kinds of people off my lease," he said. "We've got about a hundred acres. . . . Sometimes it's people who don't know what they're doing, don't know what the stakes mean . . . other times it's people who know *exactly* what it is—I came up on two men once, and one of them ran and dove into the marsh, then came up and said they were lost or something. . . . I'm usually pretty nice about asking them to move on, but Bonnie's raising Cain, madder'n fire. . . .

"One time, two, three years ago, we found a beautiful wooden table, a dining-room table the storms had washed out and left on the north end of Permuda Island and we decided to salvage it, take it home. It was up in the brush in the edge, and I got out of the boat, started walking over to it, got within fifteen feet of that table, saw something big and black sitting right on top of it, and finally I saw it moving and I realized it was a great big water moccasin. Decided we didn't need that table so bad after all!"

"Anyone ever live out on Permuda?" I asked him.

He said a family lived out there in the 1940s and '50s, as caretakers for a New York City owner who kept it for a hunting preserve. The caretaker held the oyster lease, but, as he was doing nothing with it, Jim's father-in-law, Bill Rice, made a successful offer to buy it. He took a $700 check to the man, who then asked if Rice would take him to town to cash it, which he did. After the caretaker supplied himself with some groceries and some whiskey, he returned home—he wasn't living on Permuda at the time. The next day somebody found him in his home dead, and none of that cash, almost

$700, was anywhere around. "They never did connect the dots, figure out what happened," Jim said. "Some people think he had a few too many drinks, fell asleep with the heater on high and then died as natural a death as could be had under those strange circumstances. Perhaps the first person who found him that next day found the money too and took it. And the fellow who reported him dead was the *second* person to come upon him."

On a cold late-January day one year later, Jim, at that time president of the North Carolina Shellfish Growers Association, his mother-in-law Bernice Rice, and I sat down together in the den there at Rice Farm. We talked some more about Permuda Island, and as we did they called the names of other, even smaller spots thereabouts: a little island across from Permuda toward the Topsail beach called "Devil's Woodyard," an oyster rock called "Elbow," another small islet named "Strawberry Island." And we spoke about oystering, about the potential introduction of Asian oysters into North Carolina shellfishing grounds, and about the battle over Permuda Island.

Knowing that freshwater rushing into our estuaries, particularly after an inch or two of rain inland, is constantly affecting salinity levels, I said, "Jim, we all like salty oysters. But what do the oysters like?"

"They'll grow in ocean water, thirty-five [parts per thousand]," Jim said. "We run in the thirties out here—I've seen it as high as forty out here, when it's really a drought—they seem to like a little bit fresher, seem to like the teens. If you get below ten parts per thousand they will survive for a period of time, but they won't thrive. I've seen em survive down to five parts per thousand, Wilson Bay being the case. Wilson Bay in Jacksonville, tried to grow em up there. They did real well one year when we had the drought—course the salinity went up—and then I put some up there a couple years ago as an experiment, and they all died. Had a lot of freshwater and sometimes we didn't have any salinity and sometimes we had five. They just died."

For some years now scientific study has engendered a public discussion, if not outright debate, concerning the potential introduction of the "Asian oyster," *ariakensis*, into North Carolina's shellfishing grounds—a supposedly faster-growing and Dermo-disease-resistant oyster that would replenish our massively depleted native-oyster (*Crassotrea virginica*) stocks. No one these days was having any trouble reading the report our native oysters have given us: in the winter of 1898–99, the state had its record oyster harvest, 2,450,000 bushels; in 2002, only 46,000 bushels were landed.

Some politicians have warmed to the idea. Carolina oystermen, though, have not.

Bernice Rice said her late husband Bill was afraid the Asians would, in fact, introduce disease that would kill our native oysters. And such concern and uncertainty has leapt state lines. Jim said: "Maryland is just about ready to bring em in, 'cause the Chesapeake Bay is in such bad shape. Virginia is saying, wait a minute, now, we don't want you to do this, you know. Delaware is saying the same thing, and now I understand even Rhode Island's complaining." Jim was not sure the introduction of *ariakensis* in the Chesapeake would lead to their populating North Carolina's sounds—he thought they would more likely migrate northward. Yet he voiced his own fears about this toying with the species pool, saying tersely: "It's almost a *Jurassic Park* kind of thing.

"It's like: this is the *savior*, but it's not—I don't think it's going to save anything. I can grow our oysters, cultured oysters, just as quickly as you can grow an *ariakensis*. I've got some huge oysters that're eighteen months old, and they're *that big*, and they taste better, and they look better."

Once, after a Marine Fisheries event up in Morehead City, Jim brought some *ariakensis* home. When I asked what they were like, Bernice Rice immediately started laughing at my question, saying "I wouldn't taste em!" And at this Jim smiled, as he mostly does, and recalled:

"So I went up there to a meeting and I was a little late so I didn't get to taste em, so Mike Marshall, he's at Marine Fisheries, Mike said, 'Well, Jim, we got some leftovers, if you want to take some home,' and I said 'Okay.' Brought em back here.

"My dog loves oysters, and we eat oysters out here, roast em right outside here. My dog'll just sit by the table and you just keep feeding him oysters. He won't stop. And if you don't give him one he'll just sit there and whine and bark. We have a big rack. I put about a half a bushel of my oysters on the rack, and I put that peck of *ariakensis* on the rack, and you can tell by looking at em they're different. And we roasted em, we always roast em over an open fire. And I tasted one and I didn't really like it—just didn't like it. I didn't like the looks of it, kind of a pinkish, orangeish color, with a black gill. Had a couple and I just didn't want any more, and I tried to give one to my dog Milt and he put it in his mouth and *spit it out*!"

Jim believed back in 2002 that the question was settled, till he read something recently about *ariakensis* doing well at a taste test in Maryland and that "they were selling em and doing super.

"I thought, my God, they must really need oysters *badly* up there!

"I thought we had put it to bed, but lo and behold they [scientists] get another 200,000 [dollars] and we're getting more oysters . . . and I wouldn't be surprised if they didn't have another batch *coming in next summer!*"

Another serious dust-up in Rice Farm's immediate area was the battle over Permuda Island's fate, which started in 1982 when the Rices, Lena Ritter and all the other Stump Sounders learned of a proposed 383-condominium and marina development for Permuda, a developer's plans to build a cause-way through Topsail Island's soundside marshes—which ultimately did happen—and then construct a mile of condominiums on the island—which did not.

"I think Bill and I found out about it before anybody," Bernice said. "We were just amazed at the buildings they could put on there, and they had it drawn out from one end to the other."

"Course Lena was organizing a lot of things," Jim said. "She did a *good job*—we had a couple cookouts here trying to raise money, had an auction at Holly Ridge, trying to raise money so we could pay a lawyer. Hired a lawyer from Wilmington—he did a pretty good job too.

"Just about all the kids getting married within the same couple years, every time you had a wedding going on, you'd have all these politicians showing up—at our weddings, 'cause of the cookouts here. They knew the whole neighborhood was coming, for the wedding, so they came here. They got to come to the wedding, do a little politicking on the side.

"Then the developers changed plans, and they were going to put two-story structures, duplexes and triplexes. But, even then, I'm sure that during hurricanes, Permuda Island would flood all the way over."

The shellfishermen ultimately prevailed: though Onslow County went for development, the state of North Carolina refused to allow it on Permuda Island, honoring the fishing grounds and the fragility of the area, and the Nature Conservancy then bought the island in 1987 for $1.7 million and later sold it to the state. In an era when every grain of barrier-island sand that could be built upon *was* being built upon, and when much of our 4,000-mile estuarine shoreline was being aggressively marketed as *inner banks*, the placing of Permuda Island in public trust and the saving of Stump Sound's oyster waters ranked as a major, not minor, miracle.

"We all just put in together," said Bernice Rice.

As for the marsh-road out to Permuda, the remnant of that quashed project, Jim said: "We're trying to get the causeway taken out, open the thing up a little bit. Right now where the bridge was is probably a span of water not much wider than this room, maybe twenty-five, thirty feet. Going to take out about 150 feet. It's about eight to ten feet deep there (where the bridge was), so all the water just rushes through there. If they take the 150 feet there, it should kind of level things out . . . and I think it *will* help the oysters. What you need to have for oysters is food and flow—water flowing brings food."

*Natives on burlap,*
*December 2005*

Elsewhere in the Sound Country, help for the native oyster has come in the form of restored oyster reefs. Working with the state's Division of Marine Fisheries, the Nature Conservancy has recently built twenty-six reefs, each over a hundred square yards, spread across a forty-five-acre area in Pamlico Sound, and has begun an oyster-shell recycling program on the Outer Banks like the one the Coastal Federation and the state have planned for Morris Landing and Stump Sound. Between 30,000 and 40,000 bushels of oyster shells have gone into five Coastal Federation reefs in recent years, in such diverse spots as Hoop Pole Creek in Bogue Sound, Williston Creek in Jarrett Bay, Hewlett's Creek in Masonborough Sound, Everett Bay in Stump Sound, and Alligator Bay, just northeast of Stump.

Behind Jim and Bonnie Swartzenberg's tireless efforts and their hopefulness about Stump Sound's future and in Rice Farm's mariculture as a healthy part of it, indeed, behind the good cheer and great spirits I found at Rice Farm lay a terrible irony, one almost beyond belief: out on the Intracoastal Waterway in 2000, while transferring oysters from polluted waters to the clean grounds of Stump Sound, Jim and Bonnie and her eighty-seven-year-old father Bill Rice in their heavily-laden boat were swamped by a passing yacht, which neither noticed them nor stopped.

Shellfish champion, Rice Farm patriarch, lifelong Stump Sounder Bill Rice drowned.

On my way home after my first time out at Rice Farm I carried fifty or so of Jim and Bonnie's gourmet oysters, the mica-like fringe of new shell still on many of them, something one would never see in the real wild, and two 100-count bags of their clams. In Holly Ridge I passed the closed-up night-club Jess's Mess, the pink paint of its formerly garish exterior now nicely faded, and I got to thinking of how I would nevermore see such a funky place in the well-groomed Triangle of central Carolina, nor would I ever find there a dead-solid, real-deal pool hall like Beaufort's Royal James, the RJ, where the barmaid's outfit the night before had been a formfitting sequined deep-woods camouflage dress.

*How long would the truehearted, the headstrong, and the downhome last?*

*How long the native oysters?*

I headed west with the sights and the aromatic salt-marsh smell of the Sound Country filling my head, all the way back to the red-clay hills that were so near and yet so far from the *spartina*, the Spanish moss, and the seawinds singing in the pines.

# Money Island

*Ful ofte in herte*
*he rolleth*
*up and doun*
*The beautee of thise*
*floryns newe*
*and brighte.*
*[And in his mind*
*he rolls both*
*up and down*
*The beauty of*
*those florins*
*new and bright.]*
*—Geoffrey Chaucer,*
*The Pardoner's*
*Tale (ca. 1395)*

Up and over the drawbridge, with its pale-green bridge-tender's house, one booms east across the waterway toward old Wrightsville Beach, tires whining over the green metalgrate roadway, a welcome sign then appearing just over the bridge on stout, marsh-middled Harbor Island, a dredged-up interposition once known as The Hammocks that lies between the waterway and Banks Channel, beyond which is the seabeach itself. On Harbor, a chalk tower called Seapath now looms over marshes and creeks to the south, but, closer by, one is beckoned by the bright terracotta-tin-topped MOI restaurant—"middle of the island," a legend explains. Under the MOI roof, a fish market also offers, collaterally, immodestly spiced sauces of all cultures, even as its exceptionally appointed near-neighbor spirits store, the Lighthouse, proffers beers of all peoples. Here prevails a certain jollity.

From the top of the bridge, if one had but turned and looked quickly shot-straight a mile down the waterway to the south, one might have gotten a scant glance of the lean, little, storied strand of beach at the mouth of Bradley Creek, a spot long known as Money Island.

We were seated at a long table, six to a side, in a Chapel Hill bistro in the fall of 2003. Tall, striking Musette Morgan of Memphis, whose mother hailed from Raleigh, was reenacting scenes of protocol from her teenage years, such as her mother's languorous moan when calling her to the telephone, "Mew-*zay*-ette!" and making visiting novelist Pat Conroy howl with delight. After a spell this entertainment passed, and she and I got to talking about Wrightsville waters.

"You know about Money Island, don't you?"

"Heard of it," I said. "Why?"

"We *own* it!" she said excitedly. "My family does. Just a big sandbar now, really. But I love all those tales about Captain Kidd burying treasure out there—I'll send you some clippings when I get back to Memphis."

Musette was as good as her word. If anyone ever turns up treasure there, I hope 'tis she.

---

On the eighth of April 1939, the Associated Press moved a story with a Wilmington, North Carolina, dateline. O. E. Parker and W. S. Northrop of Wilmington had been out scavenging around and looking for scrap metal on Money Island in Greenville Sound, between Wrightsville Beach and the mainland, when they turned up an enormous iron chest with a correspondingly large lock on the front.

The chest was empty, its oak-planked lining inside all but rotted away.

Was this part of Captain Kidd's vaunted buried treasure? A pair of chests of gold coins and silver laid for safekeeping here on a Carolinian inner island in what was then *terra obscura*, just before his arrest in New York and subsequent hanging in London in 1701? At his execution, the pirate Kidd's noose broke twice before a third rope caught and held and did him in, after which his captors tarred his body and hung it in chains beside the Thames—he never would get back to New Hanover County, North Carolina, to lift his loot.

The finding of that iron chest in 1939 sent the AP writer inquiring after pirate lore from one Andrew Jackson Howell Jr., Presbyterian minister retired, who thirty-one years earlier had published *Money Island*, a "story of buried treasure on Money Island . . . the mysterious little island that blinks in the sunlight and tries to hide its secret." In Howell's work, only the first page appeared to be in his own voice, whereas dozens of subsequent pages represented themselves as the manuscript of one Jonathan Landstone, who in turn wrote that he (Landstone) had heard the tale from his grandfather about his grandfather's *father*, Captain John Redfield, a trusted confederate of Captain William Kidd the Pirate.

Landstone's story:

Overburdened with Spanish plunder from the Caribbean, Captain Kidd made a plan with his closest collaborator, Redfield, to take a longboat into shore from where their ship was lying at anchor off North Carolina, and to carry with them two chests of gold and silver for burial on Money Island. After a specified time, they would split this treasure, with the first one back to it taking half and leaving half for the other. Redfield, by Kidd's plan, would leave the ship, build a house ashore, and live there proximate to the treasure spot, a place to be known only to the two men who dug the hole and buried the booty.

Redfield stayed on in this locale, devising himself a home called "Rindout." But a handful of Kidd's sailors, suspicious of their leaders, soon jumped ship and made their way back to that part of the Carolina coast, found Redfield and confronted him. They would have knowledge of the treasure's burial place, they demanded. Redfield was intransigent—his word to Captain Kidd was bond, and he would not give up anything about the treasure without written word ordering such from Kidd himself.

In at least one version of this tale, the frustrated shipjumpers then killed Redfield in cold blood, a counterproductive act to be sure, dead men being

*Money Island,*
*about 1920*

famously legendary then as now for telling no tales. In Landstone's version, though, as passed on by Reverend Howell, Redfield fared better.

The pirates, one Brisbau their leader, took both Redfield and his wife captive, clapped them in chains, and after days and weeks of fruitless scouring of the woods around Rindout for treasure, returned to their craft. They sailed, their cruise a ruse to destabilize Captain Redfield and break the secret out of him, then to go back to Money Island and claim the prize.

Yet Brisbau's ensemble touched in Charleston, where now *they* were imprisoned, while the Redfields were freed. Tale-teller Landstone had had it on best authority from his grandfather that Captain Redfield "determined to settle down to an honest, industrious life." He apparently acquired wealth, though from industry or industries unknown, and never went back to Rindout or Money Island.

The grandfather did go, twice, though, as far as turning up Captain Kidd's lost loot, his trips were washouts both times. And Howell, or rather his stand-in narrator, heard all this on good authority "when I was a boy in the early forties." The 1840s, that is. Nice work, for the real Andrew Howell Jr. was born in 1869. Yet, back inside the little novel, the teller of the tale of the tale, that is to say the *boy in the early forties*, wound up joining old Landstone out on Money Island and after much yarnspinning and digging of holes finally unearthing a gaggle of "blackened gold coins . . . all corroded and misshapen through the action of the salty mud in which they had lain, and the disturbance caused by the roots of the trees." All that was left was for the narrator to lament his poor judgment in the years since the treasure hunt, allowing as how he should have been living in luxury had he only used his treasure wisely—this was written by a Presbyterian preacher, after all!

Would that we could pass old Howell a doubloon or two and direct him to the nearest crow's nest—no telling what he'd see or hear next. Even had Reverend Howell foresworn buccaneering fiction and laid off inventing legends of the Spanish main, other stories—all told for true since his early twentieth-century novel—fed the mill of pirate lore grist aplenty and kept it a-going, grinding exceeding fine.

Mullet men came upon gold doubloons on the beaches of Money Island.

An old oysterman named Hezekiah, claimed one John Frederick Newber of Bradley Creek, found a pirate chest "under an oyster rock in Greenville Sound," loaded it onto his mule-cart, and quit being a waterman for the rest of his days.

Intracoastal Waterway dredgers sliced into Money Island's edge as they created the channel seventy-five years ago, and, lo, what turned up in their dredge pipes? Pieces of eight!

Some tales loosely associated with Money Island and its storied treasure dated not to the Golden Age of Piracy in the early eighteenth century, but to the Civil War. One told of blockade-runners offloading gold by the keg-full when threatened with capture. Where, though? How proximate to Money? Reverend Howell also threw into his novel the tale of a Confederate naval officer on the verge of building a home on Greenville Sound, the prospect of which prompted *sub rosa* nocturnal excavations on the site prior to the officer's house-building work—locals recalled there once having been an old inn for Portuguese sailors on the *very spot* and, further, believed the inn's cellar to have been a hiding place for buried money.

Well, why not? Secreted plunder shows up as the core of the plot in works such as Stevenson's *Treasure Island*, Poe's *Gold Bug*, Haggard's *King Solomon's Mines*, and Hammett's *Maltese Falcon*, not to mention Faulkner's *Intruder in the Dust* and Chaucer's *Pardoner's Tale*, and artfully so. Dreams of finding limitless treasure and sea chests of gold send divers after sunken ships, build casinos in the desert, fuel lotteries in states peopled by otherwise sensible citizens, and underwrite Hollywood and all the silver screens that light dances upon daily and nightly in every big-shouldered city, in every sprawling suburb, shopping mall, whistlestop and tanktown in America.

Back in Reverend Howell's day, someone acting on behalf of the preacher's estate took time in the 1940s to draft a letter to the RKO Motion Picture Corporation, making RKO aware of the preacher's novel and offering it as a potential film property. Like Landstone's grandfather's trips out to Money Island, this entreaty came to naught. For Hollywood already had *Treasure Island*, *Captain Blood*, and *The Sea Hawk* on celluloid and in the can. In a letter now archived at the gorgeous old Italianate, iron-fenced Latimer House on Third Street in Wilmington, the RKO man who wrote in replying to the reverend's representative said only:

"I have read *Money Island* with considerable interest. It is a fine yarn, but is nothing I can make into a picture at the present time."

## ROAN ISLAND

"Roan Island?" said the old timberman in Pender County's Canetuck Township. "That's a bad place to get to."

Roan Island sits mighty low in the water at one of eastern Carolina's great drains, the confluence of the Cape Fear River and the Black River just a few miles northwest of Wilmington. Outside of its immediate swampy area, Roan is one of our state's least known inner islands—though at 2,757 acres and dimensions of four miles by a mile and a half, it is about as large as one of our best known, Harkers Island up in Carteret.

Owing to a January 1998 land-preservation deal, the big swamp island has now come into the common weal. The North Carolina Nature Conservancy bought 2,132 acres of Roan from its longtime owner, Wilmington's Corbett Farming Company, with a $1 million Natural Heritage Trust Fund Grant. Corbett Package Company donated the remaining 625 acres to the conservancy, which then transferred the whole of Roan Island to the state's Wildlife Resources Commission for management as a public game land.

Not a bad place, now—just a bad place *to get to*.

Only a boat will get you there. No bridge touches it, and only a handful of rough, private lanes even lead to within sight of it.

As you drive down into the stout neck of land between the Cape Fear and the Black, you can feel, and see beyond the broad fields, the land dropping away below and before you, and the names of the three lanes in that neck reveal its character: Steel Trap Road, Light Wood Knot Road, Canetuck Road. In late fall the tall cypress along the creeks stand out a rusty gold beyond the great eastern farm fields, and Ann and Cary and I were bound one November afternoon right down to the center of that land above Roan Island, through fields that were not so very long ago swamps themselves, till Lyon's Creek was worked into Lyon's Canal and the drained swamps and branches were worked into farms.

Ted Brown, an affable forester we came upon along Heading Bluff Road south of Currie, said of Lyon's Canal: "If it hadn't a been dug, there wouldn't *be* any farming in this whole section—it'd *all* be swamp."

We enjoyed as best we could a near-vertical put-in of our jonboat at the Heading Bluff Road bridge over Lyon's, a maneuver that thanks to gravity was a piece of cake, albeit an unleavened and thin-sliced one. Our jonboat-

*What seas what*
*shores what grey*
*rocks and what*
*islands*
*What water lapping*
*the bow*
*And scent of*
*pine and the*
*woodthrush*
*singing through*
*the fog*
*What images return*
*O my daughter.*
*—T. S. Eliot, Marina*
*(1930)*

*Roan Island, 1998*

ing was in the dug-out creek for a mile or more, and then the last mile to the Thoroughfare (that runs between the Cape Fear and Black Rivers on Roan's upper end) we were in all-swamp on what remained of the natural creek, passing three and a half to four-foot cypress, a few palmettos, and sycamore on the way down. Whenever we killed the little Johnson outboard and just floated, we would hear a kingfisher splitting the air somewhere near, and woodpeckers aplenty were out knocking and chopping away at the swamp forest, their tattoos carrying sharply through the woods as if they were calling it to order.

If they were, it was the order of a primitive nature. For Roan Island at the Thoroughfare was a jungle, the vine-tangled capital of the Cape Fear lowlands and the Black River valley, a wild, wet spot harboring alligator and bear, deer and otter, songbird and wild turkey, as well as the more ancient, millennial cypress for which the Black is justifiably celebrated. Roan was now the anchor for the Nature Conservancy's basin-wide Black River protection effort, the lower end of its wildlife corridor, the last lonesome land before the big riverport Wilmington downstream. The conservancy's Fred Annand called this island "a real treasure . . . the result of careful management and its isolated location at the junction of a blackwater and brownwater river," acknowledging that Roan Island's confluent position made it a unique environmental gauging station. Here was the southeastern Carolina analogue to the Nature Conservancy's bottomland conservation work farther north in the Roanoke River valley.

It had come to us North Carolinians with a cost, though, and not just the one represented by the price tag. Those dozens who had braved the wild island and learned it and negotiated its trackless interior—some of them for nearly forty years—as members of the Roan Island Hunting Club now lamented not only the passing of their hunt but also the stewardship it entailed. To the press they worried aloud that the absence of a *bona fide* hunting club and its posted signs and its patrols would lead to free reign for poachers and the concomitant diminishment of the island's deer. Somehow, the state would have to honor the club's late and longstanding presence with a strong stewardship of its own.

Much to reflect upon, as Ann and I brought the jonboat out of the swampy tangles, out from the pure reflection of forest in the blackwater of Lyon's Creek into the openness of the Thoroughfare, and plied it first down toward the Black and after awhile up toward the Cape Fear, spooking the occasional wood ducks, alarming a turtle out for some late-season Sunday sunning right off its log. We weren't in the middle of nowhere, for we had company aplenty: cardinals, crows, buzzards. And along Roan's overgrown banks the big trees loomed.

When I spoke later with Eddie Corbett—whose Wilmington firm made the Roan deal with Annand—he marveled over one of the big island's biggest trees, a low-country wonder he'd spotted from the air a few years ago. He described a doubletrunked cypress growing up like a tuning fork, with each of the twin trunks appearing to Corbett from his helicopter's eye view to be a good *eight feet* in diameter.

"Did you ever walk to it?" I asked.

"No—o-o-o," he said. "It'd take *GPS* to find that thing. I've flown over the island a couple times since then in a small plane, and I've looked for that cypress. Didn't see it either time. I don't know but, with the storms and all, it might've blown down. No *telling* how big the *main* trunk below that pair might be!"

It was Corbett who directed me to Milvin Marshall, the aged timberman who by Corbett's reckoning knew Roan Island just about better than anyone. Marshall lived by himself on the Heading Bluff Road hard by Lyon's Canal, not far from where Ann and I had put in the previous fall, and he had a high-pitched, lively and emphatic voice, kind of like Walter Brennan when excited. Yes, he answered my question, he *did* have a recollection or two from his Roan Island tenure many years ago.

"We cut timber all over Roan's Island, off and on for ten years or so, we sure did," he said, "except in the middle where we couldn't get it out. Cypress, black gum too, and sweet gum, tupelo gum . . . some elm, a few sycamore along the riverbanks."

Milvin Marshall and his brother Hailey used to rough it on Roan at the mouth of Black River, where they had themselves a twelve-by-twelve camp. "We'd go down there by boat, stay maybe a week at a time. Carried meal for corncakes, and eggs . . . set a trot line, catch cats, skin em and eat em."

"Any other fish?" I asked.

"Perch, trout, largemouth bass. We'd kill squirrels in the winter time, or coons, anything we could get. We fared good!" he laughed. "We were just as healthy as bulls!"

No wonder. These waters were legendary fishing grounds, as Carolina Beach outdoorsman Richard Cecelski said: "That whole area's known for monster cats!"

"How about bear?" I asked Milvin Marshall. "Run across many of them?"

"Never—wadn't bothered by bear. Had some bobcats, though."

Of his main reason for being out there in the wildcat woods, Marshall said: "We used to work timber from Elizabethtown right on down, on Roan's Island for Corbett, for Southern Box. We'd deliver it to Wilmington."

When I asked him the name of his company, he just laughed again.

"Didn't have no *name* . . . just Marshall brothers, I guess."

Working Roan Island, "Somebody *might've* had a dinky train on there," he said, but he wasn't very sure about that. For the Marshalls the work was always by boat and by hand; they cut timber into three-foot and five-foot blocks, then rowed it out and rafted it up—and the rafts they made of Roan timber were enormous, their biggest topping out at 89,000 board feet. To drift downriver, he said, it would take "three-and-a-half to four tides to carry em to Wilmington." For the Roan Island and lower Black River swamps are at sea level, and the Black is known to be tidal as far upriver as Point Caswell, most of ten miles *above* the Black's confluence with the Thoroughfare.

"I wish I had it now, that timber, the price it is now. I'd be *heeled* over—with *money*!"

Marshall's fondness for the isolated island, though, went far beyond the woodsman's economy he'd once been part and parcel of. "Nice scenery," he said. "*Wild* territory. There're big cypress shells, where they couldn't get to it, and a six-foot cypress would be common. Been twenty years since I been out there," he said. "Used to be a lot of deer, coons, possums—I don't know what's out there now."

Years back, when he had known it, he had indeed known it well. "Never got lost," he said. "I was like a coon . . . raised up here in Canetuck. More of a varmint than anything else . . . we were tough as alligators."

I asked him to give me some soundings on the footing in the island's interior, and Marshall said: "Well, there's some high ground along Cape Fear River, along the Thoroughfare. But you haven't got a whole terrible lot of high ground." Bottomland hardwoods took what high ground there was, in a lazy-*C* from about a half-mile east of Lyon's Creek's mouth into the Thoroughfare around to where the Thoroughfare hit Cape Fear River and then about a mile downriver to the east. On maps of Roan Island a couple of marshes showed up as old rice fields: one along the Black just above the confluence with the Cape Fear, another farther up the Black and filling a tooth-shaped loop between Peachtree Landing and the Thoroughfare's mouth.

As for putting a small Roan-bound boat in anywhere even vaguely proximate to that island, somewhere closer than the Riegel Course Road ramp five or six miles up the Cape Fear, or closer even than the Heading Bluff Road bridge, Milvin Marshall laughed yet again and said, "Well, I don't know—where you were on Lyon's Creek, that might be the nearest point."

So by the old timber-drifter's estimation we had done as well as we might have, and had been to the head of the beast if not yet to its belly. Ann and Cary and I rode on home to the piedmont, into a big, bright red-and-

*Frank A. Thompson
and men loading
naval stores onto
barge, Eagles Island,
across the Cape
Fear River from
Wilmington, N.C.,
early twentieth
century*

gold sunset, with a taste of Roan and with a taste of Bladen County as well—a tin of Houston's blistered peanuts. A circumnavigation of Roan Island would have to wait, as would a laying of hands on that mythical doubletrunked cypress. That was all right, I thought, and it was stuff enough for springtime dreams to be made on.

### EAGLES, CAMPBELL, AND KEG ISLANDS

On below Roan Island, the Cape Fear and its distributary the Brunswick made Eagles Island, 2,300 acres of marsh and swamp forest on the west bank of the Cape Fear, across the river from downtown Wilmington. The great gray battleship *North Carolina* now lay snug in its cut in the island's upper part, put there by the pennies, nickels and dimes of Tar Heel schoolchildren two generations ago, and thousands of shorebirds in migration stop and seek shelter in the diked dredge-spoil impoundments comprising Eagles's lower third. Little but the tops of pilings at the river's edge gave evidence of all the warehousing and commerce that once went on over there, of the ferryboat *John Knox* daily moving workmen and goods back and forth to and from such establishments as the Dunn Brothers Company, whose riverfront wall once proclaimed its interests to be "MOLASSES COFFEE RICE" or Frank A. Thompson's cooperage and shipping shed for "TAR, PITCH & TURPENTINE."

Downriver past Dram Tree Point—a huge mossy cypress marking the outbound mariner's last sight of home, the incoming sailor's spot for celebratory drink—lay Campbell Island, 300 acres on the west side of the modern shipping channel, and, just below it, Keg Island on the channel's east side. Named to honor Revolutionary War General William Campbell (1745– 81), who commanded the American force at the Battle of Kings Mountain and later wrote succinctly "The victory was complete to a wish," Campbell formerly carried the name Crane. Not to be confused with Eagles Island's earlier name, Cranes.

This island may have been the November 1663 meeting place of an Indian king and an English explorer, Captain William Hilton, who wrote of that Cape Fear council:

> For a further teftimony of their love and good will towards us, they prefented to us two very handfom proper young *Indian* women, the talleft that we have feen in this Countrey; which we fuppofed to be the Kings Daughters, or perfons of fome great account amongft them. Thefe young women were ready to come into our Boat; one of them crouding in, was hardly perfwaded to go out again. We prefented to the King a Hatchet and several Beads, alfo Beads to the young women and to the chief men, and to the reft of the *Indians*, as far as our Beads would go: they promifed us in four days to come on board our Ship, and fo departed from us. When we left the place, which was prefently, we called it *Mount-Bonny*, becaufe we had there concluded a firm Peace.

No record exists that Hilton took the women, however eager, sailing away with him back to Barbados.

James Sprunt, writing in 1896, still referred to Campbell as Big Island, site of a former lighthouse that had been discontinued during "the late war," a battery having been built in its place. Sprunt forecast "a fortune waiting for some enterprising truck farmer" who would take up and till the island's rich alluvial soil, though undercut his proposal immediately by railing on about the "millions of fat rice birds" then roosting on Campbell Island after devouring the rice from nearby Cape Fear River plantations.

Gangs of men and boys firing constantly at the avian raiders, he reported, made no dent on this ravenous population. Yet Sprunt turned again, concluding this passage with a salute to the birds he otherwise termed "toothsome little pests": "For a dainty supper, a fat rice bird is perhaps the most delicious morsel that ever tickled the palate of an epicure."

### BATTERY ISLAND

One cool sunny morning in May 2003, Walker Golder of the National Audubon Society took Coastkeeper Ted Wilgus and me for a boat ride down the Cape Fear River from the Carolina Beach State Park docks all the way to Battery Island, just off Southport. Golder has been haunting the lower Cape Fear since his student days at the University of North Carolina at Wilmington, since Audubon leased Battery Island from the state of North Carolina and Wilmington's master naturalist James Parnell started managing it. Parnell's graduate students would do thesis work on the colonial waterbirds—pelicans, all the small herons, along with the one-tenth of ibis in North America nesting there—and help warden the island.

"Back in the mid-eighties, we used to have to run so many people off Battery Island for disturbing the place and the birds, ten or twelve a week, half a dozen a weekend," the dark-haired, good-natured birdman said in the truck on our way to the river landing at Carolina Beach State Park. "Used to have to deal with photographers in the trees, with news crews walking through the island. Now, it's not a dozen a season—occasionally we encounter somebody, but it's pretty rare."

The reason?

"Southport has embraced the sanctuary program," he continued, "and the media emphasize that people can ride *around* the islands but are *not* to beach their boats and get out on them. One person could wipe out hundreds and hundreds of birds . . . one dog could do a tremendous amount of damage."

At Carolina Beach State Park, we launched the seventeen-foot runabout, a center-console, and made off downriver, the day in the sixties, the wind blowing ten to fifteen out of the north, at our backs as we headed south. First we cruised past North Pelican Island, where the big and gorgeously ungainly-looking birds regarded us with a complete, implacable indifference. It was a posture the brown sentinels could easily afford, for there were no mammalian predators on the islands of the lower Cape Fear and, though gulls go after terns and oystercatchers, no bird bothers pelicans.

Pelicans were nesting in Ocracoke, Golder said, as far back as 1928, but set up a colony on the lower Cape Fear more recently. Of the 4,100 breeding pairs that comprised North Carolina's pelican flock, 500 pairs nested right

*Pelican young,*
*June 2002*

here in the lower Cape Fear, making do off plentiful menhaden and thread-fin herring.

At Ferry Slip Island, an undiked dredge-spoil island, we beached and got out. "Birds prefer this—terns like it bare," Walker said. He had barged a tractor out to Ferry Slip back in February to scrape it clean, giving the same treatment to South Pelican Island downriver, only to see much of their sandy land grassed over "almost immediately" by April. Everything this energetic man had his hands on, and had his wit and keen eye focused upon, had to do with the protection and improvement, wherever possible, of the nesting and living space of the state's colonial waterbirds.

"The beaches are getting all the sand that the Corps of Engineers dredges up," he said. "Not much available for bird habitat." Ferry Slip, just then at five acres, had gotten its last sand in 1990—Walker, wanting to maintain a seven-acre footprint for the island, said he was hoping for a big dump of sand sometime in 2003 or '04. (Two years later, Walker would report that both Ferry Slip and South Pelican had benefited from a project finished in December 2004, and that both islands were back up in size to approximately seven acres. "We were really, really glad to finally get the sand.")

We pushed on, now crossing the river to look in closely on Price's Creek Lighthouse on the west side. Price's Creek Light, a small brick tower only twenty feet tall, sat there as it has since 1851, though it was now dwarfed by the industrial works around it—just a few yards upriver loomed the huge trestling of an Archer-Daniels-Midland dock. One might find it hauntingly hard to believe that Price's Light here had been an important communications link for the Confederacy, *the* link to signal Fort Fisher across the lower Cape Fear, the fortress with the two-mile pounders that had kept the Union blockade at bay and allowed the blockade-runners to operate and keep Wilmington open—the *last* Southern port to open after Vicksburg fell in July 1863—and therefore keep the rebel nation going for most of two years more. So we paused in the boat to wonder that the fate of the long-gone Confederacy once hung, in part, on what the candles in Price's Creek's iron lantern said, or *didn't* say. There before us the diminutive lighthouse stood *prima facie*, needing no verification whatsoever from us, simply being its own fact, its own witness, mute and dwarfed yet extant still, any window lights it might once have had long since broken out, a nice home for a barn owl if a barn owl would but have it.

Downriver, just off Southport, lay Battery Island.

Only ten acres of Battery Island's hundred were what one might call *high ground*, yet to this small spot yearly flew 8,000 or 9,000 ibis. The ibis arrive around Eastertide, as early as the first of April and as late as the twenty-first, in flights of 50 to 500 birds a mile high, way above Cape Fear country. This year, 2003, Walker Golder said they had returned from Latin America in force on the twelfth of April, in five or six great flocks, the birds' wings first flashing in the sun and then, as they came dropping down to the island, the wind whistling through their wings as they fell out of the sky.

A single cedar here would sport fifty to sixty nests, the trees becoming not merely laden but literally packed beak by tailfeather with birds. The original island, the "north colony" so called, had only a few cedars and one lone palmetto growing on it—the "south colony" was where this phenomenon of birds were, in a little maritime forest grown up where the Corps had dumped dredged sand over half a century ago. Red cedar and yaupon and toothache tree succeeded here, a couple of black cherry trees, and no myrtle at all. One could hear the high-pitched cheeping of the young even over the boat's engine, and Walker said, "When they get a little bigger you can hear it from well out in the channel."

On a narrow beach along the river side of the island were terrapin tracks—a diamondback went crawling up away from the water. Large geo-tubes of sand lay at the waterline here, the third season they had been employed to stem Battery's loss of land to the wash of the channel, which was severe: as much as 120 twenty feet in places, an average of 70 to 80 feet.

Away from the river's channel, on the back side of Battery *spartina* spread out, and one saw *baccyru* (sea oxeye), and bright red-and-yellow gallardia. In the middle of the island, though, the ibis had done some denuding, creating nearly a dozen open sandy patches, ranging from a quarter-acre to a half-acre in size. "Anything the birds can break off or pull up, ibises will use for nests."

Midday in late May—"Only half the birds are here," Walker said. "The others, the mates, are out foraging." There was some evidence, he said, that the females did most of the feeding during the first couple of weeks the ibis had young. It took a bird to know a bird—with good humor, Walker allowed that his graduate studies had led him into the skies. "I got in a plane and followed them, just to see how far they'd go!"

Thus did Walker Golder become the premier sky-tracker of the white ibis.

And track them he did. First circling the south colony in a Cessna 182 at an altitude of nearly a thousand feet, Walker would then pick out a random individual or flock of ibis and stay with it till it touched down, the working assumption, he said, being that the first landing site was also going to be the feeding site. Over twelve weeks during the nesting season back in 1988, he watched arrivals and departures of over 80,000 birds, morning and evening, and found that, whereas ibis flew as far as four miles to feed within the saltwater environment, they flew many times that distance to find freshwater food—particularly the crawdaddy, or crayfish, craved by nestlings in their first two weeks of life.

Walker tracked the ibis to the southwest reaches of Orton's Pond, the old plantation watering hole. He tracked them to Town Creek, north of Orton's, which emptied into the Cape Fear just upriver of Campbell and Keg Islands and, then, well north of that, up to Indian Creek above Eagles Island. He tracked them to upper Lockwood's Folly River. And he flew above them and tracked them on what must have been *the* epic flight, to a point beyond Lake Waccamaw, forty-three miles west-northwest of Battery Island!

Every winged thing caught his eye. An anhinga may have recently nested on Battery, he said, a possible first. Forty crows scavenged here, not enough to "really put a dent in the ibis population." In the wintertime marsh hawks and owls moved in, and the marsh was full, too, of clapper rails. This latter-day Audubon smiled as he recalled the "slow moving bird" he used to hunt around Wrightsville and Masonborough well north of here.

"It's beautiful to be out hunting them in the marsh, in the fall."

The white ibis, though, was his first love, and he was due a certain amount of paternal pride over the bird's booming success breeding in the lower Cape Fear. The numbers of nests on Battery Island told the tale: in May 1983 there were 3,737 white ibis nests, with 637 of another eight species of wading birds; in May 1984, 4,839 white ibis nests, 852 of the other eight; and in 1988, 6,072 white ibis nests, 1,025 of the other eight. By 2004 the counts had grown enormously—11,504 white ibis nests were built on Battery Island, followed by the tricolored heron, 292; great egret, 95; little blue heron, 86; and black-crowned night heron, 32.

When the 2004 Governor's Award for Wildlife Conservationist of the Year went to the birdman of Battery Island, to this man who has crafted and guided the waterbird sanctuary program throughout the Sound Country, the only one in the whole state of North Carolina to be at all surprised was Walker Golder himself.

---

We snuck through the shallows to the marshes of Striking and Shell Bed Islands. Below us lay a marsh maze, an intricate estuarine map, the Smith, or Bald Head, Island wetlands, and in it a pair of old seabeach ridges: now the islands called Middle and Bluff. Behind the barrier beach a couple miles off to our right sat North and No Name Islands, then another marsh, Zeke's Island, and then the main river channel and the north wind's chop that would bang us all the way back upriver to Carolina Beach. Before we were well out in the big Cape Fear again, though, I watched and wondered about the waters rolling over and breaking lightly upon what appeared to be a dark stone walkway, running from just above Shell Bed Island on to the north.

The Rocks.

Owing its existence to the 1761 hurricane that opened New Inlet seven miles above Cape Fear, the Rocks was a gargantuan underwater seawall paralleling the banks, intended to keep the Atlantic from continuing to shoal the Cape Fear River's channel—in short, an attempt to effect the closure of New Inlet, which for many decades had served as a popular, much-used shortcut for Cape Fear commercial craft bound for the North, but by the mid-nineteenth century was deemed too much a threat to the main channel. River historian James Sprunt called the Rocks "a continuous line of log and brush mattresses sunk and loaded with stone laid entirely across the New Inlet." The Corps of Engineers had started this work in 1873, and, after laying that foundation of mattresses, had spent years dropping marine limestone quarried from along the Northeast Cape Fear River into the New Inlet deep, wrapping it all up in June 1879.

Nowadays, one seeing the waters ripple and wash over the top of the Rocks would not quickly leap to the realization that the old breakwater below might be anywhere from 75 to 120 feet wide at its base, or that the base might lie as much as 37 feet below the high water. The Rocks ran 4,800 feet, from the top of the Smith Island marshes up toward Zeke's Island, on whose north shore a crescent-shaped two-gun Confederate battery once lay, and Federal Point, where the ferries that now crossed the river from Southport came in and docked.

On Zeke's Island as far back as the 1880s, the Davis family operated quite a considerable fishery, pulling in on one September 1880 haul 16,000 mullets that, once salted, strained the staves of eighty barrels. The May 12, 1883, *Wilmington Star* reported that the Davis fishery comprised four or five families, six houses, a pen with 600 terrapins, and much poultry ("150 chickens, to say nothing of geese, ducks, etc."). W. E. Davis and his sons fished every day at five in the morning and again at five in the evening, getting fish from traps into sharpies, hoisting them from the sharpies onto rolling stock there to move them on a railway across the narrow island to the river side, and then putting the fish onto boats bound upriver for Wilmington and market. What fish they couldn't sell they pressed for oil, then dried, cut and ground up and bagged the remains for fertilizer.

On November 12, 1900, "a new gasoline launch, the *Morning Star*, named after the well known morning newspaper here . . . arrived yesterday by freight over the Seaboard Air Line Railroad, from Racine, Wisconsin, where it was manufactured," according to Wilmington's *Evening Dispatch*, which added that one of the *Morning Star*'s five owners, Captain George Warren, would run her from Wilmington downriver to Zeke's Island, to haul fish back up from this quintet's fishery there.

Prominent Wilmingtonians, rabble-rousing Mayor A. M. Waddell among them, around the turn of the last century made the trip to Zeke's Island for sportfishing as well, finding the sheephead and trout around the Rocks particularly fine. One August 1902 party came back to Wilmington and told of catching an eighteen-inch pig fish—"the largest we ever heard of," said the *Wilmington Messenger*. This group's only complaint, it seemed, was "sandflies in great swarms."

---

Through a glass, one standing in the cedars on Battery Island might have witnessed the making of that underwater wall, or, later, all that fishing up around Zeke's Island. Indeed, one transcending mortality and leaning up here against one of Battery Island's short, dense, wind-sheared cedars might have taken in quite a lot from this riverside vantage. Might've spied, through a glass, even darkly, those Spaniards out on Bald Head Island in the 1520s, recovering from the first New World shipwreck by building the first New World ship. Or seen Stede Bonnet the Gentleman Pirate staving off Colonel William Rhett of Charleston, till the boats of both mariners foundered in the lower Cape Fear, the tidal flow righting Rhett before Bonnet and the Charlestonian getting the better of the Barbadian brigand, who met the noose and discovered eternity in the mud below the seawall at White Point Gardens in Charleston.

The former vice president, nullifier, and Southern rebel before the fact John Caldwell Calhoun, who died in Washington, D.C., on the last day of March 1850, made his final journey past the islands of the lower Cape Fear. Temporarily entombed in the Congressional Cemetery and now borne south by train, Calhoun's remains (encoffined in a Rhode Island–made Fisk Metallic Burial Case) arrived at the railroad depot in Wilmington about two o'clock on Wednesday afternoon, April 24, 1850. Stores closed, ships in port struck colors to half mast, churchbells tolled, and guns fired, as Senator Calhoun's procession—despite inclement weather, the largest ever seen in Wilmington—moved slowly down Front Street to the black-crepe-and-bunting-draped steamer *Nina*, which was lying at Market Street dock awaiting the casket and the three Calhoun sons who accompanied it. At half past three, the *Nina* bore the Calhoun party away from the Custom House wharf down the Cape Fear River, right past Battery Island, out to the open ocean and on to Charleston, where Calhoun found his narrow bed beneath a tall granite slab across Church Street from tawny, columned St. Philip's.

Ships built in Wilmington for the navy of the Confederate States of America in the 1860s and, much later, of the United States of America in the 1910s and 1940s would come down the narrow Cape Fear channel just a few yards from these ibis-filled cedars. Blockade-runners in the service of the Confederacy, like Captain John N. Maffitt who once charted southeastern waters for the U.S. Coast Survey, would cruise up these same reaches, though their imports were not always to the good of the Old South—the blockade-running *Kate* in 1862 brought yellow jack up from Nassau and right past Battery Island and on into Wilmington, where the fever laid nearly 450 souls in the grave.

Eleven years before that plague, though, a lighter pawstroke of nature kept a huge theatrical troupe—sixty strong—belowdecks and seasick on a mailship bound from Wilmington to Charleston for a show. Impresario Phineas Taylor Barnum, the company's manager, hung below with them, but his Scandinavian star, a coloratura soprano, did not, choosing instead to stay up on the ship's open deck for the entire journey, through what was later remembered as "the most tempestuous voyage ever encountered by these boats."

Was she not moved to song when, in passing, she saw the small cedars swaying in the wind, where so many thousands of ibis had clustered over time and ridden out more storms like this than even Time itself could count, and thought of Sweden and home? She would have amazed even the birds that knew the course and flew all the way to their Battery Island home from South America and caught the sunlight like clouds and then fell from a mile high right down out of the sky and into the middle of the little islet's cedar thicket. Whatever birds were hidden there when she stood on the mailboat's deck and passed their scant redoubt, she may have felt she had found kindred spirits way down in Caroline, and spoken to them through the storm with song. For she was Jenny Lind, the singer folks called the "Swedish Nightingale," and if she sang out over the rolling river in passing that day and if music can ride the very waves and if song can live on through centuries and outlast empires, then listen well in such a spot and hear the melodies at the heart of the inner isles, and, hearing them, join, and sing on.

# Coda

*This thou*
*perceivest, which*
*makes thy love*
*more strong*
*To love that well*
*which thou must*
*leave ere long.*
*—William*
*Shakespeare,*
*Sonnet 73*

In deepest yesteryear the oncoming Atlantic drowned streams and created sounds, turned hillocks on the plain into hammocks in the marsh, leaving us hundreds of islands as it flooded a whole coastal plain below the one we know, a terrace now beneath Carolina's vast inland sea, one that no one shall view again for another 100,000 years.

These inner islands are not rocks, nor metals hammered hard at Vulcan's stithy and made final for all time—they are simply mud and sands, or shells, or swamps, massed for moments mere. We may stand and stride upon them and take their measure, feel the brevity of their moments (how like our own), and perhaps feel too some sense of kinship between animate and inanimate, the kinship of all ephemera.

*Harbor Island, 1998*

## Selected Inner Islands Sources

**MACHELHE ISLAND**

The Pasquotank River and life around it at The Narrows are well documented in such texts as the *Pasquotank Historical Society Yearbook*, vol. 1 (N.p.: n.p., 1954–55), vol. 2 (N.p.: n.p., 1956–57, edited by John Elliott Wood), and vol. 3 (Baltimore: Gateway Press, 1975, compiled and edited by Lou N. Overman and Edna M. Shannonhouse); *On the Shores of the Pasquotank: The Architectural History of Elizabeth City and Pasquotank County, North Carolina* (Elizabeth City, N.C.: Museum of the Albemarle, 1989), by Thomas R. Butchko; *A Pictorial History of Elizabeth City, N.C.* (Elizabeth City, N.C.: Carolina Printing Co. of Elizabeth City, n.d.), compiled and edited by Edward Fearing and Gloria J. Berry, and *Elizabeth City Days Gone By* (Elizabeth City, N.C.: Flowers Printing, Second Printing, 2000), compiled by Jane Von Schaaf and Marian Stokes, both books with photographs provided by Fred L. Fearing. Don Pendergraft of the Museum of the Albemarle has been particularly insightful in answering numerous queries.

**DURANT ISLAND**

Sue and Peter Thomson of Elizabeth City told me the kayaker story one evening in Kitty Hawk in April 2000. The lives of Ann Marwood Durant and George Durant are discussed in the *Dictionary of North Carolina Biography*, vol. 2 (Chapel Hill: University of North Carolina Press, 1986), edited by William S. Powell. Robert Anthony Jr., curator of the North Carolina Collection, UNC–Chapel Hill, has fielded my questions about the Durants, their antique family Bible, and many other matters of eastern Caroliniana. Pocosin artists Feather and Willy Phillips of Fort Landing, N.C., have generously cosponsored much of my eastern Tyrrell and Alligator River explorations, including Durant Island.

**HERIOTS ILE, BATTS GRAVE**

Colonel Creecy's *Grandfather's Tales of North Carolina History* (Raleigh, N.C.: Edwards & Broughton, 1901) holds his "Legend of Batz's Grave." Thomas Harriot's *A briefe and true report of the new found land of Virginia* (London: Theodore de Bry, 1588) and John William Shirley's *Thomas Harriot: A Biography* (Oxford and New York: Clarendon Press, 1983) inform us about the man whose name originally—in English—adhered to this island. William S. Powell's "Carolana and the Incomparable Roanoke" (*North Carolina Historical Review* 51, no. 1 [January 1974]) and Elizabeth Gregory McPherson's "Nathaniell Batts: Landholder on Pasquotank River, 1660" (*North Carolina Historical Review* 43, no. 1 [Winter 1966]) discuss the man whose name succeeded Harriott's and stayed with the island till it drowned. Vincent J. Bellis, Stanley R. Riggs, and Michael P. O'Connor wrote about Batts Grave in *Estuarine Shoreline Erosion in the Albemarle-Pamlico Region of North Carolina* (Raleigh: Sea Grant Program, North Carolina State University, 1975), and Professor Bellis discussed their fieldwork in correspondence to me on March 10, 2001.

### THE PURCHACE ILES

Jerry Leath Mills, with whom I boated the Roanoke River and lower Purchace Islands, wrote of Samuel Purchas for the *American National Biography* (New York: Oxford University Press, 1999). From the North Carolina Nature Conservancy's Merrill Lynch, Sam Pearsall, Jeff Horton, Jeffrey Smith DeBlieu, Fred Annand, and Katherine Skinner I have gained much awareness of the Roanoke and its basin. Lynch's "Roanoke River Preserve Design Project" (typescript, North Carolina Natural Heritage Program and North Carolina Nature Conservancy, 1981), a thorough inventory, is also a monument to this man's industry and inspiration toward the preservation of North Carolina wilderness.

### THE CURRITUCKS

Henry Beasley Ansell's handwritten recollections and memories of nineteenth-century Currituck, run to three volumes in UNC–Chapel Hill's Southern Historical Collection. Nathaniel Holmes Bishop recalled his floating through Currituck in *Voyage of the Paper Canoe: A Geographical Journey of 2500 Miles, from Quebec to Mexico, during the Years 1874–75* (Boston: Lee and Shepard, 1878). Further reports of old Currituck appear in *A North Carolina Naturalist, H. H. Brimley: Selections from His Writings*, edited by Eugene P. Odom (Chapel Hill: University of North Carolina Press, 1949), and Alexander Hunter, in *Virginia and North Carolina*, vol. 1 of *The Huntsman in the South* (New York: Neale Pub. Co., 1908), gives perhaps the best contemporary overview of the old huntclub era, before market hunting was outlawed. T. Gilbert Pearson also wrote of market hunting in the very early 1900s, and of St. Clair Lewark in particular, and Lewark's 1921 trial for the killing of Derwood Gallop was covered devotedly by two Elizabeth City, N.C., newspapers: the *Daily Advance* and the *Independent*. Maxwell Bloomfield wrote of Joseph Palmer Knapp in Supplement 5 (1951–55) of the *Dictionary of American Biography* (New York: Charles Scribner's Sons, 1977). Sarah Downing, assistant curator at the Outer Banks History Center, Manteo, N.C., provided me with several items on Currituck's gunning history, including *Prospectus of the Kitty Hawk Bay Sportsman's Club* (ca. 1881); Travis Morris, "History of the Monkey Island Club," *Journal of the Currituck County Historical Society* (Barco, N.C.: Graphics & Photography Department, Currituck County High School, 1976); and *The Heritage of Currituck County, North Carolina*, edited by Jo Anna Heath Bates (Winston-Salem, N.C.: Albemarle Genealogical Society, Currituck County Historical

Society, and Hunter Publishing Co., 1985), 34–36. Dew's Quarter Island owner Richard Thurmond Chatham's papers are in the Southern Historical Collection, UNC–Chapel Hill (#4701); Frank Borden Hanes Sr. wrote me on August 2, 2004, about times spent at Dew's. More on Currituck's rich and complex hunting history is in *Waterfowl Heritage: North Carolina Decoys and Gunning Lore* by William Neal Conoley Jr., with photography by Ken Taylor (Wendell, N.C.: Webfoot, 1982). Eddie Nickens wrote of a recent outing in "The Swan Island Club" (*Shooting Sportsman* 10, no. 5 [September/October 1998]). Tim Cooper, refuge manager, provided information about Mackay Island National Wildlife Refuge; with Ducks Unlimited, the refuge staged the October 6, 2005, dedication of the Knapp memorial and trail at Live Oak Point. Barbara and Wilson Snowden of Currituck graciously opened their soundside home to us for a research and photography outing to Mackay and Knotts Islands.

## A ROSE FOR ROANOKE

David Stick unravels the yarn of yarns, that of the 1587 Lost Colony, clearly and elegantly in *Roanoke Island: The Beginnings of English America* (Chapel Hill: University of North Carolina Press, 1983). Concerning the Holland case, Cindy Bland Perry, who worked on *The Lost Colony* in the summer of 1967, wrote me of her firsthand recollections on August 2, 2004. The *Raleigh News and Observer*'s Sarah Avery published "The Lost Colony Murder," a thirty-years-later retrospective on the cold case in the paper on July 6, 1997. A copy of the 1921 silent film about the Lost Colony—authored by Mabel Evans Jones, directed by Elizabeth Berkeley Grimball, and entitled simply *North Carolina Pictorial History*—is in the North Carolina Collection, UNC–Chapel Hill. In *Paradise Preserved* (Chapel Hill: University of North Carolina Press, 1965), William S. Powell chronicles various modern efforts to memorialize the Lost Colony. The tale of playwright Paul Green's having taken a break from second-season *Lost Colony* rehearsals and engaged with others in a brief archaeological dig near Wanchese appeared in the *Dare County Times*, July 1, 1938. The substantial 1979 excavation dig and its results are reported in detail in David Sutton Phelps's *Archaeology of the Tillett Site: The First Fishing Community at Wanchese, Roanoke Island* (Greenville, N.C.: Archaeological Laboratory, Department of Sociology, Anthropology and Economics, East Carolina University, 1984). Two other significant texts of interest to seekers after Roanoke are Marjorie Hudson's *Searching for Virginia Dare* (Wilmington, N.C.: Coastal Carolina Press, 2001) and E. Thomson Shields and Charles R. Ewen's coedited work *Searching for the Roanoke Colonies* (Raleigh: North Carolina Office of Archives and History, 2003). Suzanne Godley of Roanoke Island Festival Park on Ice Plant Island has been a friend of this project, as has KaeLi Spiers, curator of the Outer Banks History Center at Roanoke Island Festival Park. Professor William Stott, director of UNC–Chapel Hill's Albemarle Ecological Field Site in Manteo, has also been helpful and keenly inquisitive in many conversations about the inner islands. Longtime cohorts John Foley and Scott Bradley reminisced about the old Drafty Tavern, and noted author and Cape Hatteras Coastkeeper Jan DeBlieu confirmed the vanished wayside's location.

### BEHIND OCRACOKE

Storytellers Merle and Donald Davis kindly opened their Ocracoke home, Swamp Turtle, to us at the beginning of this work. John Weske and Micou Browne invited us right into the birdbanding world and their island tours of duty. Cap'n Norman Miller skillfully got us to Beacon Island and Shell Castle Island—and back. Documentary evocation of Shell Castle's turn-of-the-nineteenth-century heyday lies in *The John Gray Blount Papers*, vol. 2 (1959), 1790–95, edited by Alice Barnwell Keith; vol. 3 (1965), 1796–1802, edited by William H. Masterson; and vol. 4 (1982), 1803–33, edited by David T. Morgan (Raleigh: North Carolina Department of Cultural Resources, Division of Archives and History). My brief narrative of historic events at Shell Castle is informed by the *Blount Papers* and by scholar Phillip Horne McGuinn's excellent telling of the huge story of this small place in his M.A. thesis for the Department of History, East Carolina University: "Shell Castle, a North Carolina Entrepôt, 1789–1820: A Historical and Archaeological Investigation" (2000). In *To Ocracoke: Boyhood Summers on the Outer Banks* (Columbia, N.C.: Sweet Bay Tree Books, 2000), Fred M. Mallison portrays Pamlico River and soundside life in the 1930s. Ocracoke Preservation Society director Julie Howard has advised me well about the island. I continue to learn about Pamlico Sound from waterman James Barrie Gaskill and from Ocracoke-to-Portsmouth navigator Rudy Austin as well. Alton Ballance's *Ocracokers* (Chapel Hill: University of North Carolina Press, 1989) is a first-rate depiction of historic and contemporary Ocracoke and its watery surrounds. Don Dixon, Marti Jones, and their daughter Shane shared Serendipity cottage on Silver Lake with us the last of June 2002, a most productive musical and literary week.

### TO THE CASTLE

Historian David S. Cecelski's interview, "Odell Spain: My Way of Life," with Spain's valuable memories of fishing at the now-drowned Brant Island, appeared in the September 13, 1998, *Raleigh News and Observer*. Cecelski gave me the H. H. Brimley photograph of Castle Island and the Pamlico River oyster-fleet circa 1890, and North Carolina Collection gallery keeper Neil Fulghum made available the Wheelock painting *Little Washington*, which so well portrays Castle Island in the Civil War. David McNaught, then Pamlico–Tar River Foundation director, showed me the river's edge in detail late one night in 1989. Estuarium director Blount Rumley and artist Whiting Tolar, Tom Stroud of Partnership for the Sounds, along with Lawrence Behr and Matt Hollar, have answered frequent queries about Castle Island and the Pamlico. A good general history is *Washington and the Pamlico*, edited by Ursula Fogleman Loy and Pauline Marion Worthy (Washington, N.C.: Washington–

Beaufort County Bicentennial Commission, 1976). Jerry Leath Mills and his wife Rachel have welcomed us into their Washington home innumerable times and have taught us a fortune about this town and its waters.

## NORTH CORE SOUND

Dr. John Robert Kindell, Ann's father, has taken us boating all over North Core Sound and for nearly twenty years has answered thousands of questions about life and history hereabouts. Don and Katie Morris launched us out into the sound, on ferryboat and smallcraft both, from their Atlantic landing, and their daughter Kari now carries on with Morris Marina. Artist Lucille Truitt of Oriental told me much about Hog Island, including the story of Neva Gaskill Spencer, and Cedar Islander Paul Smith provided documentary materials relating to this Lupton, N.C., tragedy, on which master Carteret County storyteller Rodney Kemp also conferred. Lawrence Earley recorded decoy carver Julian Hamilton Jr.'s recollection of running across North Core Sound in terrible weather in "A Core Sound Memoir" (*Wildlife in North Carolina*, November 1985). Jack Dudley has charted this world in his *Carteret Waterfowl Heritage* (1993). Other North Core books of interest include *Cedar Island Fisher Folk*, by Jean Day (N.p.: Golden Age Press, 1994); *Sailing with Grandpa*, by Sonny Williamson (Marshallberg, N.C.: Grandma Publications, 1987); and *Riddle of the Lost Colony*, by Melvin Robinson (N.p.: n.p., 1946).

## SOUTH CORE AND BACK SOUNDS

Concerning Davis Island, Mark and Penny Hooper of Hooper Seafood, Smyrna, N.C., have hosted us on more than one occasion. John Humber spoke with me about Robert Lee Humber Jr., his father, about Davis Island, and about Humber's world federalist efforts, some of which are written of in Joseph Preston Baratta's *From World Federalism to Global Governance*, vol. 1 of *The Politics of World Federation* (Westport, Conn.: Praeger, 2004). J. M. Brown, Dennis Chadwick and Robin Chadwick, Sonny Williamson and Jenny Williamson, Lida Pigott Burney and David Burney, Bryan Blake and Barbara Garrity-Blake all helped us get to, and learn more of, Browns Island. Similarly, Karen Willis Amspacher and Pam Morris of Core Sound Waterfowl Museum have informed us well of modern Harkers Island. More revealing works about this area include Joel Hancock's *Strengthened by the Storm: The Coming of the Mormons to Harkers Island, N.C., 1897–1909* (Morehead City, N.C.: Campbell & Campbell, 1988); John R. Maiolo's *Hard Times and a Nickel a Bucket: Struggle and Survival in North Carolina's Shrimp Industry* (Chapel Hill, N.C.: Chapel Hill Press, 2004); Carmine Prioli's *Hope for a Good Season: The C'ae Bankers of Harkers Island*, with photography by Edwin Martin (Asheboro, N.C.: Down Home Press, 1998); Barbara Garrity-Blake and Susan West's *Fish House Opera* (Mystic, Conn.: Mystic Seaport Press, 2003); and Ulrich Mack's photography collection *Island People* (Boston: Boston University, 2000).

## THE VIEW FROM BIRD SHOAL

Patricia Cary Kindell, Ann's mother, and Carl Spangler have taken us boating all over Newport River and eastern Bogue Sound in both *Lady Jane* and *Luna*, and have advised us well on many topics related to this project. Corinne Webb Geer of Morehead City both fielded our inquiries about Phillips Island and advanced others on our behalf. Lockwood Phillips of the *Carteret County News-Times* has answered many a query, as have Business Editor Mark Hibbs and Managing Editor Beth Blake. Charles O. Pitts Jr. authored "The Island" series about Phillips Island in the *News-Times* (September 22 and 29, and October 6, 1993). Richard Ogus, longtime master of the *Cape Hatteras*, kindly gave us the captain's tour of his ship one Pivers Island evening years ago. Among the works of real interest are Jean Bruyere Kell's *The Old Port Town: Beaufort, North Carolina* (Beaufort, N.C.: n.p., 1980); Scott Taylor's *Coastal Waters: Images of North Carolina* (Wilmington, N.C.: Coastal Carolina Press, 2000); and Rachel Carson's *The Edge of the Sea* (Boston: Houghton Mifflin, 1955). Friends who have helped us in Carteret County include Michael and Corliss Bradley, Scott Taylor and Lenore Meadows, and Table 13; Connie Mason of the North Carolina Maritime Museum; Jimm Prest of Langdon House; Daryl Farrington Walker; Cap'n Jim Rumfelt; Steve Desper; David Robert; and the Folks at the Royal James.

## THE DEFENSE OF HUGGINS ISLAND

Hammocks Beach State Park rangers Sam Bland, Kevin Bleck, and Sean McElhone have all provided me with much help and information about Huggins Island. I was fortunate enough to visit the island in the company of Todd Miller, director, North Carolina Coastal Federation, and Bill Holman, director, North Carolina Clean Water Management Trust Fund, along with the boards of directors for both groups. Paul Branch, Fort Macon State Park ranger/historian, has written the significant manuscript "Report on the Huggins Island Battery" (1999). Poet Peter Makuck of Pine Knoll Shores has given us many a wonderful lyric about Bogue Sound and other watery environs in such works as *The Sunken Lightship* (1990), *Against Distance* (1997), and *Off-Season in the Promised Land* (2005) (Rochester, N.Y.: BOA Editions).

## PERMUDA ISLAND

Rice Farm's (and J&B Aquafood's) Jim Swartzenberg, Bonnie Rice Swartzenberg, and Bernice Rice generously discussed Permuda Island, Stump Sound, and oyster gardening in those waters. More information on North Carolina's oyster restoration efforts has come from the North Carolina Coastal Federation (NCCF), particularly from longtime Cape Fear Coastkeeper Ted Wilgus and Cape Lookout Coastkeeper Frank Tursi, tireless defenders of the Carolina shores. The NCCF's *Oyster Restoration and Protection Plan: A Blueprint for Action, 2003–2008* is available at <http://www.nccoast.org/publication/oysterplan/index—html>. More on the Permuda Island Coastal Reserve can be found at <http://www.ncnerr.org/pubsiteinfo/site info/permuda/permuda.html>.

## MONEY ISLAND

Musette Morgan of Memphis gave me old clippings and fresh enthusiasm about Money Island. I have found Reverend Andrew J. Howell Jr.'s *Money Island* (Wilmington, N.C.: Commercial Printing Co., 1908) and more in the archives at the Lower Cape Fear Historical Society, Wilmington, N.C.

## THE CAPE FEARS

Informants for Roan Island included Eddie Corbett, Corbett Farming Company, Wilmington; Fred Annand, North Carolina Nature Conservancy, Durham; Milvin Marshall, Canetuck; and Eddie Nickens, Raleigh. An important early work on the Cape Fear River is *A relation of a discovery lately made on the coast of Florida (from lat. 31. to 33 deg. 45 min. north-lat) by William Hilton commander, and commissioner with Capt. Anthony Long, and Peter Fabian, in the ship Adventure* (London: Printed by J. C. for S. Miller, 1664). David Robert gave me James Sprunt's colorful *Tales and Traditions of the Lower Cape Fear, 1661–1896* (Wilmington, N.C.: LeGwin Brothers, 1896). Walker Golder, deputy director of Audubon North Carolina, wrote the M.S. thesis "Foraging Flight Activity of Adult White Ibises at a Southeastern North Carolina Colony" (Department of Biology, UNC–Wilmington, 1990); his leadership of Audubon's Coastal Sanctuaries and Important Bird Areas is signal. Richard Lawrence of the North Carolina Underwater Archaeology Branch, Fort Fisher, Kure Beach, N.C., wrote about the Rocks in "A Historical Overview and Archaeological Assessment of the Cape Fear River's New Inlet," which appeared in *Underwater Archaeology*, edited by Stephen R. James Jr. and Camille Stanley (Society for Historical Archaeology, 1996). Lawrence also graciously provided me with archival newspaper transcripts about the lower Cape Fear from the collection of the noted journalist-historian Bill Reaves. Family and friends who have helped us in the Wilmington, Wrightsville, and Southport areas also include my cousin Eugene Edwards and his wife Elizabeth; Richard Wright; Jenny Wright; Harper and Plunkett Peterson; and Camilla Herlevich, director, North Carolina Coastal Land Trust.

# Acknowledgments

The writing of this book was generously supported by a Chapman Fellowship and a Spray-Randleigh Fellowship, both at the Institute for the Arts and Humanities, and by a grant from the University Research Council—all of which are programs of our alma mater, the University of North Carolina at Chapel Hill.

Portions of the text initially appeared, in slightly different form, in *Wildlife in North Carolina*, Official Educational Publication of the North Carolina Wildlife Resources Commission, under editors Jim Dean, Lawrence Earley, and Rodney Sutton. *North Carolina Literary Review* editor Margaret Bauer published "Ode to Neva May" in *NCLR*'s Coastal Issue, Summer 2005.

We have made constant reference to the works of three wonderful North Carolina historians: David Stick (his classic *The Outer Banks of North Carolina*, as well as the more recent *Roanoke Island*); William S. Powell (*The North Carolina Gazetteer*); and David S. Cecelski (*A Historian's Coast* and *The Waterman's Song*). And we have never left home, or the dock, without the *GMCO Chartbook* or the state of North Carolina's yearly updated *Coastal Boating Guide*.

In Wilson Library at UNC–Chapel Hill, we have continued to find unstinting research support and encouragement from North Carolina Collection (NCC) curator Robert Anthony Jr. and staff members Nick Graham, Harry McKown, Eileen McGrath, and Jill Wagy; in NCC's Gallery, from Neil Fulghum and Linda Jacobson; and in NCC's Photographic Archives, from Stephen Fletcher, Keith Longiotti, Fred Stipe, and Jane Witten. At East Carolina University in Greenville, more help and advice has come from Maritime Studies director Tim Runyan and North Carolina Collection director Maury York. Charles G. (Terry) Zug III counseled us on pottery.

At the University of North Carolina Press, Editor-in-Chief David Perry supported this exploration from the very first mention of it, and Pam Upton, Paula Wald, Rich Hendel, Heidi Perov, Kathy Ketterman, Gina Mahalek, Meagan Bonnell, David Hines, and many others have again helped us to make a book. Michael Southern drafted the maps.

Valuable research and logistical help has come our way in Elizabeth City and the northeast from Russ Haddad, George Jackson and Blair Jackson, Don Pendergraft, and Penny Leary-Smith and in Beaufort from David Robert, Jim Rumfelt, and Bill Garlick and Isa Cherren. My cohorts Jack Herrick, Don Dixon, Jim Wann, David Cecelski, and Michael McFee have joined in on many a jaunt, and they—and their wives, Lynn Davis, Marti Jones, Patricia Miller Wann, Laura Hanson, and Belinda McFee—have listened to many a tale. Other compatriots who have helped keep us on course include John Shelton Reed and Dale Vollberg Reed, Jane Oliver and

Jim Byrum, and Rachel V. Mills and Jerry Leath Mills. The sage and inimitable outdoorsman-scholar J. L. Mills has yet again given equal measures of expert editorial advice and grand companionship, as he has so graciously done for nearly forty years.

To all of these people, and to all those who speak through these pages, we offer our deepest thanks, to all the living and the dead.

M.B.S. III

A.C.S.

# Illustration Credits

# Maps

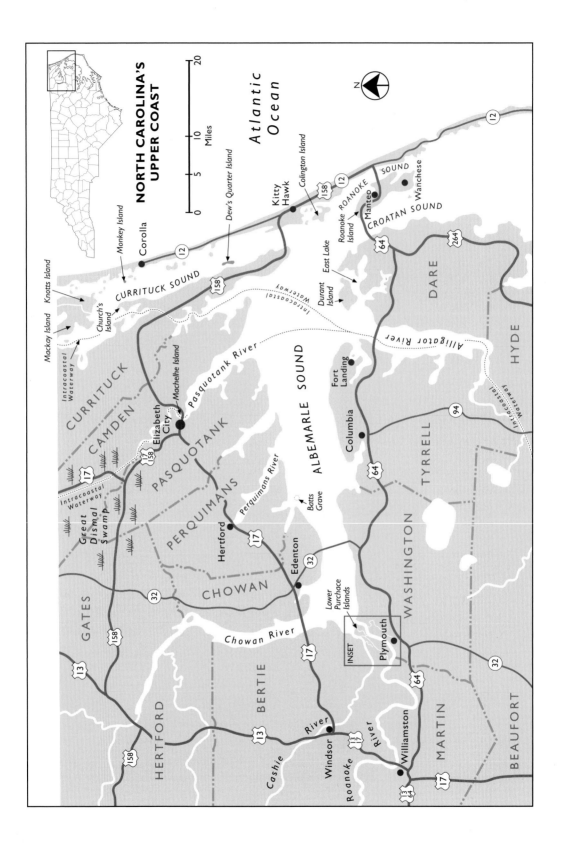

NORTH CAROLINA'S
UPPER COAST

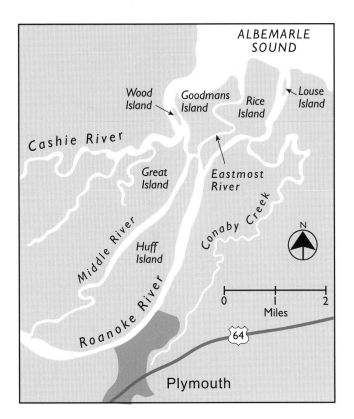

LOWER PURCHACE ISLANDS

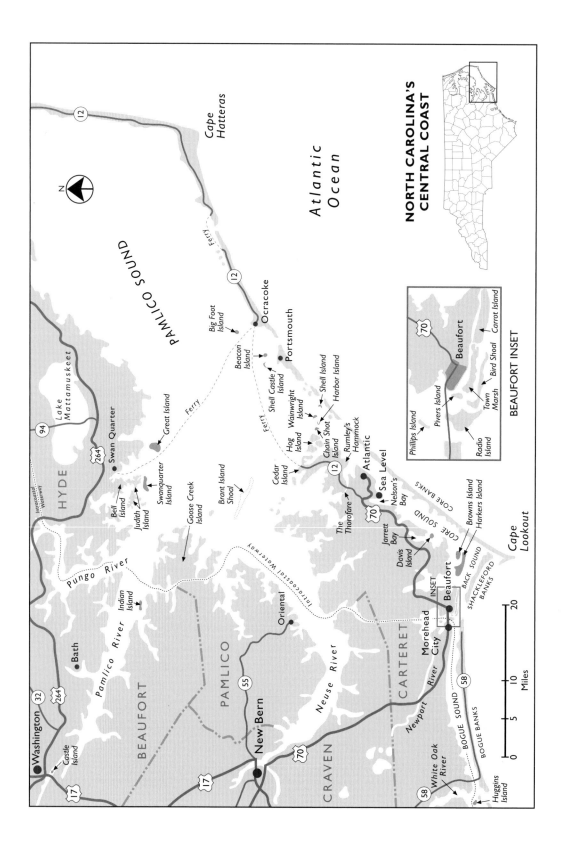

NORTH CAROLINA'S
CENTRAL COAST

BEAUFORT INSET

Atlantic
Ocean

Cape Hatteras

PAMLICO SOUND

Ocracoke

Portsmouth

Beacon Island

Big Foot Island

Shell Castle Island

Wainwright Island

Shell Island

Harbor Island

Hog Island

Chain Shot Island

Rumley's Hammock

Cedar Island

Atlantic

Sea Level

Nelson's Bay

Great Island

Swan Quarter

Lake Mattamuskeet

HYDE

Bell Island

Judith Island

Swanquarter Island

Goose Island

Brant Island Shoal

The Thorofare

Jarrett Bay

Davis Island

CORE BANKS

Browns Island

Harkers Island

CORE SOUND

BACK SOUND

SHACKLEFORD BANKS

Cape Lookout

BEAUFORT

Pamlico River

Bath

Pungo River

Indian Island

Washington

Castle Island

PAMLICO

Oriental

New Bern

Neuse River

CRAVEN

CARTERET

Morehead City

Beaufort

INSET

Newport River

BOGUE SOUND

White Oak River

BOGUE BANKS

Huggins Island

Intracoastal Waterway

Intracoastal Waterway

Ferry

Ferry

Ferry

N

Phillips Island

Pivers Island

Town Marsh

Bird Shoal

Carrot Island

Beaufort

Radio Island

12

12

94

264

264

32

17

17

55

70

70

70

58

58

0   5   10   20
Miles

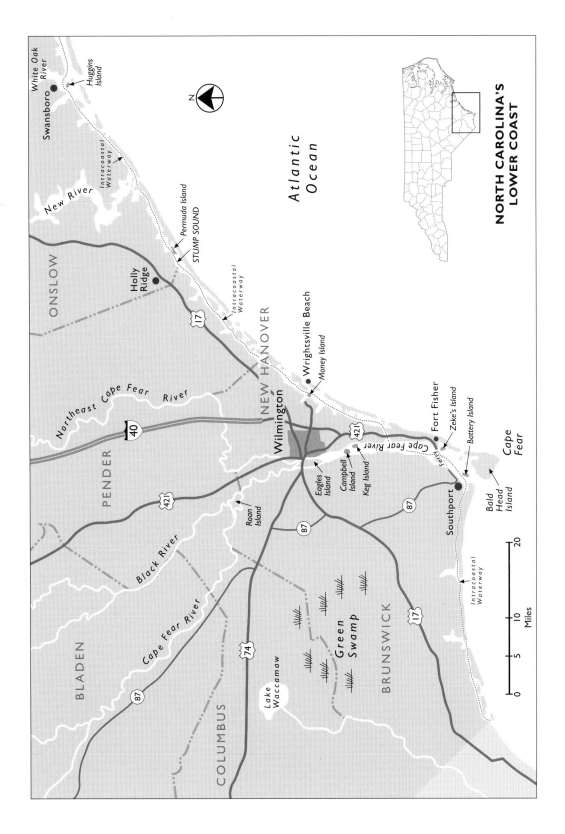

NORTH CAROLINA'S
LOWER COAST

# Index